CANTINFLAS AND THE
CHAOS OF MEXICAN MODERNITY

Cantinflas and the Chaos of Mexican Modernity

Jeffrey M. Pilcher

SR
BOOKS

A Scholarly Resources Inc. Imprint
Wilmington, Delaware

Scholarly Resources Inc.
104 Greenhill Avenue
Wilmington, DE 19805-1897
www.scholarly.com

Library of Congress Cataloging-in-Publication Data
Pilcher, Jeffrey M., 1965–
   Cantinflas and the chaos of Mexican modernity / Jeffrey M. Pilcher.
     p. cm (Latin American silhouettes)
   Includes bibliographical references and index.
   ISBN 0-8420-2769-6 (alk. paper)—ISBN 0-8420-2771-8 (paper : alk. paper)
    1. Cantinflas, 1911–   2. Entertainers—Mexican—Biography. I. Title. II.
Series.

PN2318.C3 P55   2000
791'.092—dc21
[B]   00-041331

To W.H.B.

ABOUT THE AUTHOR

Jeffrey M. Pilcher received his Ph.D. in Mexican cultural history from Texas Christian University in 1993. His first book, *¡Que vivan los tamales! Food and the Making of Mexican Identity* (1998), won the Thomas F. McGann Prize of the Rocky Mountain Council for Latin American Studies. Currently he is writing a history of the modernization of Mexico City's meat supply and editing a forthcoming volume on the human tradition in Mexico. He teaches at The Citadel in Charleston, South Carolina.

CONTENTS

ILLUSTRATIONS

ACKNOWLEDGMENTS

Writing a biography of Mexico's most incomprehensible comic seemed, at times, to be a hopeless undertaking for a self-confessed *gacho*. I made it this far only with the help of countless *chavos* and *changuitas* who took the trouble of explaining the *detalles* of Mexican life. Some of the best lessons came from anonymous *peladitos,* and I only hope they found me a polite *paco.* Other tutors lingered in their discussions of Mexican culture—often over a *copita* or two—and it is a pleasure to thank them individually.

This book is dedicated to my dissertation adviser, William H. Beezley, who steered me away from the historical profession's worst *cantinflismos.* John Mraz contributed some of the best ideas in the book, and it would doubtless have been better still if I had listened to more of them. Judy Ewell and Drew Wood read the entire manuscript and provided many thoughtful suggestions, as did Eduardo Moreno Laparde, Roberto Moreno Laparde, and Beatriz Moreno de Mejía, who saved me from countless factual errors concerning their renowned uncle. I also received valuable comments and criticisms from Rob Buffington, Linda Curcio-Nagy, Matt Esposito, Seth Fein, Charles Harris, John Hart, Joanne Hershfield, Keith Knapp, Glen Kuecker, Sonya Lipsett-Rivera, Victor Macías, Colin MacLachlan, Michael Meyer, Vincent Peloso, Karen Racine, Anne Rubenstein, Ray Sadler, Pedro Santoni, Alex Saragoza, Ann Marie Stock, Heather Thiessen-Reilly, Julia Tuñón, Paul Vanderwood, and Eric Zolov. And for special translating services—that is, explaining the jokes—I thank Pedro de Aguinaga, Elba Andrade, María Arbeláez, Linda Curcio-Nagy, Sonya Lipsett-Rivera, Epifanio López, Zarela Martínez, Victor Nava, Sergio Rivera Ayala, and Carlos Schaefer.

This study could not have been finished without the assistance of the Filmoteca of the Universidad Nacional Autónoma de México and, in particular, of Salvador Plancarte, who provided copies of rare films; Antonia Rojas and her staff, who efficiently answered all my questions; and Diego and Denise, who let me interrupt Barney to watch Cantinflas. Once again I am indebted to the archivists and librarians of the Archivo General de la Nación, the Archivo Histórico de la Ciudad de México, the Cineteca Nacional, the Instituto Nacional de Antropología e Historia, the Instituto Nacional de Bellas Artes y Literatura, the Hemeroteca Lerdo de Tejeda and the Hemeroteca Nacional in Mexico City, the Library of Congress in Washington, DC, and the Daniels Library in Charleston. I received much-appreciated technical support from Tim and research assistance from Donna, Jeanne, and Dr. Mush. At Scholarly Resources, Rick Hopper encouraged me from the beginning, and Michelle Slavin, Deborah Lynes, and her staff did a splendid job editing the manuscript. With all this magnificent help, I have only myself to blame if the punch line falls flat.

Jeffrey M. Pilcher
Sullivan's Island, South Carolina

CHRONOLOGY

1911 Born (August 12) in Mexico City. Revolution toppled the dictatorship of Porfirio Díaz. Francisco I. Madero elected president.

1930 Began theatrical career in the Carpa Sotelo in Azcapotzalco.

1933 Moved to Tacuba to work at the Carpa Valentina, owned by the father of Valentina Ivanova.

1934 Left the Carpa Valentina to work in Mexico City at the Salón Rojo and Salón Mayab. Married Valentina Ivanova (October 27). Lázaro Cárdenas elected president. Samuel Ramos published *Profile of Man and Culture in Mexico.*

1936 Opened the Follies Bergère. Appeared in first movie, *No te engañes, corazón.*

1937 Had first starring roles with Manuel Medel in *Así es mi tierra* and *Aguila o sol.*

1939 Filmed the feature-length *El signo de la muerte* and the shorts *Siempre listo en tinieblas, Jengibre contra dinamita,* and *Cantinflas boxeador.*

1940 Filmed the international blockbuster *Ahí está el detalle* and the shorts *Cantinflas ruletero* and *Cantinflas y su prima.* Manuel Avila Camacho elected president.

1941 Filmed *Ni sangre, ni arena* and *El gendarme desconocido.*

1942 Filmed *Los tres mosqueteros* and *El circo.* Elected president of the Asociación Nacional de Actores, ANDA.

1943 Filmed *Romeo y Julieta.*

1944 Filmed *Gran Hotel.* Began movement to gain ANDA's autonomy from the national cinema union, STIC.

1945 Filmed *Un día con el diablo.* Union struggle continued despite presidential decree in actors' favor.

1946 Filmed *Soy un prófugo.* Spoke in defiance of STIC at the Esperanza Iris Theater. Miguel Alemán elected president.

1947 Filmed *¡A volar joven!*

1948 Filmed *El supersabio* and *El mago.*

1949 Filmed *Puerta, joven.* Staged *Bonjour, Mexique,* renamed *Cantinflas en Paris,* at the Esperanza Iris Theater.

1950 Filmed *El siete machos* and *El bombero atómico.*

1951 Filmed *Si yo fuera diputado.*

1952 Filmed *El señor fotógrafo.* Adolfo Ruiz Cortines elected president.

1953 Filmed *Un caballero a la medida.* Staged *Yo, Colón* at the Insurgentes Theater.

1954 Filmed *Abajo el telón.*

1955 Filmed *Around the World in 80 Days* in Europe, Asia, and Hollywood.

1956 Filmed *El bolero de Raquel.*

1957 Won the Golden Globe for best comic actor.

1958 Filmed *Ama a tu prójimo* and *Sube y baja.* Adolfo López Mateos elected president.

1960 Adopted Mario Arturo Moreno Ivanova. Filmed *Pepe* in Las Vegas and Mexico and *El analfabeto* in Mexico.

1962 Filmed *El extra.*

1963 Filmed *Entrega inmediata.*

1964 Filmed *El padrecito.* Gustavo Díaz Ordaz elected president.

1965 Filmed *El señor doctor.*

1966 Wife Valentina died (January 5). Filmed *Su excelencia.*

1968 Filmed *Por mis pistolas.* Mexican army crushed student protesters in the Plaza of Three Cultures, Tlatelolco.

1969 Filmed *Un Quijote sin mancha.*

1970 Filmed *El profe.* Luis Echeverría elected president.

1972 Filmed *Don Quijote cabalga de nuevo* in Spain.

1973 Filmed *Conserje en condominio.*

1975 Filmed *El ministro y yo.*

1977 Filmed *Patrullero 777.*

1981 Filmed *El barrendero.*

1993 Died (April 20) in Mexico City.

INTRODUCTION

The cold-blooded killer fascinates decent people everywhere, and spectators fill the courtroom when such a criminal is brought to justice. The murder trial of Leonardo del Paso in 1940 did not disappoint the crowds who turned out to see one of the most reprehensible outcasts of Mexican society. The accused appeared every inch the "gangsta," with baggy pants tied low on his hips, a long white shirt, a tattered scarf, and an undersized hat perched above his unshaven face. Gesticulating madly while speaking in a repetitive voice riddled with street slang, he looked guiltier with every word. He admitted under oath to shooting the victim, denied all remorse, contradicted the public defender's alibis, and insulted the judge. Law-abiding citizens cheered when the jury found him guilty and recommended the death penalty. But the criminal not only escaped punishment, he also became one of the most celebrated figures in Mexico, because the drama took place in a movie, *Ahí está el detalle* (That's the point), the hit comedy of 1940. Mario Moreno, the star known as Cantinflas, turned the courtroom upside down with his nonsense language, babbling away until even the judge and lawyers began to parrot his insane speech. In episodes such as this one, Cantinflas embodied the chaos of Mexican society in its quest for modernity.

From early in his career, critics compared Mario Moreno to another great film comic, Charlie Chaplin. Cantinflas and the Tramp both represented the human debris of industrialization, rootless migrants to the big city who survived by their wits in a bewildering and coldhearted environment. Both were masters of physical comedy and possessed an innate geniality that elicited sympathy for their underdog status. But while Chaplin had a knack for transformation—turning bread rolls into dancing girls in *The Gold Rush* (1925) and changing himself into a machine in *Modern Times* (1936)—Cantinflas was always content with his place, and a carefully defined place at that. Unlike the Tramp, who appeared as an anonymous denizen of an unnamed metropolis, Cantinflas was identified with a particular neighborhood, Tepito, site of the notorious thieves' market of Mexico City during the 1930s. Careful attention to historical context therefore reveals much about Moreno and his Mexico. He never made a counterpart to *Modern Times*, for example, because the circumstances of industrial development in Mexico differed sharply from those in Britain and the United States. The repetitive factory labor that Chaplin found so dehumanizing was an unattainable dream for countless Mexicans, who were forced instead to seek a precarious livelihood in service as bootblacks or street sweeps.

A more appropriate analogy for Moreno is, therefore, the malevolent verbal humor of Groucho Marx rather than the silent comedy of Chaplin. Speaking in a lower-class New York accent, Groucho constantly deflated the pretensions of the rich and powerful while resisting any personal desire for upward mobility. Psychologist René Cisneros observed a similar rejection of linguistic and social rules in the multiple layers of Cantinflas's double-talk. The comedian jumbled together multiple conversations while alternating between forms of deference and defiance in order to undermine the legitimacy of authority. For instance, in the courtroom scene of *Ahí está el detalle* when the prosecuting attorney called him "stupid" out of frustration with his refusal to give a straight answer, Cantinflas replied, "We . . . ll. Don't get insulting. Your honor . . . I . . . protes . . . Why don't you get out of here, buddy . . . ? It's so upsetting, your honor. He should not be insulting. And since you're the big wig around here . . . if he would be so kind as to treat me with respect . . . that . . . Why don't you scram, buddy?"[1] By failing to address the judge consistently, calling him first "your honor" and then "big wig," Cantinflas emphasized the artificiality of distinctions within Mexico's social hierarchy. Moreover, he constantly beguiled the objects of his humor, drawing them into this carnivalesque, upside-down world in spite of themselves. At the judge's insistence, the attorney excused himself, whereupon Cantinflas replied, "You are an *excusado* [toilet]."

Yet while Groucho was always an outsider, unwilling to join any club that would admit him, Mario Moreno became a symbol of Mexican national identity comparable to John Wayne in the United States. Of course, Cantinflas did not resemble the Duke's idealized cowboy figure, standing tall and shooting straight; indeed, the two characters could scarcely have been farther apart. For just that reason, Cantinflas offers an excellent portrait of Mexican self-image during a transitional moment from a traditional agrarian society to an industrial urban one. As a shiftless migrant from the provinces, Cantinflas provided an object lesson in adaptation for millions of his countrymen entering the urban economy in the mid–twentieth century. He symbolized the underdog who triumphed through trickery over more powerful opponents—including those from the United States. Instead of speaking slowly like John Wayne, Cantinflas taught that when confronted by "the policeman whose hat you stepped on or the boss whose shirt front you just spilled catsup down, the [common man's] defense is to talk, talk, talk."[2] He inhabited not a mythically pure Anglo Saxon frontier but a racially mixed urban society in which Native Americans intermingled and intermarried with Europeans and Africans. His trademark whiskers, exactly the reverse of Chaplin's narrow mustache, were discrete tufts of hair situated like dimples over the corners of his mouth. This inability to grow a proper mustache immediately revealed the indigenous blood in Cantinflas, making him a mestizo, the modern exemplar of Mexican national identity.

Moreover, unlike the Duke or comparable Mexican icons such as Jorge Negrete or Pedro Armendáriz, Cantinflas acknowledged the ambivalent nature of masculinity and thereby conveyed some of the emotional introspection of James Dean. As a student of Method acting, Dean eschewed theatrical conventions and used dramatic roles as a form of psychoanalytic performance intended to reveal authentic patterns of human behavior. He disturbed and captivated audiences, in ways that John Wayne never did, by playing troubled and sexually insecure characters. Mexican film historian Emilio García Riera attributed Mario Moreno's success precisely to his lack of dramatic artifice. "Cantinflas is the first *real and living* personage in a cinema characterized by cheap histrionics."[3] In the Mexican comedian's films, the precarious nature of masculine identity emerged most clearly through his pantomime of macho posturing in which he talked himself into trouble, only to slink coyly away from the fight. While best known for his talk, Moreno made his act work through the slink, timed perfectly, with a pause, a provocative backward gesture, then a quick rush to safety. This madcap performance of bravado, oscillating wildly between courage and cowardice, offered Mexican men a momentary release through laughter from the psychic demands and anxieties of masculine behavior. The inept misogyny of Cantinflas also struck a familiar chord among women, who often suffered physical abuse from the excesses of machismo, particularly at a time when modernity was unsettling established gender roles.[4]

Movie stardom ensured Mario Moreno a central role in constructing modern identities in Mexico and throughout the Spanish-speaking world. Social hierarchies, speech patterns, ethnic identities, and masculine forms of behavior all crumbled before his chaotic humor, to be reformulated in revolutionary new ways. His performances were viewed, imitated, discussed, and internalized by an entire generation, the first to experience the homogenizing effects of mass media throughout the republic. His status as the most popular film star of the 1940s, the "golden age" of Mexican cinema, magnified his influence on the national consciousness. Moreover, the length of his cinema career, stretching from 1936 to 1981, and the regularity of his movie production, generally one a year for a total of forty-two feature films, made him an inevitable landmark on the modern Mexican scene. In 1992, the Royal Academy of the Spanish Language formally acknowledged his status as an institution in the Hispanic world by adding to its dictionary the verb *cantinflear,* meaning to talk a lot without saying anything.

Mexican filmgoers naturally applied their own cultural references to Cantinflas, perceiving him in three basic roles: the *pelado,* the demagogue, and the capitalist. Mario Moreno began his acting career about 1930 in the improvised *carpa* (tent) theater, a Mexican version of vaudeville, playing the stock character of the country bumpkin who is bewildered by the big city but far wiser than the supposedly urbane people around him. This universal comic figure acquired a Mexican face in the colonial period as a member of the racially mixed urban underclass of mestizos, who were excluded from both elite Spanish society and Native American communities. Colonial stereotypes depicted mestizos as depraved mongrels—drunken, lazy, lecherous, and criminal—whose only possessions were the ragged clothes on their backs and their inflated egos. Yet, after the Wars of Independence abolished the caste system and then the Revolution of 1910 overthrew the Eurocentric elite, the formerly disdained mestizos were suddenly enshrined as a "cosmic race," and Cantinflas, the theatrical and film representative of the pelado, became an unofficial spokesman of the national identity.

A second role situated Cantinflas in the tradition of rabble-rousing Mexican politicians, famous for their meaningless torrent of promises. Writing of the 1930s, in a style similar to that of Cantinflas, journalist Salvador Novo described the "dawning of a wordy era, confused, oratorical, promising without accountability, which prudent journalists would call 'demagogic.' The sensitive antenna that received this new vibration; that gave the key of humor through which this new era released its repression, would be called Cantinflas."[5] The comedian's best work was in portraying the powerful union boss and Marxist intellectual Vicente Lombardo Toledano. From the stage of the Follies Bergère, Moreno performed a weekly ritual of comic deflation, satirizing the labor leader's dialectical materialist rhetoric with his own nonsense language. Cantinflas actually entered the national political discourse in 1937 when Lombardo publicly acknowledged this parody by suggesting that a union rival debate with the comic, who responded by announcing, "Comrades, there are moments in life that are truly momentary."[6]

Cantinflas's dual identity as bumpkin and politician was juxtaposed against a third vision of Mario Moreno as a member of the bourgeoisie. Mexico's foremost cultural critic, Carlos Monsiváis, interpreted this capitalist Cantinflas as a crucial element of the hegemony exercised by Mexico's postrevolutionary state, which sanitized the genuinely threatening urban proletariat into a harmless, even cute, prankster known diminutively as the *peladito*.[7] Sociologist Roger Bartra described Cantinflas's humor as a palliative of the Mexican working class that actually helped to entrap them in a corrupt union bureaucracy. "The verbal confusion of Cantinflas, rather than serving to criticize the demagogy of the politicians, actually legitimizes it. . . . The pelado lives in a world that, in order to function, needs to be oiled regularly:

thus, a shifting society is built in which, at any moment, everything can lose meaning, and civility becomes slick and lubri-
cious. When things freeze up, it is necessary to smear them with
what in Europe is called the 'Mexican ointment': a bribe."[8]

These public images of Cantinflas as plebeian, politician, and
plutocrat were as contradictory as his language because rather
than changing over time in a linear fashion—a simple case of
selling out his working-class humor to the media establishment
and the Mexican state—all three interpretations were valid
simultaneously throughout his film career. Because of his phe-
nomenal box office success and despite the long-standing rejection of critics, Moreno infused elements of popular culture,
derived from the improvisational acting style of the street theater, into every movie he made. But at the same time, the culti-
vation of a personal brand name was essential to his success,
just as it has been to modern celebrities such as Madonna and
Michael Jordan. Some of the first movies Moreno made were
paid advertisements for Canada Dry ginger ale, Eveready batteries, and General Motors automobiles. And from early in his career, journalists took pains to reassure middle-class readers that
while Cantinflas represented the lowest levels of society, Mario
Moreno was quite respectable in real life.[9] The actor, in turn,
parlayed his celebrity status into the role of a social and political commentator. The evolution of Cantinflas's image thus offers
a multifaceted reflection of Mexico's changing society. By placing his films in historical context, one can gain valuable perspectives on the contested terrain of popular culture, battled
over by the common people, the cultural industries, and the
Mexican state.

The blending of politics and mass media has become so universal in the modern world that it is virtually impossible to separate, for example, Ronald Reagan's political biography from his
interpretation of the role of president of the United States,
scripted by speechwriter Peggy Noonan and the Westinghouse
Corporation. In much the same way, Mario Moreno assumed the
role of the Mexican "people" as defined by screenwriters and
advertisers as well as by the people themselves. The character
of Cantinflas, in turn, helped to shape the expectations and
identity of the Mexican people—and of Mario Moreno. The actor
had noticed this fusion of himself and the character Cantinflas as

early as 1938, when an interviewer complained about his nonsense language. He responded by saying it would be difficult to
interview Moreno alone "because if Mario Moreno had 'inflated'
[soplar] Cantinflas, Cantinflas 'squeals on' [same verb] Mario
Moreno. . . . Now if you want to interview both, well 'we're' at
your service."[10] A dual biography, examining the tension between actor and character, is therefore essential to understanding
Moreno and his place in Mexican history. In an effort to separate
these two—at times inextricably linked—personages, the text
will explicitly distinguish between references to the actor Mario
Moreno and to the character Cantinflas.

These multiple subjects, Moreno, Cantinflas, and, by extension, all of Mexico, appear so confusing partly because their
common object, modernity, has been equally elusive. For more
than a century, Mexicans of all political stances have shared the
common goal of building a "modern" nation, without actually
agreeing on what that means. There was some consensus on
what Mexico lacked in comparison with Europe and the United
States—industry and democracy—although business leaders
sought to emulate Britain and France while socialists looked to
the Soviet Union as a model. Moreover, as Marshal Berman has
explained, modernity was itself a moving target because of the
logic of capitalism, in which the eternal cycles of production
and consumption required a constant process of creative destruction. The dynamism of boom and bust, essential to the capitalist economy, took a heavy toll on people forced to adapt to
new and alienating forms of industrial labor and urban living,
who enjoyed moments of prosperity only to face another turn
of the business cycle with its attendant unemployment and
poverty. And through it all, Mexicans' goal of modernity has remained just beyond reach.[11]

In describing the lives and times of Mario Moreno and Cantinflas, this book pays special attention to the question of audience reception. It does so not in a linear fashion but rather by
laying out the multiple loops of feedback between star and society through which Cantinflas came to personify the Mexican
pueblo. Miguel Covarrubias perceived the actor as a reflection of
the people when he wrote in 1938, "Cantinflas impersonates the
class-conscious man of the city's lower classes."[12] The belief that
cinema mirrored society may also have motivated the remark by

a UCLA professor in 1941 that "when in Mexico one can see 'cantinflas' everywhere."[13] Reciprocally, Cantinflas began to shape the Mexican people as they repeated his jokes, mimicked his speech, and identified with his character. Already in 1942, Adolfo Fernández Bustamante observed that "his sayings and picturesque phrases are repeated not only by the low pueblo, but also by the middle class, and on occasion even by [elite] cultured persons."[14]

Another loop of feedback, between the improvised theater and the mass media, confused still further the audience reception of Cantinflas. Although Moreno drew upon long-standing traditions in popular culture, he adapted his comedy to the contradictions of modern life. The Mexican capital was in flux throughout the twentieth century as it grew from a pleasant city of three hundred thousand residents to a sprawling monster of more than fifteen million. Carpa theaters flourished in the 1930s in the old Barrio Latino, a brothel district on the west side of the city that had been demolished during recent urban renewal. Although an improvement over prostitution, the popular theaters were still viewed with suspicion by municipal authorities, who closed them down in the following two decades, replacing them with movie houses.[15] This process of destruction and renewal, so characteristic of the industrial world, was the lifeblood of Cantinflas, the pelado linking the countryside and the city without fitting properly in either place. His nonsense language eloquently expressed the contradictions of modernity as "the palpitating moment of everything that wants to be that which it cannot be."[16]

Giving attention to audience reception can also help resolve the perennial disputes over the social functions of humor. Henri Bergson considered humor to have the didactic purpose of ridiculing inappropriate behavior and thereby helping to maintain the social order. Sigmund Freud meanwhile saw laughter as a temporary release of inhibitions through expressions of hostility or obscenity. Both interpretations implied forms of social control, either directly through coercion or indirectly by providing an escape valve for political dissatisfaction that might otherwise be expressed in more constructive forms of protest. As the Caribbean dictator said in Graham Greene's novel *The Comedians,* "I am in favor of jokes. They have political value. Jokes are a release for the cowardly and the impotent."[17] Moreno indeed told jokes in support of Mexico's authoritarian regime, but Cantinflas's subversive language made the reception of that same message problematic. In this way the comic character exemplified the liberating power of carnival to turn the world upside down, as Mikhail Bakhtin showed in his study of the French Renaissance novelist François Rabelais.[18] After all, Moreno began his career in a lively political theater that constituted one of the most powerful and democratic elements of Mexican civil society in the Revolution of 1910.

Moreno's remarkable success throughout the Spanish-speaking world adds further complexity to the question of his reception. At first glance, Cantinflas seemed unlikely to become a regional star because his chaotic street slang was largely incomprehensible outside of Mexico City. Yet that ambiguity was precisely one of the secrets to his success. His jokes were at once simpleminded and laden with multiple meanings, accommodating differences of regional dialect and personal taste. Audiences throughout Latin America join in laughing at his movies, but when asked to explain the jokes, they frequently offer differing interpretations. Aging residents of Mexico City catch specific references to the neighborhood of Tepito or to the carpa theater of the 1930s that are lost on their children or foreigners. But anybody who understands Spanish can find, or imagine, humor in his chaotic wordplay and expressive gestures.[19] The knowledge that this laughter was shared by diverse regions helped Mexicans to imagine a national community in the 1940s, while the success of Cantinflas's humor throughout the Spanish-speaking world planted a seed for a transnational Latin American cultural industry that reached fruition in the 1990s.[20]

But not all Mexicans were laughing; as early as the mid-1940s, haughty reviewers had begun to attack Cantinflas as a symbol of the lowbrow taste endemic to Mexico's working class. Ilan Stavans dubbed this split between popular acceptance and critical rejection the "riddle of Cantinflas," and he attributed it to Moreno's consistently vulgar yet distinctively Mexican humor. Carlos Monsiváis, for example, found social relevance in the films Moreno made in the late 1930s and early 1940s but considered the rest inanely repetitive sequels. In perhaps the most insightful periodization of Moreno's career, John Mraz located the turning point much later, at about 1960, when his films became "preachy, tedious, and humorless . . . [taking] on social roles he had earlier critiqued to lecture from the pulpits of a priest, a doctor, a professor, a diplomat, a politician, and a policeman."[21]

The first three chapters of this book examine the formative period of Moreno's career, up to the mid-1940s. Chapter 1 contains a thematic discussion of the roots of Cantinflas in Mexican popular culture. The pelado character was a staple of the carpa theater, and Moreno borrowed the various aspects of his character, including the chaotic verbiage, the tavern humor, the political discourses, and the gender transgressions, from folklore, comic strips, and contemporary actors. Chapter 2 describes Moreno's attempts to modify his stage character for a more general cinema audience. The character Cantinflas was very much a collaborative effort in the late 1930s, using dialogue from diverse screenwriters, directors, and journalists while also incorporating Moreno's own improvisations. This experimental period produced what many see as some of his most interesting films, but the working-class jokes and frankly homoerotic behavior proved too threatening for middle-class viewers. Chapter 3 relates how Moreno finally arrived, with *Ahí está el detalle,* at a successful formula, less avant-garde and more commercially oriented, that brought him genuine stardom. His career therefore represented a synthesis of popular culture and the media industry, but a tense one still marked by internal contradictions. Moreover, although he received almost universal applause in the Spanish-speaking world, his character failed to gain acceptance in the United States, in part because of the difficulty translating his nonsense discourses, but also because he refused to play to Hollywood stereotypes of the Mexican.

The second stage of his career, running from the mid-1940s to the mid-1950s, marked his incorporation into Mexico's governing elite. Chapter 4 describes the peculiar reversal of roles that transformed a comic specializing in parodies of labor bosses into a union leader in his own right. Moreno's political career began with a struggle by the Mexican screen actors' guild to gain independence from the corrupt directors of the national entertainment workers' federation, but it soon became conflated with a larger struggle for union democracy. Although he negotiated

serious issues, Moreno never escaped from the comic shadow of
Cantinflas in the eyes of labor leaders, the media, and the public. Simply put, whatever Moreno said sounded to the public
like just another Cantinflas joke, demonstrating that although
the union victory assured Moreno undisputed control over the
production of Cantinflas movies, he could not control the audience reception of that character. And when the ruling elite tried
to take advantage of the political capital inherent in his popular appeal, the gap between what he said and what people
heard widened still farther. Chapter 5 examines the ways in
which Moreno began, about 1950, to make films in support of
the government's program of industrialization. Justified with the
rhetoric of social revolution, the plan actually promoted "trickle-
down" growth by restricting pay raises for workers and concentrating capital with investors. Associating with a regime that
co-opted or repressed working-class leaders to ensure the success of this development policy caused the millionaire actor
gradually to lose touch with the lives of common people, although without losing their affection.

While at the peak of his international fame, performing in
the blockbuster *Around the World in 80 Days* (1956), Moreno
set the stage for the final betrayal of his character, Cantinflas.
Chapter 6 recounts his Hollywood adventures, first in the role of
Passepartout, the valet who accompanied Phileas Fogg on his
global journey. Playing opposite David Niven's stuffy English
gentleman allowed Moreno to recreate through physical humor
the carnivalesque atmosphere of *Ahí está el detalle* even without
the Spanish-language wordplay. The film's enormous success
tempted Moreno to make a second movie in the United States,
Pepe (1960), which contained all of the extravagance but none
of the charm of his previous effort. Supremely confident of his
improvisational skill, Moreno took little interest in the script,
and so almost by default he sacrificed his beloved character to
Hollywood stereotypes. The final chapter narrates his return
home after the failure of *Pepe*. Sensing that the pelado from the
1930s no longer resonated with Mexican reality three decades
later, Moreno attempted to recapture his youth through a facelift
and juvenile scripts, but these tactics only succeeded in making
him a parody of his former self. Moreover, he had become tied

so closely to the ruling party that he was unable to respond to the common people, and his final movies appeared to many as stilted and preachy.

Through it all, Moreno retained his popularity with the Mexican people, largely through the power of his personality. From the very beginning, critics spoke with wonder of his tremendous charisma, and even the harshest reviewers had to concede his "magnetism for dominating the public."[22] The most common word used to describe him, *genial,* perhaps best conveys the extent of his charm. The English cognate "genial," with its sense of warmth and cheerfulness, certainly applied to Cantinflas, but in Spanish the term meant far more. It implied a literal genius— as one reviewer put it, "He is a genius of grace"—in addition to a sense of magnificence or grandeur.[23] Finally, and appropriately for Cantinflas, the word conveyed an ironic meaning—the brilliant ideas of a lunatic. But he was a lunatic who embodied the quixotic Mexican quest for modernity, that social panacea that always remained just beyond reach.

1

FROM VALE COYOTE
TO THE CARPA VALENTINA

Modernity—that complex of industrial capitalism and urban-ization, which pulled migrants from the provinces into a frenzied city life of trolley cars, factory labor, mass-market newspapers, weekend sports, and motion pictures—arrived in Mexico about the turn of the twentieth century, with destabiliz-ing consequences for traditional society. On a personal level, this meant that in 1900, Soledad Reyes Guízar, a debutante from Michoacán, married beneath her, a postal employee from San Luis Potosí named Pedro Moreno Esquivel. Without the assis-tance of her disapproving family, they moved through a succes-sion of tenement houses in Mexico City and Guadalajara. After ten years of marriage and six pregnancies, the couple lived with their three surviving children in Colonia Guerrero, a working-class barrio on the northwest side of Mexico City. Their apart-ment was convenient, just up Santa María la Redonda from the National Post Office, if not quiet, because of the bustling nightlife centered on Plaza Garibaldi, a few blocks away. And in that home, at about 12:30 on the night of August 12, 1911, was born the future king of Mexican popular theater and cinema, Mario Moreno Reyes.

Cantinflas made his debut some twenty years later in one of the provisional tent theaters, known as carpas in Mexico, clus-tered around Plaza Garibaldi and other working-class neighbor-hoods. According to legend, his distinctive manner of speaking developed by accident, when the inexperienced actor forgot his lines in a fit of stage fright and began mumbling incoherent nonsense. The audience laughed more at the babbling than they

1

The pelado and the city slicker, stock figures of the carpa theater, portrayed by Mario Moreno "Cantinflas" and Manuel Medel. Aguila o sol, *production still. Courtesy: Cineteca Nacional.*

had at the jokes, and he continued the practice for the rest of his career. The name Cantinflas was equally meaningless, a slurred remark made some evening by a drunk in the crowd. In this unconscious way, Moreno tapped deep traditions within Mexican popular culture. Success in the carpa depended above all on creating a distinctive personality from a standard cast of characters common to popular theaters everywhere: country bumpkins, city slickers, cops, queers, harlots, and shrews. Cantinflas proved to be an inspired name for the character of the town drunk because it combined the word "cantina" with a slang term for getting drunk, "te inflas" (inflate yourself), in some apparently secret code the exact meaning of which was open to endless speculation. His nonsense humor also permitted a multitude of interpretations, so that the diverse regional cultures that compose the Mexican nation, and indeed the entire Hispanic world, could claim him as their own.

The stage on which both Mario Moreno and Cantinflas played was the epic Revolution of 1910, which began in opposition to the dictator Porfirio Díaz and continued to dominate Mexican life for the rest of the twentieth century. Díaz first became president in 1876 through a revolution dedicated to "effective suffrage and no reelection," then proceeded to gain reelection on seven consecutive occasions, from 1884 to 1910. During that long tenure, he invited foreign capitalists to develop the Mexican economy, to the chagrin of local businessmen unable to compete with the imported technology and tax rebates of the outsiders. The country achieved rapid economic growth, enriching an elite minority, but poverty remained widespread in urban slums and rural villages. The Porfirian state co-opted or repressed opposition through a policy of *pan o palo* (bread or the club), enforced by the dreaded *rurales* (rural police). Francisco I. Madero, the son of a wealthy family, protested the sham of democracy and the perpetual reelection, and when Díaz promised an honest election and then reneged in 1910, Madero called for a revolution using the dictator's old slogan. The insurgency triumphed, bringing Madero to the presidency but also revealing the country's deep social divisions. Civil war continued for much of the decade as rival factions fought to control Mexico's destiny. The victorious generals finally restored peace in 1920 and began implementing revolutionary reforms, providing land to the peasants, allowing unions in the factories, and reserving the national wealth for the Mexican people.

This chapter examines thematically the roots of Cantinflas in Mexican popular culture. It begins with the tavern culture of eighteenth-century Mexico City, a racially mixed, often violent society, comprising large numbers of recent migrants from the countryside. Although these spiritual ancestors of Cantinflas stood at the very bottom of a social hierarchy, they nevertheless had as much concern for personal dignity as the highest noble. Everyday social interactions entailed struggles for rank, and plebeians developed elaborate word games using double entendres with sexual connotations to outwit and thereby undermine the honor of their social superiors. This peculiar language, which later became the hallmark of Cantinflas, is described in the second section of this chapter. Colonial contests of honor resurfaced in twentieth-century Mexican political discourse, as the next section illustrates. The political theater became an vital part of Mexican civil society, as Mario Moreno and other actors portraying members of the lower classes publicly discussed government scandals that print journalists dared not mention. By defusing their critiques through humor, comedians and their audiences intervened in political debates while avoiding the worst effects of censorship. The theatrical treatment of a social revolution in gender roles that Mexico was undergoing in the first half of the twentieth century forms the basis for another section of the chapter. Also examined are the aesthetic sensibility and improvisational skills that Mario Moreno acquired while working in this popular theater and carried with him through his entire film career. The conclusion then summarizes Cantinflas's lineage in popular culture by tracing the evolution of the trickster archetype throughout Mexican history.

Plebeian Culture in the City of Palaces

Although the apparatus of modern life, from factories and cinemas to streetcars and sports, proliferated in Mexico only at the end of the nineteenth century, the country experienced the first social disruptions of modernity a hundred years earlier in the late colonial period. A bonanza of silver mining and agricultural exports brought unprecedented wealth to the merchants of New Spain and their Bourbon kings. Migrants from the countryside flooded into Mexico City, but only a third of its 137,000 residents could find regular employment. The rest lived precariously from day labor, petty commerce, begging, or criminal activities and slept in overcrowded tenements or in the streets. This urban underclass of mixed racial heritage also entertained itself in public, laughing at puppet shows and street theaters, drinking in makeshift taverns, and making love in the shadows. Both the patterns of plebeian culture and the methods designed by Bourbon officials to police them continued in force a century and a half later when Cantinflas arrived on the scene.[1]

The Spanish conquistadors had founded Mexico City on the ruins of the Aztec capital, which inadvertently ensured the mixing of races despite legal attempts at segregation. The city center, called the *traza,* was laid down in a grid pattern of roughly thirteen square blocks reserved for European settlers and their African slaves. The viceroy's palace and the cathedral, monuments to the colonial authority of the Spanish crown and the Catholic Church, stood on the central plaza, flanked by noble mansions, religious cloisters, and apartment buildings. Just outside the traza lay the winding streets and adobe dwellings of San Juan Tenochtitlan, whose Native American residents entered the Spanish sector daily for labor and commerce. With few European women in residence in the early days, colonists took wives, or more often concubines, from their Indian and African servants. Elite society accepted the fiction that legitimate children of Spanish-Indian marriages were Creoles, a term for Europeans of pure blood born in the Americas. But mestizo children without a Spanish patron were either raised as Indians in their mothers' native barrio or joined an urban underclass of mixed-race, *castas,* of which Cantinflas later became an exemplar. Miscegenation continued until ethnicity was more a function of wealth and culture than physical characteristics, and established Creole families became obsessed with genealogy, both to demonstrate their own racial purity and to distinguish themselves from the street people known as *léperos.* To keep the lower classes in their place, the elite devised an elaborate hierarchy of castas, comprising every conceivable racial combination, with derogatory labels such as "coyote mestizo." The colonial policy of divide and rule seemed all the more urgent as léperos penetrated the heart of the traza, establishing their thieves' market in the Plaza del Volador, just across from the viceroy's palace.[2]

Migration from the countryside multiplied this floating population of castas to alarming proportions toward the end of the eighteenth century. Fleeing from rural poverty and hunger, the newcomers had trouble finding steady work in the trades, private service, the textile workshops, or the Royal Tobacco Manufactory. Unable to make ends meet, even by peddling or scavenging, many turned to crime; police records revealed that nearly half of those arrested in 1796 had been born outside the city. Urban services meanwhile strained to accommodate the influx of people. Apartment houses and humble shacks were subdivided among growing crowds of tenants; without indoor kitchens, tenants took meals in the streets; aqueducts carrying fresh water to poor neighborhoods began to run dry; and waste disposal proved completely inadequate to clear filth from the streets. The character of Cantinflas, as an unwashed country bumpkin who lived by his wits, had thus become a familiar figure in Bourbon Mexico City.[3]

The social life of plebeian men, and many women, centered on the city's taverns, which numbered about sixteen hundred (more than half of which were unlicensed) and which were particularly common in streets and alleys just outside the traza. The largest of these establishments served five to six hundred customers at a time, opening early for workers on their way to the six o'clock morning shift. Oftentimes craftsmen never made it to work and spent the entire day drinking *pulque,* the fermented juice of the agave plant, while musicians played rowdy tunes. At times the establishments quieted down long enough for the reading of a satiric poem critical of colonial authorities. Drinking formed an essential part of the plebeian sense of community, and it was considered rude to walk out of a tavern—far better to be carried. Cantinflas later made this alcoholic performance a standard part of his act, as did young boys of the colonial period who participated vicariously in this tavern culture through a popular game of playing drunk in the streets.[4]

Colonial authorities sought to limit such disorderly conduct by encouraging theatergoing as a wholesome alternative to bar hopping. Early missionary friars used passion plays and other

dramatic performances to instruct Native Americans in the doctrines of Catholicism, and the Royal Hospital of the Indians established a theater, later known as the Coliseum, to help support
its charitable functions. Meanwhile, popular comic troupes
played informal neighborhood *corrales* (open-air theaters), and
satirical puppet shows proliferated on Calle Ensinas and in numerous alleys. Street performances were always boisterous affairs, but even the legitimate playhouse, intended to civilize
natives and castas, often degenerated into a carnivalesque spectacle of catcalls, fist fights, and disorderliness. Eighteenth-
century Bourbon officials tried to restore order by enforcing
moral standards for actors and actresses, renowned for their disreputable behavior, and by arresting disruptive members of the
audience. But restrictions on the formal theater merely heightened the rowdiness of popular alternatives.[5]

The Bourbon reformers also tried to force beggars to contribute to society, thereby replacing religious charity with the
poorhouse. Begging, an honorable tradition in medieval Catholicism, exemplified the ideal of poverty in imitation of Christ.
Moreover, giving alms to the poor counted as one of the classic
good works allowing the forgiveness of sins. Notwithstanding
the acceptance of begging, later colonial society distinguished
the worthy poor unable to earn a living from outsiders who had
no legitimate claim on the community. The Bourbons, in their
tireless quest for greater productivity, began drafting the urban
poor for public works projects. In 1774 the viceroy prohibited
begging entirely and ordered the aged, infirm, and needy into
a newly founded Hospital of the Poor, which soon gained a
reputation as a jail for idlers. Thus Cantinflas's scorn for work
was as much a desire to avoid conscript labor as a simple case
of laziness. Nevertheless, one institution established by the Bourbons and appreciated by the poor was the Monte de Piedad
(Royal Pawnshop), founded in 1775 to extend low-interest loans
to people who were regularly forced to pawn their clothes to
buy food and other necessities—a service that is still performed
to the present day.[6]

The devastating Wars of Independence and the political
chaos of the early republic interrupted the Bourbon reforms, but
by the time Porfirio Díaz assumed the presidency in 1876, the
quest had resumed for order and progress. When the dictator

finally left office in 1911, the capital had tripled in size to 470,000 inhabitants, transforming the urban landscape of the colonial traza. Wealthy families that had survived the nineteenth-century upheavals, along with their arriviste counterparts, moved west into European-style mansions along the fashionable Paseo de la Reforma, leaving the decaying colonial palaces north and east of the city center to be divided into low-rent apartments. Factory owners and merchants lived in the suburban *colonias* (developments) of Roma and Condesa, and working-class housing extended north into such colonias as Guerrero, home of the Moreno Reyes family, and Tepito, a former Indian community that became the new location of the thieves' market after it was displaced by urban renewal from the Plaza del Volador.

The léperos of the colonial period became known during the Porfirian age as pelados. Literally "pealed," stripped clean, penniless, or raped, the term also implied bald or shaved, a reference to migrants from the countryside who tried to fit into the city by cutting their long hair, which was a mark of distinction in Native American communities and humiliating to lose. Like their eighteenth-century forerunners, the pelados lived a precarious existence, always looking for their next meal and a flophouse in which to sleep. The elite believed that they drank pulque to excess, bathed not at all, and composed, in the words of the Catholic newspaper *El Tiempo,* "one of the most vile underclasses in the world, as dirty as it is insolent."[7] The Porfirian police carried on the Bourbon campaign of repression, enacting a law in 1897 against so-called *rateros* (petty thieves) that served as a pretext for arresting thousands of loiterers and beggars, many of them children under the age of ten. The material conditions that gave birth to Cantinflas thus reached deep into Mexican history, and his distinctive manner of speech also drew on long-established popular forms.

The Language of the Vacilada

Nobel laureate Octavio Paz lamented the Mexican tendency to mask reality through dissembling speech and empty politesse. Whereas Spaniards often spoke with brutal directness—as the saying goes, "al pan, pan, y al vino, vino," calling bread and wine by their names—Mexicans contrived infinite stratagems for disguising their intentions and concealing their natures. The poet attributed this linguistic camouflage to a history of colonial subjugation and a fear of shame or embarrassment. Because the social pecking order depended on public recognition of honor, every personal encounter and every spoken word comprised a ritualized duel for status. But the phrases and gestures of deference inevitably contained the means of their own subversion; the verbal jousts that established hierarchies could also liberate people from them through the *vacilada,* a carnivalesque laughter capable of turning the world upside down. In bemoaning the apparent aggressiveness of the national character revealed by popular speech, Paz and other intellectuals overlooked the life-giving qualities of this playful, irreverent language, which was common to all Mexicans and particularly manifest in the humor of Cantinflas.[8]

About 1930, the very moment that Mario Moreno made his theatrical break, Carleton Beals described the vacilada as a particular mode of conduct founded on extravagant individualism. Artistic expressions of the vacilada included the reckless exaggerations and whimsical distortions of the Baroque age in New Spain and the satiric caricatures of the national period. Beals observed that outsiders often dismissed such vaciladas as passionate, willful, and irrational. "The Mexican's approach to life, death, and sex, an approach dominated by the vacilada, is shot through with poetic irresponsibility; it defies direct logic, takes serious things lightly, and insignificant things with great gravity. This is a gracious and self-protective distortion, a creative destruction of values cherished by the European mind."[9] The peculiar logic of the vacilada made sense given the social conditions of New Spain.

Colonial society ranked individuals in an elaborate hierarchy of *calidad* (quality) based on racial purity, noble status, wealth and occupation, and personal honor. Knighthood, or its religious counterpart in one of the holy orders, constituted prima facie evidence of calidad, but even caballeros had to remain vigilant to preserve their reputations. Masculine honor depended primarily on safeguarding the sexual purity of female relatives, to avoid contamination of the bloodline, whereas feminine virtue resided in chastity and modest behavior. Any form of public disrespect hinted at sexual impropriety or lack of family honor, making members of the elite extremely sensitive to outward signs of deference. They addressed subordinates with the familiar "tu" and demanded the formal "Usted" in response. Body language also communicated respect, and the failure to doff one's hat and maintain a submissive posture in the presence of superiors or, worse still, making rude gestures showed extreme contempt. Nobles considered honor to be an exclusive privilege of rank, but plebeians nevertheless insisted on maintaining their dignity. Even the poorest mestizo could claim a measure of calidad based on a reputation for honest work and could thereby assure himself legitimate standing within the community.[10]

Plebeian Mexicans jostled for rank and belittled authority through vaciladas, which confused the language of deference, debasing the mighty and exalting the insignificant. The principal expression of linguistic subversion came in the form of *albures,* double-entendres with obscene allusions, used as assertions of superior masculinity in verbal contests of one-upmanship that Cantinflas later mastered. Anthropologist John M. Ingham recorded a number of modern examples from a rural community in central Mexico. "A friend named Martín may be greeted, '¡Hola Martín Cholano!'—the significant syllables being *in-cho* (I swell) and *ano* (anus). When a friend refers to another as *vale* (pal), the other may say, 'No me digas vale porque mi leche se me sale' (Don't call me pal, because my milk will come out)."[11] By implying passive homosexuality, albures robbed their victims of masculinity, thereby allowing clever plebeians to gain status at the expense of witless nabobs—but at the risk of violence, which often resulted from such challenges to honor.[12]

Albures also provided a means of subverting civil and ecclesiastical authorities. Eighteenth-century Inquisitors denounced the widespread performance of lewd songs and dances mocking church officials, the holy sacraments, and the Ten Commandments. One popular ditty proclaimed that the brothers of the Order of San Juan de Dios "are such pigs they grab the women and grope their bacon."[13] During the Wars of Independence, from 1810 to 1821, the patriotic pamphleteer José Joaquín

Fernández de Lizardi used the vocabulary of the poor, so rich in double entendres, as a way of evading Spanish censorship. His broadsheets bore seemingly innocuous titles, such as "There Are Many Shepherds Who Shall Dance in Bethlehem"—a covert way of saying that royalist priests would end up in the Belén prison. Lizardi wove these pamphlets into a picaresque narrative published in 1816 as Mexico's first novel, *El Periquillo Sarniento* (The Itching Parrot), thus creating high literature from the street language that Cantinflas eventually made his own.

Irreverent attacks on the social hierarchy and political authority continued as a staple of popular culture long after Mexico gained independence in 1821. The *títeres,* or puppet theater, provided one of the most widespread forms of popular expression, as puppet masters traveled the countryside, giving performances at saint's day festivals in towns and villages. The most famous troupe of the nineteenth century, the Rosete Aranda brothers, featured the puppet Vale Coyote, a "coyote" mestizo "pal" whose name betrayed his common origins. The "Discourse of Vale Coyote" employed the same halting, nonsensical language later adopted by Cantinflas to parody the patriotic speeches made by government officials throughout the republic on the anniversary of independence. It began with a series of cheers: "Viva the peace! Viva the faith! Viva the grace and doctrine! Viva the 36th of September of 1814! Viva all the Herods of the fatherland and *viva yo!*"[14] The final cry, literally meaning "long live me," could more accurately be translated as "up yours!"

A more recent antecedent to Cantinflas appeared in the Sunday morning comics of *El Universal,* beginning on September 25, 1927, under the title "Vaciladas de Chupamirto." The author, Jesús Acosta, named his character "myrtle sucker," a slang term for the hummingbird, a perennial trickster in Mexican folklore. As a pelado from Tepito, Chupamirto engaged in endless wordplay, giving literal interpretations to slang as a means of destabilizing the social hierarchy. When a well-dressed bourgeois instructed the vagabond to make his car shine like glass (échale vidrio a mi coche), he covered the driver's seat with broken glass. On another occasion, Chupamirto discovered a wallet on the street, then cursed with disappointment when it contained no money, just a health department credential. But the next time a policeman caught him feeling up a young woman, he whipped out the badge and announced with disdain, "Look, ox, that's why I'm the meat inspector."[15]

Chupamirto represented the petty thief from Tepito, and his dialect mimicked the thieves' patois of that notorious barrio. To evade police informers, members of this criminal underworld—and their honest but equally harassed neighbors—perfected the art of verbal misdirection, going far beyond the usual range of albures. This popular idiom seemed extremely limited by normal linguistic measures, using at most three of the ten possible tenses in Spanish and avoiding the subjunctive mood entirely. Nevertheless, speakers conjugated verbs in such an arbitrary and strange manner that all statements appeared contingent and doubtful. Everyday vocabulary was likewise reduced to a minimum, for example, blurring distinctions of color down to the three primaries, with no gradations in between. But pelados drew on a seemingly infinite number of terms for useful concepts such as money (*lana* and *luz,* literally wool and light), cops (*tecolotes* and *Don Nalgas,* respectively, owls and "Mr. Buttocks"), and chumps (*pacos, bartolos, zurumatos*). Individual words were also compressed, syllables dropped out randomly, and sounds changed. The letter "b" came out as a slurred "g" so instead of greeting someone with "buenos días," a pelado mumbled a simple "güeno." The dialect of Tepito reached the pinnacle of incomprehensibility with the so-called *arte-acá* (art of the here), in which the words for "here" and "there" became so interchanged and confused that outsiders had no hope of deciphering the secret code.[16]

Mario Moreno drew on this popular language in creating the speech of Cantinflas. He coined many slang words, most notably *gacho* (nincompoop), but his signature phrase "ahí está el detalle" came straight off the streets. Pelados used this saying in countless situations: to describe a difficult problem, to signal the unclear part of an explanation, to indicate a woman they were chasing, or as a euphemism for a marijuana cigarette. Another typical Cantinflas vacilada consisted of alternating between respect and familiarity in his extended dialogues with authority figures. Cantinflas subverted the social hierarchy with body language as well as speech; the ongoing joke of his drooping pants threatened at every moment to reveal his buttocks, one of the most offensive gestures in Mexican popular culture. These malicious actions were nevertheless redeemed by his genial smile and good-humored nature.[17]

Indeed, although often associated with short-tempered plebeians, albures were common to all social classes and only rarely resulted in violence. Poetry tournaments of the colonial period had rules specifically ordering "the elimination, even in humorous passages, of a false playing on words susceptible of double meaning; only one meaning may be used, leaving the other implicit in the sound of the word"—a clear indication that even dignified academics resorted to such puns.[18] A playful interrogation of language, stretching grammatical rules and inverting semantic content, composes the everyday poetry of Mexican speech; for example, confusion has spread far beyond Tepito from the tendency to use the word *hasta* to mean "beginning at" as well as the more proper "until."[19] Puns appeared prominently in political as well as social humor, especially the popular theater that emerged during the Revolution of 1910 as one of the foundations of Mexican civil society.

Political Theater in a Revolutionary Society

From the flat top of his boat hat to the silver tip of his walking stick, Leopoldo Beristáin looked every inch the bourgeois, and therefore completely out of place in the working-class barrio of Peralvillo. But each day he passed under the dragon-emblazoned marquee of the María Guerrero Theater, popularly known as the "María Tepache" for the numerous taverns that lined the street. After changing from his smartly tailored summer suit into white cotton pajamas, he went out on stage to be greeted by affectionate cries of "Cuatezón" (Big Drinking Buddy). Beristáin acted the part of the inebriated Indian from Xochimilco, a theatrical village idiot and the prototype for Cantinflas's character. "El Cuatezón" delighted audiences with trenchant political commentary slurred into his drunken discourse, but the crowds were no mere passive recipients of his satire. They boisterously joined in the conversation, helping to make the so-called frivolous theater one of the most influential and democratic voices of Mexico's revolutionary society.

Clifford Geertz coined the term "theater state" to describe the government of nineteenth-century Bali, where political authority derived from court rituals demonstrating the divine sanction of the ruling dynasty. European historians, building on Jürgen Habermas's theory of the public sphere, have likewise shown that during the Enlightenment an appreciation of operas, plays, and essays gave the middle classes the necessary confidence in their own critical judgment to claim political rights from absolute monarchs.[20] Eighteenth-century Mexican audiences also used satirical theater to claim a political voice from the repressive Bourbon regime. The New Coliseum filled to capacity in 1790 when a play about the torture and execution of the last Aztec emperor, Cuauhtémoc, slipped past a substitute censor with only a change of title, from *México rebelado* (Mexico in rebellion) to *México segunda vez conquistado* (Mexico conquered a second time). Emotions ran high as native-born Creoles and peninsular Spaniards began taking sides with the characters and shouting political commentaries under cover of the darkened playhouse. The portrayal of Cortés as a greedy and vicious brute earned the play both the rapturous applause of Mexican patriots and the wrath of Spanish officials, who immediately banned the show. In 1866, with the country occupied by the soldiers of Napoleon III, a bold theatrical company in Mexico City lampooned the French-imposed Emperor Maximilian in a comedy entitled *Aventuras de un monarca* (Adventures of a monarch).[21]

Political drama also heralded the onset of the Revolution of 1910, which toppled the dictatorship of Porfirio Díaz. The 1906 strike at the Cananea copper mine in Sonora inspired a musical called *Sangre obrera* (Workers' blood) in honor of the scores of strikers who died at the hands of Mexican police and Arizona Rangers. Meanwhile, the slavelike conditions of many workers on large plantations formed the basis for *En la hacienda* (On the hacienda). The Indian hero of this work pointedly questioned Porfirian justice with the observation that the poor knew only one law, the *ley fuga* (law of flight), under which rural policemen shot suspects in the back for supposedly fleeing arrest. Nevertheless, other theater companies supported the Porfirian regime and attacked the democratic reformer Francisco I. Madero. Congressman José Juan Tablada wrote the "zoological political tragicomedy" *Madero-Chantacler,* in which the title character, a rooster, campaigned for president on a platform calling for a whole week of Holy Mondays, the unofficial holiday dedicated to sleeping off the drunken excesses of Sunday, "and the employers will pay vacation time!" In reality, Díaz arrested his opponent and stole the election of 1910, leading Madero to issue the Plan of San Luis Potosí calling for a revolution against the dictatorship. Beristáin, who had once given a command performance for the president, enlisted his pelado character in the army to bolster federal morale. The production *Juan Soldado* denounced the Maderista rebels as a pack of assassins before mixed audiences in Mexico City, but not even the Cuatezón could stop rebel commanders Francisco "Pancho" Villa and Pascual Orozco in the field. In May 1911 the aging Díaz sailed off to a European exile.[22]

Madero returned to the campaign trail that summer to vindicate his military victory with a free and open election against a prominent Porfirian politician, General Bernardo Reyes. As campaign posters cluttered the sidewalks and speeches filled the air, another political drama unfold at the Lírico Theater, *El Tenorio Maderista,* a parody of José Zorrilla's *Don Juan Tenorio.* Partisans of Madero cheered as their hero, in the role of Don Juan, rescued Doña Inés, symbolizing the Mexican people, from the scarcely disguised Porfirio Noches. Police stood by to restrain the outrage of Porfirians during the final scene as Don Juan stood triumphant over the graves of Tyranny, Oppression, and Perpetual Government. The comedy played for an unprecedented fifty-five nights, on the wave of excitement from Madero's campaign. The playwrights, Luis G. Andrade and Leandro Blanco, followed that success with *La Presi Alegre,* a parody of *The Merry Widow,* which opened to popular acclaim on October 6, a week before the election. But unlike *El Tenorio,* with its criticism of Porfirian tyranny, this light-hearted romantic comedy, about the Presidency choosing Madero from among her many suitors, offered only the message that no political romance should last longer than the constitutional limit of one term.[23]

If the euphoria surrounding Madero's election curbed political satire in legitimate theaters, comedians maintained a vigilant watch over the new administration from improvised stages in popular barrios. An anonymous parody of Andrade and Blanco's *Tenorio Maderista* playing in one such venue treated the incoming president with neither respect nor trust. This representation of the wealthy Madero revealed his uneasy relationship with the impoverished masses by calling Doña Inés "drinking partner of my soul" and "Indian woman of my heart." She returned the favor by snubbing him with the nickname *"chaparrito"* (little shrub), a sure laugh because of his short stature. But her affectionate speech revealed, more profoundly, both popular adoration of the new president and ambivalence about his commitment to democratic principles. "Oh, Madero, I could not resist you if you would not fulfill your program of justice!" She said this in a confusion of subjunctives and double negatives that left the outcome completely in doubt. "Your seductive glance is giving me a beating *[paliza]*," she continued, with a reference to the Porfirian policy of pan o palo, "and your fascinating voice is driving me crazy and making me sick." The question of whether the new government would carry on the authoritarian traditions of the old received its answer in Madero's final couplet: "Don't get wrinkled, old leather, because I want you for a drum!"[24]

As the anonymous playwright predicted, Madero rejected social reforms and retained the services of the Porfirian army and bureaucracy. But he paid for this conservatism with his life following a military coup of February 1913, when General Victoriano Huerta seized power. Maderista partisans challenged the military dictatorship with the Constitutionalist revolution led by Generals Pancho Villa, Alvaro Obregón, and Venustiano Carranza. Meanwhile at the María Tepache in Mexico City, Beristáin and his company continued to play the *revista* (review) theater, so called because of its commentary on the daily news. "Their audience was utterly hybrid," recalled artist José Clemente Orozco, "the filthiest scum of the city mixed with intellectuals and artists, with army officers, bureaucrats, politicians, and even secretaries of state."[25] Huerta himself cultivated a friendship with the popular comedian, who had to flee into exile as a result of that friendship when the Constitutionalists triumphed in the summer of 1914. The revolution then entered its bloodiest stage in the spring of 1915 as a civil war erupted between the revolutionary armies. The brilliant tactician Obregón defeated the headstrong Villa in a series of climactic battles. Notwithstanding the defeat of the lower-class armies, the Constitution of 1917 contained radical land and labor reforms in addition to provisions for economic nationalism and secular education.

With the restoration of peace in 1920 revolutionary generals turned politicians began to implement these reforms under the critical gaze of the political theater. Obregón dedicated his presidential administration (1920–1924) to agrarian reform, the construction of rural schools, and the negotiations with foreign oil companies that had gained immense subsoil rights under Díaz and whose Mexican businesses had subsequently been subject to nationalization by the new constitution. The general was as well known for his clever jokes as for his military skill, and he kept a sense of humor while playwright Antonio Guzmán Aguilera, known as Guz Aguila, turned out a succession of political satires. One such satire was *El Jardin de Obregón,* in which the Spanish pronunciation of *jardin* (garden) punned the last name of President Warren G. Harding, with whom Obregón negotiated the petroleum question. After an unsuccessful military rebellion in 1923, Obregón's protégé, Plutarco Elías Calles, took office in 1924 and worked to strengthen the official union, the Regional Confederation of Mexican Workers (Confederación Regional Obrera Mexicana, or CROM). Union boss Luis Napoleon Morones, an enormously fat former plumber with a taste for diamond rings and flashy cars, personally accumulated a business empire as minister of industry under Calles. The CROM leader's blatant corruption provided endless material for the successor to Beristáin as Mexico's leading comic, Roberto Soto, known as "El Panzón" because of his equally huge belly. One popular comedy, *Trapitos al sol,* promised to hang the government's dirty laundry out in the sun, whereas another, *El camarada Tenorio,* revived Don Juan as a Bolshevik comrade. "El Panzón" Soto also spoofed the notoriously anticlerical governor of Tabasco, Tomás Garrido Canabal, a fierce opponent of the Catholic insurgency movement known as the Cristero Rebellion (1926–1929).

The political theater thus served as a bulwark of Mexico's civil society, educating the public and criticizing the government. During the Constitutionalist movement, Obregón had instructed theatrical companies to stage *En la hacienda* as a form of revolutionary propaganda. And when Calles ordered the exile of Guz Aguila following the rebellion of 1923, the president refused to intervene on his friend's behalf, saying, "He is more responsible

than the generals I have just shot."[26] Despite death threats from
hot-tempered generals, playwrights continually stretched the
boundaries of acceptability, and the cognoscente made a point
of attending Saturday night premieres to hear the best jokes before they were censored. On one occasion, the notoriously un-
funny President Calles attended to see himself parodied. At the
moment of truth, the crowd held its breath—Calles cracked up,
and the show went on.[27] Improvisation provided another way of
avoiding censorship, for if a joke was not present in the script,
the author could not be held responsible. The playwright's
words also fell victim to the whims of the audience, who often
took over this form of political discourse by shouting out their
own crude albures. José Clemente Orozco complained that
spectators "conducted themselves worse than at bullfights; they
pushed their way into the very performances, taking the most
familiar tone with the actors and actresses, and insulting one another and making such changes in the dialogue that no two performances were alike."[28]

But what the muralist lamented as a loss of theatrical art
opened a space for democratic action in which the lower
classes could destroy the credibility of their authoritarian rulers.
Political power in revolutionary Mexico, like personal honor in
New Spain, depended on public recognition and deference. A
general without the strength of character to order troops in battle, like a populist politician without the charisma to inspire the
masses, was as laughable as he was impotent. Such reputation
obviously derived from a subtle calculus of many variables. The
ability to laugh at oneself, as had Obregón, and to a lesser extent Calles, demonstrated an unquestioning self-confidence that
commanded respect from others. But a politician who became
the laughingstock of others and lacked the power to suppress
their mirth could not long hold onto his office.

Instability within the government heightened the possibilities
for such popular participation. The political theater gained prominence in the early days of the Madero revolution and reached its
pinnacle of influence during the Maximato (1928–1934), when a
succession of three interim presidents struggled to hold office.
The troubles began with the assassination of Obregón at a banquet celebrating his reelection as president. The general's followers accused Callista rivals of plotting the murder, and renewed

civil war threatened to destroy the ruling coalition. Vowing not to run for office again, Calles founded the National Revolutionary Party (Partido Nacional Revolucionario, PNR) to institutionalize the presidential succession, then attempted to run the system from behind the scenes. But playing the puppet master required a deft sense of balance, particularly during the interim presidency of Emilio Portes Gil, when the Obregón faction remained ascendant. Portes Gil, an agrarian leader with a hatred for the CROM, enlisted the popular theater as an ally in his struggle against Calles and his labor crony. Miguel Covarrubias wrote, "It is generally acknowledged that Soto's satire had a good deal to do with the discredit and the downfall of Morones."[29]

The power play began at the CROM national convention on December 3, 1928, within days after the interim president's inauguration. Morones opened the meeting with a blistering attack on Obregonista enemies within the new administration, and Calles followed with an imprudent promise that he would always remain loyal to the union. Roberto Soto immediately staged a parody entitled *El desmoronamiento* ("De-Morones-izing," or Slow dissolution), in which he dressed in a Roman toga and shouted between hiccups: "Viva the proletariat!" The satire was all the more devastating because "El Panzón" had been a regular guest at the orgies thrown by Morones on a Tlalpan ranch that the labor boss kept well-stocked with alcohol and prostitutes. CROM appeals to the government to suppress the revista as "detrimental" to Mexican labor backfired when the president stationed federal troops outside the Lírico Theater to prevent union toughs from disrupting the show. Portes Gil also used the humiliating spectacle to extract a public statement from Calles renouncing all claims to political authority.[30]

As the Desmoronamiento showed, the government condoned the theater in part because it could be manipulated for political purposes. Officials gave financial support to plays that were sympathetic to their cause, just as they paid off journalists for favorable reporting. Calles survived the loss of his union ally and gradually consolidated his power behind the scenes as *jefe máximo* (Maximum Chief), using political satire to decrease the independence of future presidents. Pascual Ortiz Rubio, who was inaugurated in 1930, once found a sign on the lawn of his official residence announcing: "The president lives here, the one who rules is across the street"—a reference to Calles's mansion. Unable to achieve respect, let alone independence, he woke up one morning in 1932 to read in the newspaper of his own resignation. When Abelardo Rodríguez was appointed to finish the term, Calles used albures to subvert the president's foreign relations by informing U.S. Ambassador Josephus Daniels that Señora de Rodríguez wore the pants in the first family.[31] This remark, intended to insure that Calles stayed informed of diplomatic matters, also illustrated how the personal was political in revolutionary Mexico.

Plays of Gender and Modernity

In 1925, Madame Berthe Rassimí succeeded where Emperor Napoleon III had failed, by conquering Mexico, not by force of French arms, but rather through the beauty of French legs. *Voilá le Ba-ta-clán* stormed the stages of Mexico City with a company of Parisian showgirls, strutting about in plumes and glitter and little else, leaving local men dazed and helpless. Mexican theater companies, stripped of their audiences, decided they might as well take off their clothes too and fight back through imitation. Popular troupes staged parodies of the French review with such titles as *Pataclán* and *Gataclán* (paw and cat *clán,* respectively) and featuring local beauties with bobbed hair and revealing flapper costumes. Fortunately for everyone, "El Panzón" Soto kept his clothes on, but he also joined the fad with a show called *Rataplán,* which bared the nefarious deeds of rats within the government. The *Ba-ta-clán* dancers and their local imitators, with short locks, boyish figures, and outlandish behavior, exemplified the destabilizing effects of modernization on Mexican gender roles. Revista shows generally alternated chorus lines with stand-up comedians, and this theatrical genre, which commented on the instability of social patterns, was an important source for Cantinflas's parody of macho behavior.

Social revolution and technological change liberated women from many onerous burdens of patriarchy. When peasants enlisted in the armies of Pancho Villa and Alvaro Obregón, they traveled by train throughout the republic, making comrades from different regions, expanding their affiliations from the local patria to the broader nation. Women also joined in these campaigns, most as *soldaderas* (camp followers) preparing food for the troops, but some actually participated in combat. Such revolutionary experiences empowered women to begin entering business and the professions and to demand political rights. The spread of mechanical corn mills, freeing women from the arduous and lengthy task of hand-grinding corn to make the day's tortillas, opened a space for humble peasant women to engage in petty commerce, even if their husbands later claimed the income.[32]

Inspired largely by popular culture from foreign lands— movies, sports, comics, and tourism—many middle-class young women looked to a new role model in the *chica moderna* (modern girl). Not content with the limitations of traditional womanhood, the chica moderna maintained an independent, exciting lifestyle, filled with the latest gadgets, cars, and radios purchased with her own earnings. She attracted men with stylish makeup and clothes, despite her unconventional ideas about women's liberation and companionate marriage. Mary Pickford, the most popular actress in Hollywood, exemplified this appealing attitude of a tomboy who nevertheless remained completely feminine. The art deco covers of the *Revista de Revistas* illustrated Mexican versions of this ideal, women with bobbed hair who danced the tango, played sports, and even fought bulls. The beginnings of tourism from the United States provided living examples of liberated women who defied social expectations, often without even realizing it. The popular theater depicted the gringa as an attractive blonde, unable to speak proper Spanish, who caused laughter through linguistic naïveté. One such character unintentionally declared her love for more than Mexican cuisine by saying that she liked her chiles big—a play on the hot peppers' phallic connotations.[33]

Shameless conduct was expected of foreign tourists and movie starlets, but young Mexican women who adopted the mannerisms of the chica moderna often risked their good reputation, still an essential asset in a rigidly patriarchal society. Many adventurous middle-class women took such chances in the 1920s, bobbing their hair and slipping into alleyways off Santa María la Redonda to dance the Charleston or the *danzón*. Even in the notorious Salon México, they felt secure in the observance of social distinctions, for the tramps of the third class, known as *lo del cebo* (the feedlot), were forbidden to dance into the second- or first-class sections, *manteca* (pork fat) and *mantequilla* (butter). Nevertheless, cabarets supposedly posed grave dangers to bourgeois respectability, as Federico Gamboa reminded readers in his popular novel, *Santa* (1903), which was repeatedly adapted for stage and cinema. The story told of a nice provincial girl seduced by a passing soldier, cast out by her brothers, and forced into a Mexico City brothel where she died of syphilis. If Salón México represented the pinnacle of Bohemian nightlife, its sordid depths lay on the south side of town in the "Barrio Latino." French pimps, called "Apaches," ruled the cobblestone alley of Cuauhtemotzín at the heart of this red light district and solicited for their countrywomen from under brightly colored canopies, charging a full peso for the infamous "three things." Local competitors offered only one thing but at a lower price.[34]

The difficult life of lower-class women was a favorite theme of the popular theater. One frequent skit, combining comedy with social commentary, involved the statue of Christopher Columbus on the Paseo de la Reforma coming alive to "discover" the peculiarities of modern Mexico. In one show, Columbus and his straight man, a gendarme, encountered a pair of women who challenged traditional gender roles through their names, Doña Petroleum and Señorita Howitzer.

Petroleum:	Greetings, compañeros.
Howitzer:	Greetings and social revolution.
Columbus:	Good evening compañeras.
Gendarme:	What's with this "compañeras"? Well from where do you know them?
Petroleum:	From the union. I am secretary general of the syndicate of mothers.
Gendarme:	And you?
Howitzer:	I'm with the hatters [sombrero is slang for penis, so *sombrerera* implied a prostitute].
Petroleum:	We're struggling for the emancipation of women workers, to obtain the vote, and to get drunk [*ponernos las botas*, literally to put on the boots].
Gendarme:	And the mothers, what do they want?
Petroleum:	Improved conditions and fixed working hours.
Gendarme:	Why? Do you work a lot?

Petroleum: I've got eight.
Gendarme: Eight hours of work?
Petroleum: Eight kids . . . which represents a barbaric labor.
Gendarme: And they're all alive [vivos]?
Petroleum: Some are bright [same word], the others stupid, but they all eat, and my husband is so placid.
Columbus: He doesn't work?
Petroleum: Yes, he belongs to the bums' union. And here we women are subjugated in the home and ignored in politics, and we need to aspire to enter the cabinet.
Columbus: And what role will you take in the cabinet?
Petroleum: A roll of toilet paper. To disinfect politics.[35]

Other theatrical vaciladas of gender depicted passive men and violent women. Although the punning humor of albures involved subtle allusions to homosexuality, flamboyantly gay and transvestite characters—and actors—were common on stage.[36] And no theater company was complete without an actress to play the aggressive proletarian woman. Emilia "La Trujis" Trujillo gave memorable performances in the Porfirian era of a working-class woman being dragged off to jail for drunkenness, cursing the hypocrisy of policemen who arrested poor people for consuming pulque and tequila while ignoring the rich fops getting soused on champagne and cognac. A shrewish, often drunk wife inspired some of the finest scenes from Mexico's leading pelado characters. The beautiful Lupe "La Pingüica" Rivas Cacho distorted her features into a vengeful termagant for alcoholic duets with "El Cuatezón" Beristáin. Perhaps for this reason, the near-sighted artist, José Clemente Orozco, unfairly dismissed the "actresses" of the popular theater as all "terribly old and deformed."[37] Delia Magaña and Amelia Wilhelmy dominated this role opposite "El Panzón" Soto in the early 1930s when Cantinflas arrived on the carpa stage.

The Carpa Valentina

The diverse genres of Mexican theater, from puppet shows to political satire to chorus lines, met at their lowest common denominator in the carpas. These improvised tent theaters flourished during the 1920s and 1930s in working-class barrios of the nation's capital and in many provincial cities. For just a nickel, spectators could enjoy a *tanda* (show) or two, of four acts each, including comic monologues, lewd songs and dances, acrobatic stunts, and romantic skits. The audience developed an immediate rapport with the performers on stage, freely contributing applause, suggestions, and raspberries. The carpa relied on improvisation rather than original scripts, and the artists brought their stock characters to life through their own unique personalities. This aesthetic, common to popular culture throughout the world, nurtured Mario Moreno in his early days and continued with him throughout his career.

While informal spectacles such as the corrales dated back to the colonial period, the modern carpa probably began in the 1870s with provisional theaters established for the holiday season, lasting from the Day of the Dead (November 1) presentation of *Don Juan Tenorio* through the Christmas pastoral plays. Once the city council had begun issuing permits, novelty theaters, variety salons, circuses, and *jacalones* (big shacks) operated regularly throughout the Porfiriato. By 1922 popular theaters had assumed the name of carpas and covered the boulevard of Santa María la Redonda as well as the suburban plazas of Tacuba, Tacubaya, and Azcapotzalco. Conditions inside were deplorable, with haphazard stage lights, inadvertently surrealistic backdrops, uncomfortable seats for the audience, and even worse provisions for the actors. Only the best—one in ten according to an inspector's count—offered toilets. Stagehands hung the canvas top from any available pole, including open streetlights that threw sparks across the combustible fabric. Few impresarios spent money on fire extinguishers. One official ordered a show closed because of rain pouring through holes in the tent, but with the actors' encouragement, the spectators refused to leave. The embarrassed city delegate reported that the lack of police and the character of the audience made it impossible to avoid a scandal; in other words, the show went on. Authorities were tolerant because, as one inspector concluded, "Better the carpa than the pulque shop and the tavern."[38]

Socorro Merlín has described the carnivalesque aesthetics of the carpa, which required an immediate personal rapport between performers and the audience. Although based on the medieval popular culture of feast days and marketplaces, the early carpa already reflected some elements of modern industrial society. The actors and actresses, "those admirable proletarians of the theater," worked the crowds from four o'clock until midnight, the eight-hour legal day, then another eight preparing for shows.[39] Nevertheless, their careers turned on a mere fifteen or twenty minutes performing on stage, for regular employment depended on producing rapid-fire laughs. With little time to develop subtle characterization, they needed to make an immediate impression on the crowd using iconic figures familiar to all: pelados and dandies, cops and robbers, foreigners and floozies, gays and shrews. A favorite combination, the encounter between a city slicker and a country bumpkin, was observed by Carleton Beals. The urban dweller in this skit described his motorcycle to a Native American, who offered to trade his cow for the newfangled contraption. The city fellow declined, saying: "Why, I'd look like a boob riding down Francisco Madero Avenue on a cow." The Indian agreed: "Wouldn't I be a popinjay trying to milk a motorcycle."[40]

Henry Jenkins, in his insightful book, *"What Made Pistachio Nuts?" Early Sound Comedy and the Vaudeville Aesthetic,* described the singular importance of personality for success in the improvised theater. "Performers won praise not for their ability to assume the 'cloak' of a character but rather from their ability to project a unique personality that transcended stock roles. . . . The goal was to be the [Eddie] Cantor or [Al] Jolson whom less creative artists imitated or better yet, to be the [Joe] Cook or [Bert] Wheeler who had a personality seen as so vivid and unique that no one else could imitate it with success."[41] The importance of this intangible quality for Moreno's success was confirmed by the prominent stage writer and theater critic Carlos Riva Larrauri, who spent many evenings slumming in the tents around Plaza Garibaldi. "In the carpas he was a triumph," Riva Larrauri wrote in 1938. "A triumph that, in matters of art—such art as there was—came only from personality."[42]

After Moreno became a movie star, less successful carpa performers accused him of stealing their characters, costumes, mannerisms, and skits, all of which was true and also completely irrelevant. In a theater dedicated to representing the common people, originality lay in points of style, not gross outlines. Cantinflas, like the comic strip character Chupamirto, dressed as a humble porter, with drooping pants held up by rope and a small hat in place of the usual Mexican sombrero to leave the shoulders free for carrying loads. But Moreno took Chupamirto's tattered vest and made it his signature costume, the *gabardina,* an "overcoat" consisting of scarcely more than a scarf. That thin strip of tattered wool became the most elegant topcoat in the mind of Cantinflas, and he delighted audiences each night by putting it on with an elaborate care. In the same way, a simple "mire, mire" (look, look) from Cantinflas brought more laughs than the funniest jokes told by lesser personalities. Improvisation was the most popular script in the carpa, and Moreno's disregard for lines caused much anxiety among directors when he made it into the movies. In the film *Aguila o sol* (Heads or tails, 1937), based on life in the carpa, his partner asked which skit they should perform, and Cantinflas merely shrugged, "Whatever comes out."

The details of Mario Moreno's theatrical apprenticeship remain shrouded in legend, but apparently he performed many variety theater parts before landing the role of the pelado. Although he later claimed to have studied the law or medicine, youthful acquaintances recalled that he devoted more time to the movies and billiards than to studying. At sixteen he ran off to enlist in the army and was stationed in the border town of Ciudad Juárez, where he organized a strolling theatrical company and staged *Las travesuras de Marte* (The mischief of Marty) before his father secured his discharge for being underage. Still the restless youth refused to remain at home and next tried his luck as a boxer. Carpa theaters often staged prizefights, and successful boxers such as Carlos Pavón, the Sheik of San Miguel, became the heroes of working-class neighborhoods. But Moreno had scarcely stepped into the ring before the referee began counting to ten, and after that unfortunate first encounter, he wisely devoted his physical talents to dancing. He reportedly danced the "Charleston Negro" in the company of Nacho Pérez and may also have toured as far away as Xalapa, the capital of Veracruz. His first opportunity as a comedian came around 1929 with a carpa in Cuernavaca, a resort town south of the capital, and perhaps there was born the pelado Cantinflas.[43]

In 1930, with the permission of his parents, Moreno began working regularly at the Carpa Sotelo in Azcapotzalco, a suburb northwest of Mexico City, and three years later he moved to nearby Tacuba to join the Carpa Valentina, which was named for his future wife. The theater belonged to a troupe of Russian circus performers who fled the chaos of the Civil War in 1919 by way of Vladivostok and Yokohama before arriving in the port of Manzanillo in 1923. The patriarch of the clan, Gregorio Ivanoff, had three daughters, the oldest of whom, Olga, had married a Lithuanian actor, Estanislao Shilinsky. The second daughter, Valentina, was a beautiful blonde dancer, just eighteen years old when Moreno arrived in Tacuba. She convinced her brother-in-law to work as Moreno's partner and acting coach. He apparently had much to learn, toning down his gaudy makeup and tightening his delivery. As one spectator remarked: "That Cantinflas is formidable. Too bad he laughs at his own jokes."[44]

Shilinsky also wrote skits for the company, although not always from original ideas. The most popular story, based on Hollywood's *Frankenstein* (1931), featured Moreno as the mad doctor and the company's tallest dancer as the monster, with makeup based on a publicity photo of Boris Karloff. The first time he rose from the operating table, the audience fled in terror, but they came back, again and again, for three full months, a remarkable run at the carpa. Inspired by that success, Valentina wrote a parody of Dracula, with Shilinsky as the elegant count. The skit opened with Valentina and Cantinflas arriving at Castle Dracula in response to help-wanted ads for a secretary and a night watchman. Both were hired, and the lunatic residents of the vampire's castle began parading past the front desk, giving Moreno a chance to act even crazier than the inmates. Dracula then returned to the stage in pursuit of his terrified new secretary. In the antics that followed, Cantinflas alternated rapidly through a medley of emotions: bravery, cowardice, indifference. He first imposed himself in front of the vampire, protecting Valentina, then ran frantically in circles, only to stop suddenly, puff on a cigarette, and blow smoke rings at the monster. This madcap routine so delighted audiences that Moreno made it a standard part of his repertoire—the macho act of the Mexican pelado—vacillating between a fearless street fighter and a coward hiding behind the skirts of women, with moments of calm reflection interspersed throughout. The Dracula scene reached its finale with the vampire engulfing Cantinflas in his voluminous black cape. The audience heard screams of horror, pain, then silence. Suddenly Cantinflas burst from the cape with a huge grin, shouting, "I bit him!"[45]

Headlined by the comic team of Cantinflas and Shilinsky, the Carpa Valentina was soon the biggest show in town. The local police chief reserved a regular seat under the tent, and theater lovers from Mexico City made pilgrimages to Tacuba. Moreno had meanwhile begun to court Valentina, making *piropos* (poetic gallantries) whenever she passed. One evening, as she finished her dance routine, he grabbed her arm and stole a kiss; she became indignant but secretly admired the handsome young comic. Nevertheless, her father, Gregorio, refused to accept the suitor or even to raise his salary above the starting wage of a peso and a half, despite the flush ticket receipts he was bringing in. Finally, after six months of abuse—in guttural Russian—Moreno convinced Shilinsky they should leave the small-town show and seek their fortunes in the big city.[46]

Cantinflas as Cultural Hero

Lower-class audiences at the carpa theater found a kindred spirit in the figure of Cantinflas. Since the eighteenth century, pelados had maintained a constant presence on the streets of Mexico City, stumbling about, often drunk, with dirty clothes and insolent manners. Yet these seeming fools had developed a linguistic skill for deflating the pretensions of the wealthy and powerful, and when the revista theater flourished with the Revolution of 1910, pelado characters offered the most trenchant critiques of political and social vaciladas. One can trace the evolution of Mexican national identity through the development of the archetypal character that culminated in Cantinflas.

Mexican cultural heroes, like the mestizo society they exemplify, often travel together through the national psyche in dualistic opposing pairs, representing not a simplistic clash between Native American and Hispanic civilizations but rather a complex fusion, with each side of the dichotomy suffused by elements from both cultures. For an illustration of this mental cocktail, consider the Virgin of Guadalupe and La Malinche, symbolizing two conflicting yet intertwined ideals of Mexican womanhood, the mother and the whore. Tales of the miraculous apparition of the Virgin Mary to an Indian, Juan Diego, in 1531 demonstrated to believers the Catholic mother's concern for her newly evangelized children and gradually earned her reverence as the national saint. Malinche gave an entirely different meaning to the position of mother of the Mexican people by betraying her fellow natives and serving as translator and mistress to the conquistador Cortés. All Mexican women could identify at some level with both the self-abnegating love of the Virgin and the lustfulness and treachery of Malinche. Together the two icons represented the impossibility of any woman satisfying the contradictory demands of sanctity and sexuality imposed by a patriarchal society.

The recurring masculine hero in Mexican history, Quetzalcoatl, the plumed serpent, who brought civilization to the ancient Toltecs, meanwhile found his counterpart in Tezcatlipoca, the smoking mirror, the trickster, the jaguar god, and perhaps the first Mesoamerican incarnation of Cantinflas. Pre-Hispanic myths testify to the mischievous nature of the jaguar god, causing havoc, like Cantinflas, with his voice. He often passed among the people disguised as a young warrior, beating his drum and singing. Others took up the song irresistibly and became so confused that they hurled themselves to their deaths in canyons. When the priest Topiltzin-Quetzalcoatl taught the Toltecs the skills of agriculture in return for abandoning human sacrifice, Tezcatlipoca plotted to drive out the reformer and restore the old rituals. He chose as his weapon the fermented brew pulque, intoxicating Quetzalcoatl, who slept with his own sister and departed in shame. In another guise, as a chile vendor from the Huaxtec lowlands, the trickster exposed himself in the market, enchanting the local princess and causing her to fall ill. The Toltecs, in their rage, tried to drive out the foreigner, but "he came dancing, he came dancing the captives' dance. He came showing disdain. He came vaunting himself. He came crouching."[47] These Nahuatl doublets, alternating between bravado and submission, vaunting and crouching, seem written to describe the macho act of Cantinflas. Moreover, scenes of drunkenness, indecent exposure, captivated daughters, and disapproving parents were staples of Cantinflas's oeuvre. But although Cantinflas humiliated his foes with malevolent verbal humor, he stopped far short of human sacrifice.

European folktales also contained numerous versions of the trickster, such as the clever German Till Eulenspiegel, his Italian counterpart, Giufà, and the ubiquitous village idiot. But Spaniards defined the picaresque literary genre with the classic novels *Lazarillo de Tormes* (1554) and *Guzmán de Alfarache* (1599). The picaros represented the antithesis of the idealistic heroes of chivalry, and their misadventures in the service of foppish, arrogant masters pointed out the hypocrisy of society. Unlike the noble deeds of medieval knights, the picaro's tricks were motivated by hunger alone, as were those of Cantinflas, who was always mindful of his next meal, although he did not share the anticlericalism of Lazarillo or Guzmán. Poets in the New World created Creole rogues: Mateo Rosas de Oquendo's satiric Ulysses and Alonso Carrió de la Vandera's postal inspector, whose clever tricks were read to appreciative audiences in taverns and public plazas. Female rogues, called picaras, played their pranks on suitors instead of masters and provided models for the carpa characters of Amelia Wilhelmy and Delia Magaña.[48]

José Joaquín Fernández de Lizardi founded Mexico's national literature on two recurring social types, the picaro Itching Parrot and the fop Don Catrín. The latter dedicated himself to appearances, and without a peso to spare, he swaggered down Mexico City streets in a stylish overcoat, top hat, buckled boots, golden pocket watch, and slender cane. The Parrot, by contrast, followed the picaresque tradition of a lower-class hero passing from one master to the next, pointing up hypocrisy while trying to find his next meal. In one episode, he worked for a Doctor Purgative, named for his favorite remedy, just long enough to learn his mannerisms. He then swiped the medical diploma and set up practice in another town. There he diagnosed a patient as suffering from "the effervescence of sanguinary humor oppressing the ventricles of his heart, stifling his cerebrum, because it presses with all the pondus of the blood upon the medular and the trachea."[49] Cantinflas also abused scientific discourse but not in this pedantic manner; instead he stuttered about, confusing words until not even a trained doctor could understand him. Moreover, the Parrot came from the Creole elite whereas Cantinflas represented the working-class mestizo. Nevertheless, as the keenest observer of his society, Lizardi contributed to the formation of this Mexican cultural hero.

The Rosete Aranda brothers, puppet masters of the nineteenth century, updated the picaro character for the Porfirian period in the "Discourse of Vale Coyote." The quick-witted, half-breed puppet met his social antithesis and comic partner in the arrogant society matron Doña Pascarroncita Mastuerzo de Verdega y Panza de Res y Gayverde, who sang the "Couplets of Don Simón." She announced herself haughtily on stage, intending to demonstrate her illustrious Creole heritage, but her string of names was so full of albures that the audience deflated her pride with laughter. Her paternal title, Mastuerzo, translated literally as the flower nasturtium, and was also slang for a simpleton; meanwhile, her mother's family apparently descended not from the renowned Spanish explorer Cabeza de Vaca (bull's head, a reference to a medieval battle against the Moors), but rather from Panza de Res (tripe). The wordplay between the "Discourse of Vale Coyote" and the "Couplets of Don Simón" mirrored everyday confrontations between pelados and Creoles in the streets of Mexico City and inspired some of the funniest scenes in the hit film *Ahí está el detalle*.

Decades later, Chupamirto assumed the role of the pelado in opposition to *catrín* dandies, policemen, judges, and other elite figures. The first panel of his premiere strip revealed his exaggerated macho image, clubbing a lower-class woman while a policeman remarked, "what a suave little blow that pelado is giving that old woman." In the next scene, Chupamirto swore to the officer that he would leave her *por la paz* (in peace), but the officer remained skeptical, wondering how he would evade his order. The following panel answered the question: As the pelado laid into her again, the tecolote rushed up again to demand why he had not left her in peace. Leaning on his club, casually at home in the streets of Tepito, Chupamirto replied, "okay, yeah, well, but those streets [of La Paz] are a long way from here." The cop scratched his head and admitted, "Gosh, if you haven't really made a fool of me."[50]

Mario Moreno rose to stardom in the carpa by creating a unique character from a familiar cultural hero through personality alone. There was nothing particularly original about Cantinflas, nor could there have been to succeed in a popular theater based primarily on improvised interactions with the audience. He shared mannerisms, jokes, and costumes with countless contemporary performers. His stage appearances at the Carpa Valentina with the elegant Shilinsky drew laughter because they mocked the verbal duels of honor between pelados and catrines, so common on Mexico City streets. Even his supposed innovation of cantinfleando, talking a lot without saying anything, had been the gimmick of Vale Coyote from the nineteenth-century puppet theater. Mario Moreno is remembered above all his fellow artists because he made the transition from live performance to celluloid immortality. Long after securing his fortune in cinema, Moreno clung to the shabby aesthetic baggage of the carpa, eliciting scorn from critics but assuring the loyalty of common viewers.

2

AMBIGUOUS PROFILES

Having served his theatrical apprenticeship in small town carpas, Mario Moreno returned to Mexico City in 1934 determined to see, if not his own name in lights, then that of his alter-ego, Cantinflas. The homecoming held particular significance because tent theaters had flourished on Santa María la Redonda, making the street where Moreno was born into a Mexican version of Broadway. Together with his partner, Shilinsky, he played a succession of carpa theaters, eventually rising to the legitimate stage in 1936 with the opening of the Follies Bergère. Along the way, Moreno sharpened his characterization of Cantinflas against the wit of some of Mexico's leading comics: Amelia Wilhelmy, "Chino" Herrera, "Don Catarino," and Manuel Medel. His growing popularity in the theater also allowed him to make the jump into the cinema. In just a few years, he began to leave behind his former teachers, first Shilinsky, then the others. By 1940, he had established himself as the most popular comedian in Mexico City, and his fast-talking, convoluted humor was the voice of an era.

The year of his return, 1934, was a propitious one for the carpa and contributed greatly to his success. The election of Lázaro Cárdenas as president in July revolutionized Mexican politics, transforming the party of the revolution from an alliance of generals and bureaucrats founded by Plutarco Elías Calles into a genuinely popular organization free from the grip of the former jefe máximo. Having reestablished the power of the presidency, Cárdenas wielded it to realize the promise of the revolution by distributing land to the peasants, encouraging factory workers to strike, and expropriating the national wealth from foreign capitalists. But the advent of mass politics, like other aspects of modernity, proved a mixed blessing, for Cárdenas used the party machinery to discipline the people as well as to empower them. Cantinflas became the theatrical voice of the forgotten man, the pelado, and found much to criticize in the Cárdenas administration. At first glance, it seems a credit both to the president's democratic instincts and to his sense of humor that he supported Moreno and other comedians even as they savaged his reform program. Nevertheless, careful inspection reveals a complex reality belying the populist images of both Cárdenas and Cantinflas. The political theater, in fact, spoke more for the bourgeoisie than for the pelado, and Moreno certainly worked from that slant, both from innate conservatism and in response to the radical rhetoric of leftist politicians. Meanwhile, far from heralding the arrival of Bolshevism that bourgeois critics predicted, Cardenista policies actually helped save Mexican capitalism from the crisis of the Great Depression.

Cantinflas exemplified the zeitgeist not only through his satire of Cárdenas but also because he fit the *Profile of Man and Culture in Mexico,* a celebrated book published by Samuel Ramos in 1934. Ramos described the pelado as "the most elemental and clearly defined expression of national character." Using Adlerian psychoanalysis, he diagnosed a national inferiority complex arising from the history of Spanish colonial domination. Elite Mexicans of the nineteenth century concealed their feelings of inadequacy through the slavish imitation of European fashions. The pelado, bereft of the cultural capital needed for such a gilded psychic facade, hid his low self-esteem behind a belligerent phallic obsession. This was the character that Moreno portrayed in the theater, announcing Cantinflas's virility to all the world and challenging anyone who might dispute it.

By transcending the stage to become a national icon, Cantinflas no longer remained the simple creation of Mario Moreno but rather became the product of many authors, including the philosopher Samuel Ramos. The previous chapter showed the multiple roots of Cantinflas's character in Mexican popular culture, and this one will examine the many writers who scripted his career in the crucial formative period between 1934 and 1940. Mario Moreno, of course, figured prominently in the continuing evolution of Cantinflas, for example, by toning down the clown makeup to arrive at a more attractive image. Scriptwriters

Guz Aguila, Alfredo Robledo, and Carlos León provided him with material for the stage and screen. Salvador Novo, a paradoxical combination of conservative journalist and flamboyant wit, with a literary affinity for cantinflismos, helped shape his political career. Arcady Boytler, the "Russian Rooster," a collaborator of Sergei Eisenstein, directed his first two starring roles, helping to adapt his character to the screen. Finally, the insightful film critic Xavier Villaurrutia called attention to the artistry of Moreno's portrayal of the Mexican pelado. And even as these scriptwriters set his career on course, Moreno helped Mexican cinema establish its independence from the folkloric stereotypes imposed upon it by Hollywood distributors.

Moreno achieved such wide appeal precisely because of the ambiguities within his profile of the Mexican national identity. But exploiting these social tensions on screen proved problematic at first, as middle-class audiences turned away from his crude plebeian humor. Bourgeois filmgoers found his gender transgression extremely unsettling, and some of his most artistically interesting movies were popular failures. With experience, Moreno finally captured a general audience, but however versatile the image of Cantinflas became, the attempt to encapsulate an entire nation in a single person inevitably produced contradictions that later invalidated his claim to represent the Mexican pueblo.

The Follies Bergère

The Salón Rojo (Red Salon), the first stop on Mario Moreno's journeyman tour of Mexico City, illustrated the transient life of the carpas. Located appropriately at the intersection of Pedro Moreno Street and Santa María la Redonda, about five blocks south of Moreno's childhood home, it lay in the heart of the capital's lower-class theater district. Pepé Rivero, the theater manager, possessed one of Mexico City's finest lineups, headed by Armando Soto la Marina, "Chicotito" (Uncle Boy). Moreno learned much from the star but also chafed at working in the popular comic's shadow, and within a few months, he and Shilinsky accepted an offer to perform on a rival stage. Then the mercurial "Chicotito" himself moved on to work for Alfonso Brito, a man with no experience in the theater but a prominent

position in the Cárdenas administration. Thus functioned the tu-
multuous world of the carpa during its golden age of the 1930s.

Moreno and Shilinsky did not have far to travel to find a
better offer, for their next booking lay just a short walk across
Plaza Garibaldi at the Salón Mayab. The promise of fifteen
pesos a day gave Moreno the financial security to marry
Valentina Ivanova in a civil ceremony in Tacuba on October 27,
1934, with the Catholic ritual held four days later in the chapel
of San Gabriel. Professionally, the new venue allowed him to
expand his circle of contacts and add to his repertoire. He
worked with the real life Chupamirto, José Muñoz Reyes, before
his tragic death in 1935, as well as with Jesús Martínez "Palillo"
(Toothpick), a political satirist from the Workers' Theater of
Guadalajara. Moreno also met the reigning king of Mexican albures, ventriloquist Roberto Ramírez and his puppet Conde
Boby. Fans remembered Ramírez as a lousy ventriloquist but a
brilliant comedian, who headlined three separate carpas simultaneously and was driven between the different theaters by his
personal chauffeur until one day a jealous rival stole Boby's
head. Ramírez replaced the wooden head, but it was never the
same; the act declined, he began cussing out the dummy, crying
for his old Boby, and was finally committed to an asylum.[1]

Meanwhile, the comic team of Cantinflas and Shilinsky had
moved on again, touring the provinces in 1935 before reaching
the legitimate stage in Mexico City. They performed in the
northern industrial cities of Monterrey and Torreón, the Gulf
Coast port of Veracruz, and finally Mérida, where Moreno struck
up a lasting friendship with the Yucatecan actor Daniel "Chino"
Herrera. He took his nickname from Chinese characters, such as
the laundry man of *Trapitos al sol,* but just as Moreno imitated
the slang of Tepito, Herrera could make people in Mexico City
laugh simply by speaking in the Maya-influenced dialect of his
native city. Impresario Manuel Ferrándiz finally tempted the
comic pair back to Mexico City with an offer of thirty-five pesos
to work with the renowned carpa actress Amelia Wilhelmy at
the Ofelia, next door to the fabled temple of danzón, the Salón
México. Ferrándiz also tried to raise their profile by arranging
such special performances as an Independence Eve show at the
Cine Máximo, formerly the María Guerrero Theater, where "El
Cuatezón" had played. Such bookings had their own danger, as

Moreno reportedly discovered playing a private party at the elite Salón Don Quijote when he left the dressing room, already in pelado costume but without his makeup. Returning from the restroom, he was stopped by a doorman and practically kicked out of the nightclub.[2]

José Furstenberg, a Jewish immigrant showman and partner in the Ofelia, dreamed of still greater accomplishments for Cantinflas, wanting him to cross over to the legitimate stage but without losing the popular appeal of the carpa. After signing Moreno, he purchased the abandoned shell of the Garibaldi Theater, also known as the Molino Verde (a knockoff of the Parisian Moulin Rouge), and remodeled it into the luxurious Follies Bergère. But the street address, Santa María la Redonda 41, nevertheless signaled the transgressions inside, for that number had acquired special significance in Mexican popular culture following a 1905 vice raid that captured precisely that many wealthy homosexuals at a drag ball. A few years later, during an army reorganization, the high command could not find a single soldier in all of Mexico willing to serve in the 41st Regiment and had to skip over to the 42nd. Despite his vision of Moreno's potential stardom, Furstenberg felt nervous competing against more upscale acts, such as Roberto Soto at the Lírico and his former partner, Joaquín Pardavé, now playing the Apolo. Therefore, the Follies opened on October 15, 1936, with a proper script, written by Carlos Ortega and Francisco Benítez, and a huge bill, topped by Amelia Wilhelmy and Manuel Medel, a former player at the Esperanza Iris Theater who already had a movie appearance to his credit. The show was a huge success, and Moreno asked for his first paycheck in silver coins to hand out to shoeshine and paperboys. This gesture, foreshadowing his later philanthropy, also recalled a colonial tradition of assuring that crowds turned out for viceregal pronouncements by tossing silver coins to the plebes.[3]

After the triumphant premiere, Moreno took his rightful place atop the billboard in partnership with Medel. Furstenberg had offered Shilinsky a contract but soon grew impatient with his alcoholic vagaries and fired him. The Follies' owner continued investing in the best scripts from Guz Aguila, Carlos Riva Larrauri, and Alfredo Robledo, a former writer for "El Cuatezón" who became Moreno's personal favorite. As always the revistas repeated familiar themes, such as *Los tres tenorios* (The three tenorios), with Cantinflas as Don Juan of Tepito, and *36 rojo-37 negro* ('36 red, '37 black), a parody of union activism. Miguel Covarrubias described one such labor skit, featuring Cantinflas as a union leader presenting the workers' demands for better pay and more time off, which Medel, as the capitalist, immediately agreed to as an excuse to raise prices. He then proceeded to calculate "the hours of the year in which his employees do *not* work, deducting Sundays, Holy Days, vacations, Labor Day, time out to lunch, time for meetings and so forth, cleverly juggling mathematics to obtain a total of non-working hours that leaves only four days in the year in which the employees work. Cantinflas' heart sinks lower and lower and he ends by asking the factory owner humbly to tell them how much they owe *him* for the privilege of working."[4]

Moreno made another lifelong friendship at the Follies with Mexico's most popular and flamboyant musician, Agustín Lara. Known as the *flaco de oro* (golden beanpole) for his slim frame and golden tunes, he played piano for a decade in the brothels and cabarets of Mexico City and Veracruz before becoming the star of Mexico's first radio station, XEW, in 1930. His show, *La hora íntima* (The intimate hour) featured romantic songs in an eclectic range of styles, from tango and waltz to bolero and danzón. One of the most popular, "Aventurera," even contributed to inflation in Mexico City when, upon hearing the lyrics "sell your love expensively, adventuress," the capital's prostitutes reportedly doubled their rates. In the early 1930s the "musical poet" formed his own carpa at the Politeama Theater before moving to the Follies, and Moreno spoofed him affectionately in such shows as *La hora íntima de Cantinflas* and *Cada tema con su loca* (For every song a lunatic—a pun on the Mexican saying, "Every lunatic has a program").[5]

The carpa provided both performers and material for the Mexican film industry, but already a tension was developing between the improvisational talent of the stars and the aesthetic standards of critics and screenwriters with experience in the legitimate theater. One of the first critical notices of Moreno, published a month after the Follies premiere, described him as a "genuine discovery of a great comic actor with an enormous popularity among the public addicted to the 'carpas.'" But the following month, the critic Carlos Riva Larrauri, author of the previously reviewed play, lamented the systematic refusal of Moreno and Medel to play their roles correctly. Instead they reportedly fell back on old sketches, which lacked all originality.[6] Thus began a pattern that Moreno would perpetuate throughout his cinematic career, scorning original screenplays and simply repeating the same old jokes, confident of the laughter of fans if not the approval of critics.

The Pelado under Analysis

Mexicans of the Porfirian era embraced the European aesthetic ideal of modernism as a means of understanding the social dislocations resulting from the search for progress. Just as the technocratic elite, known as *científicos,* adopted an organic view of society and looked for an almost biological evolution toward the goal of industrialization, so the modernist poets, led by Manuel Gutiérrez Nájera, explored the aesthetic delights of consumerism and the promiscuous dangers of urbanism. The Revolution of 1910 repudiated the European intellectual foundations of Porfirian society and encouraged a sense of nationalism based on indigenous traditions and spirituality. Nevertheless, the self-analysis undertaken by intellectuals in the 1920s, who called themselves *contemporáneos* (contemporaries), revisited many of the modernist concerns about industrial development and social decay. In particular, they focused on the problems of urban poverty, setting the stage for Cantinflas to play a role in the national discourse.

The journal *Contemporáneos* emerged in the 1920s as a cosmopolitan antithesis to the revolutionary nationalism of Diego Rivera's pre-Hispanic murals and José Vasconcelos's *La raza cósmica* (The cosmic race, 1927), which declared the once-scorned mestizo to be the culmination of human evolution and the embodiment of Mexican national identity. The avant-garde founders included some of Mexico's most creative and influential literary figures, who continued the search for national identity without losing touch with international trends in art and literature. José Clemente Orozco, for example, attacked Rivera for abandoning universal artistic themes in favor of quaint folkloric traditions and precious Indian subjects. Two other members of the group, the poets Xavier Villaurrutia, who became the most respected cultural critic of his generation, and Salvador Novo, a pioneer of literary journalism, helped establish the experimental theater in Mexico.

Another contributor to *Contemporáneos,* Samuel Ramos, sought to explain the Mexican national identity using Alfred Adler's psychological theory of the inferiority complex. The philosopher insisted that national renewal had to begin with an unsparing self-analysis, starting with the most elemental representation of Mexican character, the pelado. Ramos classified this urban underclass as "a most vile category of social fauna . . . a form of human rubbish from the great city." The pelado constituted a constant menace to society, according to Ramos, because "the slightest friction causes him to blow up. His explosions are verbal and reiterate his theme of self-affirmation in crude and suggestive language. He has created a dialectic of his own, a diction which abounds in ordinary words, but he gives those words a new meaning. He is an animal whose ferocious pantomimes are designed to terrify others."[7] Ramos attributed these basic elements of Cantinflas's act, the meaningless dialogue and the macho posturing, to an inferiority complex that existed not simply among the lower classes but rather in all Mexicans when confronted with the achievements of Europe and the United States. Only by abandoning such invidious comparisons would Mexicans develop the self-confidence to overcome their sense of inferiority.

Numerous critics have disagreed with Ramos, not least for his conflation of the pelado with all of Mexican society. Nor was his characterization of the urban underclass particularly original; Porfirian sociologists, such as Julio Guerrero, had already described the problems of promiscuity, violence, and alcoholism. Anthropologist Robert Redfield was meanwhile conducting research that attributed the social origins of pelado behavior to the uprooting effects of migration from the countryside. Indeed, José Vasconcelos's program of forging a "cosmic race" required the forced assimilation of rural dwellers into an urban proletariat, thereby annihilating Native American societies to make way for a Mexican national culture. Finally, Ramos's obsession with the phallic nature of lower-class albures failed to appreciate the meaning of these jokes among *cuates,* or drinking buddies. As John Ingham observed: "Usually such verbal jousting among men is not overly abusive and often is taken in good humor, each man giving as much as he gets while being careful not to go too far."[8] Nevertheless, Ramos's conclusions proved enormously influential among his contemporaries, who came to view Cantinflas as a genial expression of national character, tempering the dangerous excesses of the pelado.

Cantinflas and the Search for a Mexican Cinema

The intellectual quest for a uniquely Mexican culture, based on spiritual rather than materialist values, responded in part to the growing influence of cultural industries from the United States. Although nationalists perceived such foreign influences as jazz music and flapper fashions to be threats to traditional Mexican values, they reserved their most apocalyptic rhetoric for Hollywood films. Mexican audiences thrilled to the imported exploits of Douglas Fairbanks and Clara Bow, undermining nationalist education programs and depriving domestic filmmakers of markets. Worse still, Hollywood's control of distribution networks limited the movies Mexico could sell abroad to films that were folkloric stereotypes of Indian villages, majestic landscapes, and splendid beaches. In effect, this control of foreign distribution transformed the Mexican film industry into a cheap and convenient location site for North American producers. The revista theater offered a convenient package of Mexican folk culture that facilitated both commercialization and foreign domination. But the foremost character of the popular theater, Cantinflas, subverted those folkloric stereotypes, creating an independent urban cinema that spoke to city dwellers throughout the Spanish-speaking world.

The movies, like many other aspects of Mexican modernity, arrived in the country during the late Porfiriato, then enlisted in the Revolution of 1910. Agents of the Lumière brothers exhibited the first motion pictures in Mexico in 1896, seven months after their premiere in Paris, but a decade passed before domestic production took off. These first features concentrated on documenting President Díaz and his program of modernization, and with the outbreak of revolution, cameramen found far more exciting subjects in the campaigns of Pancho Villa and Alvaro Obregón. When the fighting had ended, filmmakers began turning out revolutionary propaganda, but nationalist cinema attracted little popular interest during the 1920s, and foreign features from Hollywood, Italy, and France dominated Mexican movie houses. The advent of sound films in the late 1920s provided a new opportunity for Mexican producers to recapture local markets with Spanish-language features. Nevertheless, the financial difficulties of the previous decade prompted filmmakers to follow the lead of Hollywood, both in content and business practices. One of the first Mexican sound films, a 1931 adaptation of Federico Gamboa's melodramatic novel *Santa* illustrated this dependence, for the producers relied on Hollywood-proven talent, both on screen with stars Donald Reed (Ernesto Guillén) and Lupita Tovar and behind the camera with actor-turned-director Antonio Moreno and Canadian cinematographer Alex Phillips.

Just as early Hollywood movies relied on vaudeville performers, such as W. C. Fields and the Marx Brothers, *Santa* drew heavily on the Mexican revista theater. Although the top-billed stars had worked in the United States film industry, the supporting cast featured one of the most popular operetta singers of the frivolous theater, Mimí Derba, as the brothel madam and a character actor with years of experience at the Ideal, Carlos Orellana, as the blind piano player who befriended Santa. The popular composer Agustín Lara, then playing at the Politeama, dedicated a danzón to Santa and also wrote a fox-trot for the movie that was danced by chorus line girls from the popular theater.

The Mexican cinema industry continued to grow in the 1930s, incorporating diverse styles, but it failed to achieve a solid financial footing. Sergei Eisenstein, the great Soviet director of *Battleship Potemkin* (1925), applied his innovative visual narrative style in filming *¡Que viva México!* (1931). Although mangled in postproduction, it profoundly influenced Mexican filmmakers, particularly in the stunning landscapes and towering clouds of the nationalist director Emilio "El Indio" Fernández and his cinematographer Gabriel Figueroa. Another Russian filmmaker, Arcady Boytler, started out in the early 1920s filming silent comedies, such as *Boytler vs. Chaplin* and *Boytler vs. Boredom*, then came to Mexico and made the classic melodrama *La mujer del puerto* (Woman of the port, 1933). In 1935, Fernando de Fuentes inaugurated CLASA studios with *¡Vamanos con Pancho Villa!* (Let's go with Pancho Villa), a revisionist view of the Revolution of 1910. Although it was an artistic success, the million-peso film failed at the box office, nearly bankrupting the new studio. The government financing for that picture was exceptional; most producers worked with low budgets, and director Juan Bustillo Oro recalled prints being rushed to their theater premieres while still wet from the laboratory.

A family melodrama, modeled on foreign genres, filmed in haste, with musicians and comedians from the revista theater thrown in haphazardly for local color—this was Mario Moreno's first experience in the cinema. Such an inauspicious beginning seemed all the more ironic given the director, Miguel Contreras Torres, one of the most distinguished figures in Mexican cinema history and one of the most nationalistic. A former revolutionary officer, he made his name with historical epics of independence heroes Simón Bolívar and José María Morelos. By contrast, *No te engañes, corazón* (Don't fool yourself, dear heart) was pure Spanish *sainete* (a comedy of manners) all the way down to the affected Castilian lisp of the actors. Filmed in August 1936, a few months before Cantinflas opened at the Follies, it starred Carlos Orellana, the music hall pianist from *Santa,* as Bonifacio Bonafé (Boniface Good Faith). A middle-class schlep with a persistent cold, he slaved as a bookkeeper for a dishonest, tyrannical manager and was ordered around at home by his nagging wife. A doctor's diagnosis of a terminal heart condition shook Bonifacio out of his middle-class lethargy, and he plundered his savings for one last night on the town. A roaring binge and a chance encounter with a bum, Cantinflas, transformed Bonifacio's life; the next day he tamed his shrewish wife, exposed his boss as a crook, and won a promotion at work before learning that the doctor had been a quack.

The highlight of the film, Bonifacio's visit to the exclusive bar and cabaret, showcased the talent of Mexico's revista theater and its rising star Cantinflas. Musical performances included the title song, "No te engañes, corazón," and the folkloric Trío Hidalguense playing guitar. Between these numbers, the diminutive comedian Don Catarino danced a parody of the tango with an enormous woman. A partner of Moreno at the Mayab and the Follies, he gave a Chaplinesque interpretation to the dandy image implied by his name, complete with bowler hat and tattered tuxedo. Comic dances were his trademark, and he stepped into the tango with an ostrich gait that belied his short legs. But even then, he could scarcely keep up with his mismatched partner. While trying to dip, he wound up dangling from her embrace, and his attempt to swing tied the couple in a corkscrew of limbs that finally recoiled, catapulting him through the air. Don Catarino struggled to his feet and bowed, his partner rolled her eyes, and the audience cheered.

Cantinflas headlined the cabaret show with a four-minute act lifted straight from the carpa stage. Critics have claimed that Contreras Torres failed to realize the comedian's full potential; nevertheless, this brief appearance contained a microcosm of his later films: an aggressive and unwanted flirt, a mock duel in defense of honor, and a nonsense speech. Cantinflas began by declaring his passion to an attractive young woman, to her obvious disgust. She finally told him to "can it," but he persisted, "It's not a can, they're sardines. Let's go fishing." Just then Shilinsky appeared as her wealthy boyfriend, demanding satisfaction for the affront. A drunken Bonifacio offered to act as second and, between hiccups, suggested either pistols or swords. The boyfriend rolled up his sleeves, declaring himself a boxing champion. Cantinflas took a couple of ineffectual swings, then Shilinsky floored him with a single punch. The pelado bounced back up, took off one of his old shoes, and held it over his opponent's nose until he rolled his eyes and collapsed from the smell. Bonifacio raised Cantinflas's arm, declaring him champion—the punch line to a well-worn carpa routine. Cantinflas announced his congressional candidacy for Majalahonda la Chica during the subsequent discourse, mixing philosophical patter with political campaigning.

The film produced only modest returns at the box office, playing for a week after its premiere on May 20, 1937, but another screen adaptation of revista acts, also filmed in August 1936, transformed the Mexican cinema industry. Fernando de Fuentes, disappointed by the commercial failure of his trenchant commentaries on the revolution, turned instead to Cinderella story lines and folkloric populism in *Allá en el Rancho Grande* (There on the big ranch). Set in Jalisco, the fabled home of mariachis and tequila, the movie alternated song and dance routines with political comedy in a typical variety show format. De Fuentes again questioned the postrevolutionary state, not by exposing the cynicism of revolutionary leaders but rather by nostalgic appeal to a largely imaginary rural past marked by respect and reciprocity between planters and peasants. The film was Mexico's first international hit, appealing to foreigners as well as urban Mexicans by the folkloric depiction of an idyllic rural lifestyle that had disappeared by 1936, if it ever existed.

The movie's commercial success inspired more than twenty imitators in the following year alone, the most original of which was Arcady Boytler's *Así es mi tierra* (My land is like this, 1937). Unlike the other ranchero comedies, Boytler brought genuine originality to the genre, subverting it in the process. The film opened, in the best tradition of Mexican nationalist cinema, with a long shot of revolutionary armies marching in silhouette before Eisensteinian towers of clouds. Boytler then cut to the General, played by Antonio R. Frausto, returning to his natal village in 1916 after four years "walking among the bullets" of revolutionary warfare. The movie was filled with nostalgia for the countryside, church bells, mariachi serenades, a fiesta dinner of *mole* (chile pepper sauce) and tequila, and for the grand finale, a *jaripeo* (rodeo) complete with an amateur bullfight. Musical numbers, such as "Pajarito enamorado" (Little lovebird) and the title song, composed by Ignacio "Tata Nacho" Fernández Esperón, added to the folkloric atmosphere. But the narrative confounded these nationalist expectations by making the General the villain of a love triangle between an hacienda owner's daughter and a local youth. When the couple eloped, the General ordered a posse to hunt them down, and only in the end did he relent and allow them to marry while he returned to fight in the revolution.

The real center of the movie was an ongoing verbal duel between the comic team of Cantinflas and Medel, further undermining the ranchero genre. Critic Xavier Villaurrutia commented on Boytler's inversion of the established formula: "The director appears more interested in the particular effects of dialogue than in the general story line; in the interpretation of the comic actors than in the serious ones, who, according to the theme of the film, should carry the more formal part of the action."[9] This subplot involved a second love triangle of Cantinflas, as a local boy, Tejón (slang for raccoon), and Medel, as a revolutionary lieutenant, Procopio, competing for the hand of a village girl, Chole. In typical carpa fashion, the actors established their characters immediately through stereotypical costumes. Cantinflas became the village idiot by donning a *guayabera* shirt with frilly ruffles and a straw sombrero shrunken to resemble a sailor's cap, whereas Medel assumed his role with a bushy Pancho Villa mustache and a huge black sombrero. But albures, rather than romance, dominated the action, with Tejón trying to defend the virtue of his town by keeping Chole away from the outsider Procopio. His behavior thus acted out a common insult among Native American villages of the colonial period: "What are you doing in my neighborhood?"[10]

Sparks flew between the pair from the moment the rebel column entered town. During the fiesta scene, as Procopio danced with Chole, Tejón cut in, more to defend local honor than from any interest in the girl. When the rebel objected, Tejón aggressively welcomed the opportunity to step outside and settle the dispute, but only until Procopio drew his pistols. He then reverted to village idiot—wondering why they were going out *there* when the party was in *here*—and thus evaded the fight. As the love triangle unfolded in the main narrative, Tejón continued his campaign to frustrate the romance between Procopio and Chole. When the couple sat in a hayloft, he climbed up behind them and made strange animal noises. Later he insisted on drinking water from Chole's *jarro,* an obvious sexual innuendo; Procopio responded by smashing the earthenware jar rather than share the girl's favors. Verbal insult merged with trick photography at one point, when Tejón watched Procopio's face transformed into that of an ox. Finally, at the amateur bullfight, they took turns jumping clumsily away from the animal's horns, but the battle ended in a draw as both were carried out of the ring on stretchers.

The tension between narrative levels spilled over to disrupt the nationalist subtext as well, thus confusing the film's assessment of the revolution. Boytler at first seemed to follow de Fuentes in depicting it as an alien force disrupting the idyllic village life, for example, when the General threatened the young lovers' happiness. Moreover, Tejón, a classic fool, criticized the revolutionary for trying to rise above his station. When the General failed to acknowledge a serenade in his honor, Tejón played an off-key ditty reminding him of youthful days in the village. "Hey fancy yeast bun [cocol], you don't remember when you were just dark bread [chimisclán], and now that you have your sesame seeds [ajonjolí], you don't even want to remember who I am." But after lampooning the revolution, Boytler included a stock Pancho Villa scene of the hero riding up and making a production of dismounting, only this time it was Tejón, on a donkey. If not quite up to speed on his cavalry charger, he had wrapped cartridge belts across his chest and exchanged the little sailor hat for a more dignified sombrero. Procopio, looking on with scorn, asked where he was headed. "To the revolution," Tejón replied. "I'm going to steal Adelita away from you." The General welcomed him into the ranks with a bear hug, and they rode out of town. Along the way, Tejón came up to Procopio and asked if he still bore a grudge, "because we'll be walking into the bullets." Procopio finally recognized him as a brother, a pact sealed with a bottle of tequila, and then they staggered off to the revolution, slightly tipsy, Tejón still on his donkey. Boytler thereby redeemed the comic fool by enlisting him in a patriotic cause, in a scene combining elements of Sancho Panza and John Wayne.

Another stock figure from revolutionary lore, the Licenciado, or urban intellectual who wrote manifestos for the insurgent peasants, further complicated the film's many subtexts. The part was played by Luis G. Barreiro, a former revista actor described by Emilio García Riera as "the last Porfirian lounge lizard [lagartijo] of the national cinema."[11] He tinged the film's nostalgia with cynicism by laughing at the General's vision of bucolic rural life. His educated phrases contrasted sharply with the inarticulate stumbling of Tejón, who admitted, "I hear you speak and it makes me jealous, because suddenly I say what I don't want to, and I don't want to say what I say, and all is chaos [relajo]."

The interchange between Tejón and the Licenciado added to the plot a third romantic triangle, this one the most unsettling of all because it subverted the conventions of heterosexuality. Samuel Ramos described the sexual power struggles implicit in pelado humor, which carried over from the rural culture of Tejón. During the fiesta scene, the Licenciado tried to seduce a young village girl, fondling her feet under the table, but she pulled away, leaving him stroking Tejón instead. When somebody called upon the Licenciado for a toast, the local prankster embarrassed the lawyer by informing the crowd that he was occupied with *pierna* (thigh). The Licenciado looked for revenge by insisting that Tejón give the toast, confident that he would be unable to give an eloquent speech. The uneducated local opened with a standard Cantinflas line: "There are moments in life in which . . ." then wandered off through a succession of false starts before winning applause for his practical conclusion, "What happened to the beans?" Later in the film, Tejón remarked to the Licenciado that "from the profile you look just like a girlfriend I once had."

In his first two film appearances, a bit part in *No te engañes, corazón* and as the star of *Así es mi tierra*, Mario Moreno worked within the established genres of Mexican cinema, family melodrama and ranchero comedy. Yet he had already begun to subvert traditional forms by transforming those films into vehicles for his personal brand of anarchic comedy. Just as vaudeville stars like the Marx Brothers unsettled Hollywood narratives, Moreno infiltrated carpa humor into Mexican cinema. Indeed, he continued working evenings at the Follies while making both films, although it meant sleeping in a car during early morning commutes to a hacienda near Toluca for location shots on *Así es mi tierra*. The results certainly justified the effort, for as cinema historian Eduardo de la Vega Alfaro observed, it was the first Mexican comedy film worthy of the name.[12] Arcady Boytler deserved much of the credit for that accomplishment, for he reportedly needed the patience of a Franciscan to direct the mercurial actor.[13] And Boytler was not alone in shaping Moreno's public image; other writers were simultaneously helping define the political face of Cantinflas.

"The Polemic of the Century"

Cantinflas gained national attention in the summer of 1937 by rising from a humorous commentator on current events to an actual participant in the political debate. Just as "El Panzón" Soto's portrayals of Luis Morones had helped to topple the CROM boss a decade earlier, Cantinflas became the satiric counterpart and nemesis of Cardenista labor leader Vicente Lombardo Toledano. This identification with one of Mexico's most powerful politicians derived only in part from Moreno's work at the Follies Bergère. Just as important was the skillful employment of Cantinflas's image by opponents of President Cárdenas, particularly critical journalists, such as Salvador Novo. As a genial and photogenic representative of Mexico's lower classes, Cantinflas appealed to the editors of illustrated magazines as the ideal mouthpiece for attacks on the government's radical reforms. *Todo* launched Cantinflas's political career by publishing the "polemic" with Lombardo; *Vea* then appointed Cantinflas as roving reporter to comment on such issues as women's suffrage; and the most provocative of all journals, *Rotofoto,* announced his satiric presidential candidacy before being shut down by the government.[14] Both Mario Moreno and the newsmagazines benefited from this association, the former with publicity to boost his career and the latter with graphic materials supporting their conservative agendas.

Although at first Lázaro Cárdenas appeared to be simply the fourth in a line of puppets controlled by the jefe máximo, Plutarco Elías Calles, his inauguration in 1934 heralded important political changes. The new president seemed more puritanical than the administration of Abelardo Rodríguez, which was described sarcastically as "Ali Baba and the Forty Thieves." Cárdenas immediately shut down all the bars and casinos in Mexico City, including some reputedly owned by Rodríguez, providing jokes for revistas, such as *Laza los cárdenos* (Lasso the drunks).[15] At the same time, Cárdenas introduced a new sense of populism and accountability within the government. Rather than carrying out a perfunctory election campaign, he toured the countryside in 1934, listening to the needs of the people and reviving the excitement of the Maderista campaign of 1910. Not that he worried about an opposition candidate; instead he was preparing for an imminent confrontation with the jefe máximo by forging alliances with peasants and workers excluded from power by the National Revolutionary Party.

The showdown between Calles and Cárdenas began within a year and demonstrated the complexity of postrevolutionary politics and society. Elements of both left and right, within the official party and in the opposition, chose sides for a variety of reasons, often based more on local rivalries than national concerns. Calles precipitated the struggle on June 11, 1935, by condemning a wave of strikes that had been condoned by the president. A number of prominent unions mobilized in support of the administration, forming the basis for a national Cardenista labor organization, the Confederation of Mexican Workers (Confederación de Trabajadores de México, CTM), founded in February 1936 and headed by Vicente Lombardo Toledano. In addition, in the summer of 1935, Catholic conservatives led a protest march, shouting death to Calles and his rabidly anticlerical henchman, Tomás Garrido Canabal. When the military indicated its loyalty, Cárdenas began expelling Calles loyalists from the cabinet, and in April 1936 the jefe máximo was forced into exile along with CROM boss Luis Morones.[16]

With his authority secure, Cárdenas set out to fulfill the revolutionary promise of agrarian reforms and union radicalism. On the Follies stage, Moreno performed *The Miraculous Saint Lázaro,* a comparison between Moses parting the Red Sea and the Saint of Michoacán dividing the land among peasants in the form of *ejidos* (common public lands). Cárdenas distributed nearly fifty million acres to 800,000 peasants, sending the feudal society of the great landed estates into its death throes and at the same time inspiring a wave of nostalgia among the urban middle classes that assured the success of *Allá en el Rancho Grande.* The labor activism of the CTM seemed an even greater danger, and countless revistas warned of imminent Bolshevik takeover. Moreno performed *Paro general* (General strike) in 1937 as the wave of CTM strikes reached its crest. Another show featured a supposed Cardenista politician named García Lenin—"García on his father's side and Lenin by way of Moscow." Another joke asked, "What are you doing *trotskeying* along here, and who is that gorky [sounds like *gorjeo,* "chirping"] fellow?"[17]

Perhaps most controversial was the administration's program of sex education as part of an attempt to forge a secular, revolutionary consciousness in the Catholic country. This campaign provoked violent opposition, leading to the assassination of many rural teachers, and provided endless satiric material for the Follies. One revista, a fairy tale entitled *Bertoldo, Bertoldino y Cacaseno,* featured Cantinflas, Medel, and Don Catarino as agrarian radicals—the modern counterpart to medieval peasants—aspiring to marry the king's three daughters. The problem that inevitably arose in such tales was that the oldest had to marry first, and when played by Amelia Wilhelmy at her shrewish best, there were no takers. "La Wily" took the tone of a sex education instructor explaining men to her younger sisters, one of whom was played by Marina Tamayo in her theatrical debut. "A man can serve for many things . . . depending on how a woman uses him." The young princess emphatically agreed: "Yes, all men are half useful!" Wilhelmy continued: "Well, the one for me has to be a new model. . . . And I'm going to put a sign on him like they have at the pharmacy: 'For internal use only. Agitate before using.' "[18]

Moreno had truly arrived when Vicente Lombardo Toledano acknowledged his satire in the summer of 1937. While Cárdenas felt secure enough of his own popular support to tolerate the most virulent attacks from the political theater, the CTM boss risked his own prestige by descending to the level of Cantinflas. Alfonso Taracena claimed that Lombardo introduced the comic to the "temple of fame," but in fact the incident of the "Polemic of the Century" demonstrated how scriptwriters worked behind the scenes to create the image of Cantinflas. Salvador Novo, a staunch critic of Cardenismo, initiated the exchange on July 10, 1937, in his unsigned column in the illustrated magazine *Hoy.* The editorial, which described a labor union conference being held in Mexico City, began with a reference to Cantinflas and Medel practicing their oratory skills at the Follies Bergère. Although the reference was intended as a snub, Lombardo picked up on the theme in a published response to his old adversary, CROM boss Luis Morones, who had called for a public debate. "If Morones proposes to demonstrate his dialectical capabilities," Lombardo announced in *El Universal,* "he should debate with Cantinflas." At least one journalist misunderstood the reference as suggesting a debate with "Candingas," the devil.[19]

Cantinflas then intervened with an interview in *Todo,* published on August 12, under the title "The Polemic of the Century: Cantinflas vs. Morones." Ostensibly aimed at the aging CROM boss, the discourse actually attacked the powerful CTM leader, dragging him down to the comedian's level. "The first thing I thought of was to go see Lombardo to ask him with what object . . . but then I thought, well, no! Because thinking well, really, the Licenciado could not have picked anyone better to resolve the resolution of the problem . . . Because as I say, naturally, now that if he cannot fix anything and says a lot, the same thing happens with me, and we'll never reach an agreement." Cantinflas also spoofed the scientific language of dialectical materialism that Lombardo used to discuss the problems of workers. "Why has the cost of living risen? Because everything to be living has to live, that is, the principle of gravitation that comes to be the most grave thing . . . Now then, comrades, compañeros, friends . . . I implore you to explain to me what I just said."[20]

The authorship of this supposed debate remains open to question. Although attributed to Carlos León, a playwright for the Follies, the discourse may well have been the work of Salvador Novo, whose literary style of constantly inventing new words—"novovocablos"—represented an educated version of Cantinflas's verbal playfulness. In any event, Novo dedicated his next column in *Hoy,* on August 21, to a comparison between Lombaro's rhetoric that "the socialist ideal is idealistic because it begins with material goods and ends with the immaterial" and Cantinflas's nonsense speech, "Comrades, there are moments in life that are truly momentary."[21]

After this triumph over Lombardo, and with *Así es mi tierra* playing in theaters, Cantinflas became a regular contributor to bourgeois illustrated magazines. Although the actual authorship of these works cannot be determined, the reactionary themes of the Follies remained prominent. Cantinflas continued his satire of the CTM boss, for example, asking Lombardo: "Why have you changed so much since your trip to Europe? I don't recognize you." This seemingly innocuous remark served to question the union leader's masculinity and patriotism through a common albur implying that the union leader was the passive sexual partner of Soviet leader Joseph Stalin.[22] Cantinflas also broadened his social commentary, contributing a piece on women's suffrage in the magazine *Vea.* "The vote for women is a problem of bankruptcy, because that's what we'll be if women vote." Speaking of a group of suffragettes on hunger strike in the state of Sinaloa, he said, "I want to ask these insubordinate comrades, in what violent and stubborn manner they violate the sacred rights of the no less sacred and indispensable furniture called man. And I say furniture, because at any moment we are thrown out in the street, as if we hadn't paid the parking fees."[23]

Even Cantinflas supported the Cárdenas administration in its supreme nationalist triumph, the expropriation of foreign petroleum companies. What started as a labor dispute between local workers and their U.S. and British employers escalated into an international crisis after the oil companies refused to accept an arbitration decision handed down by the Mexican Supreme Court. President Cárdenas ordered the expropriation on March 18, 1938, and when the two sides could not agree on just compensation, Standard Oil of New Jersey led the producers in a boycott of Mexican petroleum. Without oil tankers, the government had little hope of paying the nearly $500 million demanded by the foreign companies, but in a remarkable outpouring of patriotic sentiment, the Mexican people volunteered their personal savings to help guarantee the nation's economic independence. Cantinflas did his part for the campaign, explaining the oil companies' duplicity in terms of milk vendors, a language comprehensible to common people in the streets: "The petroleum comes and the petroleum came. The petroleum goes and it hasn't been able to leave. Why? Ahí está el detalle. We sell it cheap, we're merchants . . . and they don't buy it. Is it adulterated? It cannot be, comrades! The petroleum is pure, refined, substantial, expropriated. And nevertheless, it's leftover. Why don't we make an effort and pay for it all at once?"[24]

The oil expropriation marked the high point of Cardenista nationalism, and the following two years served to consolidate previous reforms. The president worked first to institutionalize working-class participation in the official party, which was renamed the Mexican Revolutionary Party (Partido Revolucionario Mexicano, PRM) and reorganized into four sectors representing the military, labor, peasant, and middle-class constituencies. Meanwhile, economic troubles, arising only in part from the boycott, forced the administration to restrain union activism and encourage business productivity. But the key to the Cardenista legacy lay with the presidential succession of 1940, and as rumors began spreading in the summer of 1938 over the PRM nominee,

Cantinflas declared his candidacy in the pages of *Rotofoto*. Acknowledging his labor constituency, he waxed eloquently about the power of the strike, describing it as "something that inspires, that brings emotion, that gives you a rest." He also promised to continue the revolutionary reforms: "I will redistribute a peasant to every ejido, and a *quejido* [groan] to every peasant. I will give the vote to all women, and women to all voters."[25]

By employing political pronouncements in the cause of personal notoriety, Moreno took an imminently modern approach to constructing stardom. But such scandal mongering could backfire, as the comic discovered while performing a revista entitled *La segunda conquista (1521–1939)* (The second conquest), about the Republican refugees who took shelter in Mexico after the victory of fascist armies under General Francisco Franco in the Spanish Civil War. Although Moreno refrained from attacking the exiles directly, his humor alienated a group that included some of the most prominent intellectuals of the succeeding generation. And in an ironic twist, seven years later, when Mario Moreno was thrust into politics, these same Spaniards became a critical constituency.

"Between Two Seas"

Mario Moreno pursued a mock career in politics to gain public recognition, but at the height of his popularity he began shifting the image of Cantinflas in other directions. Perhaps he realized that if he remained simply a parody of Vicente Lombardo Toledano, he would lose his popular appeal when the labor leader fell from power. And that eventuality seemed ever more likely as conservatism gained strength in the final years of the Cárdenas administration. Moreover, by depoliticizing his alter ego, Moreno sought to rise above party politics and become a symbol of the Mexican people in general. He cultivated such an association by playing on Samuel Ramos's profile of the pelado, whether consciously or not, and contemporáneo critics returned the favor with publicity. But this attempt to represent the entire Mexican pueblo drove a wedge between the newly wealthy Mario Moreno and the still humble Cantinflas. Where on stage "El Panzón" Soto had sailed "between two seas," adjusting his act from reserved bourgeois propriety to pornographic plebeian albures, depending on the crowd, motion pictures allowed but one final take.[26] The young Moreno possessed an impressive range of facial expression, helping him bridge these competing audiences, yet over time this personality split widened until he could no longer reconcile the contradictions.

One of the first indications of this class tension between actor and character emerged in an interview with Bohemian playwright Carlos Riva Larrauri, published on October 28, 1937, in *Todo*. The page layout in the photojournal immediately conveyed the distinction between Cantinflas and his now bourgeois creator. On the far left, the "authentic peladito" glowered in makeup and tattered gabardine, drawn up to his full arrogant height, with arms folded imperiously over his chest and head tilted scornfully back. A matching photo on the far right illustrated the "intimate Cantinflas," standing in the same pose, but smiling in a bathrobe. Enclosed within these two extremes were scenes of bourgeois life: Moreno in fashionable black clothes and polished shoes, his new car and chauffeur, and finally, the height of respectability, his wedding portrait. The text continued in this vein, noting that "in portraying the authentic peladito, Cantinflas has accumulated considerable capital."[27] The interview functioned partly to demonstrate his respectability to middle-class audiences who might have avoided the premiere of *Así es mi tierra* a month earlier for fear of his plebeian carpa image.

Having "discovered" a new act, theater critics did their best to build up his character, trying with mixed success to make his ambiguity a source of interest to fashionable audiences. Miguel del Río observed in *Vea* that Mario Moreno "has been so tangled up by his character that now he doesn't know how to find which is his life, that of Mario Moreno, and which is that of Cantinflas."[28] Critics trumpeted Moreno as the premier actor of the times and the Follies Bergère as an obligatory stop for anyone in Mexico City. They also agreed on the source of his success—geniality; Riva Larrauri enthused that "apart from his grand theatrical qualities he has . . . that thing . . . personality!"[29] Inspired by such publicity, Moreno demanded a raise and walked out when Furstenberg refused to pay more than a hundred pesos a night. Without Cantinflas on the bill, ticket sales plummeted until the desperate impresario sent Eduardo Moreno, the actor's younger brother, searching for him in the provinces. Mario finally returned, for double the salary plus 25 percent of ticket revenues, but increasing wealth did not guarantee Cantinflas acceptance among the haute bourgeoisie. In May, Furstenberg booked him at the upscale Grand Casino, but his interactive carpa style did not appeal to audiences trained by the opera to keep silent during the performance. As theater critic Armando de Maria y Campos reported, "Cantinflas bombed in his first appearance before a more responsible and demanding audience."[30]

Bourgeois audiences felt particularly threatened by the carpa's relentless probing of the corrosive effects of modern life on the family, masculinity, and patriarchy—precisely the themes of Arcady Boytler's next film, *Aguila o sol*. After the rural setting of *Así es mi tierra*, Cantinflas and Medel returned home to the carpa in a screenplay written by Guz Aguila. The title characters, Polito Sol (Cantinflas), Carmelo Aguila (Medel), and Polito's girlfriend Adriana Aguila (Marina Tamayo), had grown up in the tent theater after running away from an orphanage. Their family unity was threatened by Castro (Luis G. Barreiro), their lounge-lizard manager, who wanted to sign Adriana to sing at the Principal Theater, leaving her brother and boyfriend behind. Don Hipólito (Manuel Arvide) introduced an Oedipal twist as a wealthy old man in love with Adriana who was also, unknowingly, the father of Polito. Unable to express his fears of losing Adriana, Polito joined Carmelo on a binge full of homosexual albures, then drifted off into nightmares of abandonment. Stable family life was finally restored when he awoke; Adriana assured him of her love and Castro reunited him with his father, Don Hipólito.

The film provides a unique historical document of the golden age of carpa theater under Cárdenas. Boytler's artistic panning shot made the transition between the nine-year old Adriana, singing for alms outside a theater with guitar accompaniment from her partners, and their grown-up versions performing the same number onstage. The song led into a tango in which Polito and Carmelo cut in repeatedly until in the confusion they wound up dancing together. After the next tanda, a flamenco song, the comic team interpreted the classic carpa encounter between Carmelo's city slicker, in a bowler hat and dark suit, and Polito's country bumpkin, wearing a tattered sombrero and an old sack for pants. The pelado described the hardships of urban life through a letter home to his family: "Father, send money. I'm living in the street, your Son," only to be told: "Son, watch out for cars, your Father." Later in the dialogue, Carmelo berated him for his crude and combative manner. "I'm not a fighter," Polito tried to explain. "We were singing, and I started with a Spanish folk song [bolero]. . . . Then the bootblack [same word] started up with me." Carmelo continued to goad him: "What gets me is the way you talk to the police. . . . When he says, 'Come with me,' what do you answer?" Polito: "You're not my type."

At Boytler's direction, Polito and Carmelo remained in character even when not on stage, thus destabilizing the boundaries between theater and reality. The alcoholic duet in the cantina and a cabaret dream sequence illustrated this subversive representation while highlighting their acting skills. A theater critic later asserted that nobody interpreted the vulgar drunk better than Cantinflas, not even Roberto Soto in the role of Luis Morones during an orgy at his Tlalpan ranch. "Soto presented the alcoholic at the edge of a coma, worn out from drink, while Cantinflas presents him in all of his euphoria and 'grandiloquence.'"[31] The cabaret, decorated in an exuberant tropical style complete with coconut trees, provided the ideal venue for such a performance. Polito's friends were present, Carmelo tending bar in a white tuxedo and Adriana singing a folkloric number in the flowered headdress of native women from Tehuantepec. But the euphoric binge became a nightmare of solitude when they refused to recognize him. Adriana discussed her solo career with Castro and gave Polito only a pitying smile. Carmelo showed still less sympathy, threatening to throw him out of the club for making trouble. Even the laws of nature seemed to join the conspiracy; coconuts came raining down on his head from artificial trees, and his mirror image turned him a cold shoulder. Surrounded by traitors, unable to find solace even in a bottle, Polito lashed out wildly at all around him.

Violence, alcoholism, and feelings of inarticulate inferiority combined to make Cantinflas the personification of Ramos's pelado. But where the philosopher saw only empty bravado in the aggressive language, the film critic Xavier Villaurrutia found genuine art. "From the gap between the desire to find the right words and the failure to do so gushes forth a fountain of humor." And beyond the humor, the critic discerned pathos. "Tragic in his impotence, comic in his results, the personality that Cantinflas has created in our midst is more complex than he appears superficially, and observing closely, the result is a form of tragicomedy."[32] The Oedipal struggle held particular significance in this regard, for the family provided the basis of Mexican society. Many of the character flaws Ramos described, such as lack of self worth and rootlessness, may have derived in part from lack of a stable family life. The pelado was, by definition, uprooted from the certainties of village life and thrust into the vagaries of the city. Polito joked about his absent father warning him to watching out for cars in order to laugh at his own life as an orphan. By leaving his son to Catholic charity, Don Hipólito had first deprived him of a sheltered childhood, then threatened to ruin his married life with Adriana as well. The pelado shouted, "I am your father," not only to gain mastery in a patriarchal society but also to soothe the painful lack of a family life.

The two comedians also acted out the struggle for sexual mastery in the constant give and take of albures. In taking their bows on the carpa stage, Polito stroked his partner's chin, questioning Carmelo's masculinity with the phrase, "My how you've changed." Later, the two huddled perilously close at the bar, arms around each other's shoulders, leaning perilously close until their lips practically met. Polito then gently pushed Carmelo's face back and mumbled an apology, only to move in again for another feigned kiss. The joke continued in the next scene as they staggered back up to their hotel room. Carmelo took the lead in helping prepare his partner for bed by taking his pants off. The action quickly degenerated into a mock rape scene, with Carmelo insisting that it was uncouth and unhealthy to sleep in pants, and Polito plaintively repeating, *"No me forces, Carmelo,* don't force me." He finally gave up, leaving Polito to his drunken nightmare. His reconciliation with Adriana reestablished heterosexual norms, but in the final gag a pair of coconuts knocked the comic team into an unconscious embrace.

Cantinflas and Medel transgressed gender roles even further in their next screen appearance, *El signo de la muerte* (The sign

"It's called the sacrificial stone because of the great sacrifices needed to carry it to the museum." El signo de la muerte, *production still. Courtesy: Cineteca Nacional.*

of death, 1939), which referred to one of the day signs from the Aztec calendar. The film added pre-Hispanic color to the Hollywood horror genre, with a neo-Aztec cult reviving the practice of human sacrifice to drive out the Spaniards and restore the rule of Quetzalcoatl. Moreno brought Cantinflas's lunatic language to the role of museum guide as he explained the mysteries of the ancient civilizations with a few mysteries of his own. He started the tour at the giant circular calendar stone, standing underneath, Atlas-like, in a splendid sight gag. Next he moved on to the sacrificial stone, so called because it "had to have cost great sacrifices to carry it to the National Museum." Medel played a detective investigating the murders who was propelled through the movie by an inner logic that never became entirely clear.

The film actually depicted one of the sacrifices on camera, a scene made all the more shocking when the priest tore off the maiden's dress before plunging the obsidian dagger into her naked breast. Catholicism notwithstanding, Mexicans produced a number of soft-core porn films in the 1920s, and nudity returned to the screen in the mid-1950s, but in the straight-laced days around 1940, bourgeois families recoiled in horror, no doubt attributing such degeneration to Cardenista sex education. And even the sacrificial scene seemed tame compared with the appearance of Cantinflas in drag. The film contained only two brief moments of transvestitism, the first when Cantinflas dressed as a woman to investigate the maidens' disappearance, and the second when a drunken Medel imagined himself to be the Emperor Maximilian and saw Cantinflas as his consort, Carlotta.

The outrageous nature of the film derived in part from the avant-garde artists behind the scenes. The director, Chano Urueta, had made his first Mexican feature film, *Profanación* (Profanation, 1933), about the curse of a jade collar dug up from the tomb of an Aztec lord, an indigenous version of the Hollywood mummy series. Another luminary of the period, the composer Silvestre Revueltas, had just returned from Spain, where he had fought for the Republican cause in the Civil War. In addition to the "Homenaje a García Lorca," written for the young Spanish poet murdered by the fascists, he had created a number of nationalist symphonies with pre-Hispanic roots, such as "Cuauhnáhuac." Most controversial of all the contributors to the film was the screenwriter and artistic director, Salvador Novo. Known for his anti-Cardenista political columns in a country of macho politicians, Novo behaved in an outrageously effeminate manner. Ridiculed by such albures as "Nalgador Sobo" (buttocks fondler), particularly from the muralist Diego Rivera, he responded by plucking his eyebrows. Meanwhile, he faced down opponents with the wit of a Hispanic Oscar Wilde.[33]

Novo wrote *El signo de la muerte* in part as a poke at Rivera and the sham of Indian identity among Mexico's postrevolutionary elite. An amateur Nahuatl scholar, Novo sprinkled the movie with pre-Hispanic references, such as a map illustrated with the same footprints used in ancient codices to indicate the pilgrimage from the ancestral home of Aztlan to the promised land of the eagle and serpent, Tenochtitlan. Nevertheless, Emilio García Riera dismissed the film's "total submission to a Hollywood formula: confronting a dynamic, healthy, recognizable modernity with a mysterious, ominous and gloomy antiquity. . . . In this way, the Mexican cinema did not set an image of its own pre-Hispanic past distinct from that of the 'white,' 'occidental' and

Complementary transgressions. (Top) *The sacrificial maiden with naked breasts, a shocking image for Mexico in 1939.* El signo de la muerte, *production still. Courtesy: Cineteca Nacional.* (Bottom) *Another unsettling scene for bourgeois Mexicans, Cantinflas in drag as the Empress Carlotta with Medel as Maximilian.* El signo de la muerte, *production still. Courtesy: Cineteca Nacional.*

colonialist style of Hollywood or Europe."[34] But in this case the distinguished film historian failed to appreciate Novo's satire of the neo-Aztecs among his neighbors in Coyoacán. By presenting Carlos Orellana, who had enough of a Spanish visage to star in the sainete *No te engañes, corazón,* as the millenarian Dr. Gallardo, Novo spoofed the Aztec revival championed by Rivera. The muralist had established his credentials as a leader of the postrevolutionary artistic renaissance by plastering Quetzalcoatl images in the National Palace, collecting archaeological relics, and encouraging his wife, Frida Kahlo, to dress in flowery Tehuana costumes. The irony lay in the Marxist bluster of an artist who had turned to painting Indian nudes for bourgeois patrons, thus performing a ritual cleansing of the indigenous masses that was similar, in a way, to Cantinflas's sublimation of the potentially dangerous urban pelado.

No simple reference to Novo's gender transgressions will explain the appearance of Cantinflas dressed in drag as Carlotta in *El signo de la muerte,* let alone the shocking behavior of previous movies. In considering these homoerotic allusions, one must first recall that Ramos exaggerated the sexual meaning of albures, which were often a form of good-natured humor among drinking buddies. Such playfulness undoubtedly accounts for the scenes in *Así es mi tierra,* when Tejón questioned the Licenciado's masculinity by comparing him to a former girlfriend. Viewers in the United States must also bear in mind that, generally speaking, Mexican culture has a much closer concept of personal space. Anthropologist Matthew Gutmann described a range of acceptable physical contact far in excess of comparable norms in the United States. Teenage males could walk down the street with their arms around each other's shoulders without anyone giving a second glance, although they could not hold hands as girls often did. Even greater intimacy, such as the stroking and hugging of the cantina scene in *Aguila o sol,* became acceptable while drinking. As Gutmann observed: "Such physical contact among men in no way necessarily implies romantic or sexual relations between the men, as it might in other cultural contexts."[35]

Nevertheless, Cantinflas and Medel derived humor by pushing the boundaries of gender roles, forcing the audience to laugh at the breakdown of family values that became increasingly apparent in modern urban life. Chris Straayer has defined an entire genre of temporary transvestite films, attributing their enduring success to the way they allowed the audience to cross social boundaries vicariously. However, the producers had to provide social anchors for audience members to prevent them from becoming uncomfortable. One method was to heighten the sexuality of other scenes, for example, exposing the damsel's breasts before she was sacrificed in order to offset the troubling appearance of Cantinflas in a dress. In this way the film anticipated *Some Like It Hot* (1959), which balanced the drag scenes of Tony Curtis and Jack Lemmon with visions of Marilyn Monroe.[36]

Filmmakers also took care, on the one hand, to emphasize the difference between temporary transvestites and genuine homosexuals and, on the other, to restore heterosexual gender roles by the conclusion. The cantina scene in *Aguila o sol* contained a brief appearance by a stereotypically effeminate male, allowing Cantinflas to distance himself from social transgression with a punned warning to Medel: "Watch out around here or you will be *pegado* [literally "poked," an albur implying passive homosexual behavior, but which could also mean "imitated" in their affectionate embrace]." The film ended by reconciling Cantinflas with both his girlfriend and his father, resolving the homosexual question and the Oedipal dilemma at a stroke. Moreover, the challenge of the romantic triangle, won by Medel in *Así es mi tierra,* went to Cantinflas in *El signo de la muerte.* Another cinematic convention for reassuring audiences about gender-crossing scenes, in Mexico at least, was the consumption of alcohol, which allowed the macho to drop his guard and express his emotions.

Yet these multiple provisos notwithstanding, the gender reversals reflected a carnivalesque element of the early Cantinflas, who used cross-dressing as a strategy for turning the world upside down. And with this topic he had the last laugh, for in the resolution of each film, ambiguities remained about heterosexual norms. The final scene of *Aguila o sol* placed Cantinflas and Medel in a lovers' embrace, albeit an unconscious one. The triumph of Cantinflas, stealing Medel's girl in *El signo de la muerte,* was equally ambiguous. The object of their mutual affection was not the pretty peasant girl of *Así es mi tierra* but rather a farcical Margaret Dumont character to Cantinflas's Groucho Marx. Instead of signaling his victory with a kiss, she started speaking in cantinflismos, demonstrating once again that Cantinflas was more interested in the chase than in the consummation.

Although these early movies have since become classics, with *Aguila o sol* considered by some to be the best film Moreno ever made, contemporary popular response was tepid at best. Despite favorable reviews from the critic Xavier Villaurrutia and extensive coverage in glossy magazines, none of the films played more than two weeks in the premiere theaters. *El signo de la muerte* opened over the Christmas holiday of 1939 and vanished just one week later, taking the producers Felipe Mier and Pedro Maus down with it. One cannot blame the actor for the failure of an undercapitalized production company. Nevertheless, Moreno returned to the Follies in the New Year, depressed by his foundering cinema career.

Mario Moreno was still searching for a character with mass appeal that could reconcile his popular origins with the demands of middle-class filmgoers. The gradual closing of artistic possibilities through the resolution of his ambiguous profile appalled José Clemente Orozco, who noted that the frivolous theater "degenerated (this is no paradox) and turned political—and suitable for families. It became a tourist attraction. A chorus was introduced, Tehuanas with their cups of chocolate, black-suited dandies from the villages, with sentimental and vulgar songs done by singers from Los Angeles and San Antonio, Texas, things, all of them, insupportable, and in the worst possible taste, but dear to the hearts of decent families."[37] Moreno challenged that bourgeois complacency at first, through his willingness to interpret lines from many different scriptwriters. In particular, Salvador Novo employed Cantinflas as a mouthpiece for his paradoxical satire of Cardenista radicalism and bourgeois behavior. And just as the culmination of Cárdenas's reforms ushered in a new era of conservatism, so Moreno restrained the experimentation of his early films, although on occasion, he let the androgynous nature of Cantinflas slip past the albures that questioned the masculinity of others.

3

THE DETAILS OF FAME

"A star is hiding in Cantinflas," declared Jesús "Chucho" Grovas, and as the biggest film producer in Mexico, his word carried the force of a decree. His previous blockbuster, a nostalgic musical comedy, *En tiempos de Don Porfirio* (The good old days of Don Porfirio), had earned record receipts at the Alameda Theater in April 1940. Sitting in his office at CLASA studios, he discussed ideas for the next film with his partner and director, Juan Bustillo Oro. Mario Moreno had already acquired a reputation in the cinema industry as a difficult actor, and Bustillo Oro tried to change the producer's mind by pointing out, "He's very poorly trained. Can he study a script and learn the lines?" Grovas replied, "Ask him. Let's go see him at the Garibaldi theater." Bustillo Oro wrote in his memoirs that Grovas practically had to drag him to the north side of the city. Despite the applause of the Follies audience, the director was scarcely impressed by Moreno's acting ability. "He belongs on the street corner," Bustillo Oro concluded. Grovas shot back, "That's why he's such a treasure, don't you see?"[1] Just what a treasure became apparent when *Ahí está el detalle* premiered in September 1940, smashing all previous box office records and catapulting Moreno to international stardom. But his pelado image notwithstanding, he owed his fame as much to capitalist marketing as to Cantinflas's roots in popular culture.

"Chucho" Grovas was not the first Mexican businessman to find gold in the shabby clothes of Cantinflas; a year earlier, in 1939, advertising executive Santiago Reachi had made a similar pilgrimage to Plaza Garibaldi. Reachi correctly perceived that the future of Mexican capitalism lay in the expansion of domestic markets and that the best way to entice the masses to buy consumer goods was through the example of one of their own, the pelado Cantinflas. Together they formed a production company, Posa Films, and made a series of highly successful advertising shorts for such products as General Motors cars and Canada Dry ginger ale. Reachi also understood the importance of establishing Cantinflas as a brand in its own right, decades before promotional ties between films and consumer goods became a common advertising practice. Moreno's public image was boosted still further by the mid-1940s, when Posa Films, with its exclusive star as the most popular attraction in Mexican cinema, outstripped Grovas-Oro and other film companies in both profitability and production values. As predicted in the years of Cárdenas, Cantinflas had become bourgeois, and, all the more remarkably, he had done it without sacrificing his appeal to the lower classes.

Assured of stardom throughout the Spanish-speaking world, Moreno began reaching for the "universal theme." But in attempting to conquer audiences in Europe and the United States, he had taken on a far larger challenge, one that continued to elude him for more than a decade. A number of Mexican film stars, most notably Dolores del Río, Pedro Armendáriz, and Lupe Vélez, had achieved success in Hollywood, but always by sacrificing their local character and playing to foreign stereotypes. Although Moreno received offers from Hollywood producers, he turned them down, in part because his tremendous financial success gave him an artistic independence and allowed him to refuse to sell out Cantinflas. Instead, he remained in Mexico and between 1942 and 1943 filmed a series of parodies of Alexander Dumas's *The Three Musketeers,* Charlie Chaplin's *The Circus* (1928), and William Shakespeare's *Romeo and Juliet.* Enormously popular in Mexico and Latin America, these films failed to break into the U.S. market. Language, of course, stymied his success abroad, for Cantinflas never translated well. But just as baffling for non-Hispanics was the fundamentally Mexican persona Moreno impressed on D'Artagnan, the tramp, and Romeo. Gestures and references that sent Mexico City audiences into uncontrollable fits of laughter left New York City viewers scratching their heads. If his stubbornly local character proved a barrier to success in the United States, it nevertheless endeared Cantinflas to the Mexican lower classes long after Mario Moreno had escaped from the barrios.

But the critics were not so forgiving. They took pride in his regional conquests and conflated his success with Mexico's growing prominence in international affairs. Yet the honeymoon ended when Moreno could not live up to the impossible expectations of his early fame, in particular when his films failed to win audiences in the United States and thus did not conquer Hollywood for the national cinema industry. This division between popular success and critical approbation lasted, with only occasional respite, for the rest of his career. A close analysis of the reviewers' sense of betrayal in their first unfavorable critiques reveals much about the contentious public image of Cantinflas. In trying to gain broader recognition, Moreno parodied some of the leading icons of international culture from a plebeian Mexican stance. Reviewers found this humor to be moronic and tasteless, on a level with the dripping sentimentality of an Agustín Lara song.

One might conclude that the critics had fulfilled their social function in pointing out the abuse of great art by the cultural industries, which pandered to the base instincts of the lower classes. But the critics were not, in this case, neutral observers; indeed, the most polemical opponent of Moreno, Angel Alcántara Pastor, who wrote for *El Universal* under the name of Duende Filme (Film Goblin), was involved in a rival production company. Moreover, sociologist Pierre Bourdieu has criticized the western aesthetic tradition based on distinctions of taste, such as Aristotle's judgment of tragedy as being refined and comedy as merely vulgar. The bourgeoisie scorned the simple pleasures of the masses in order to establish itself as a cultured elite, worthy of holding political and economic power because of its superior taste. Over time, contempt for Cantinflas became a credential of membership in Mexico's intelligentsia.[2]

Fame also swept up the character of Cantinflas as Moreno used his films to reflect on changes within his own life. The contests of masculinity he had waged with Medel by way of albures, rivalries over women, and homoerotic scenes were replaced by a new plotline—still unsettling to traditional gender roles—in which Cantinflas became the object of romantic desire. His movies between 1940 and 1944 usually featured two female leads, one plebeian, the other wealthy, fighting for his attention— just as actresses began vying to boost their careers by appearing as his costar. Cantinflas invariably chose the common girl, reaffirming his ties to Mexican popular culture. These films also explored the ambiguity of identity within Mexico's social hierarchy by having the pelado mistaken for popular heroes and authority figures. Although one might interpret these films as unrealistic depictions of revolutionary social mobility, a chronic delusion of Moreno's later years, his 1940s roles as bullfighter, bourgeois, policeman, and dancer still seemed more characteristic of his earlier carnivalesque spirit, turning the world upside down.

The Pelado Salesman

The new consumer society, which introduced factory-made textiles to the British proletariat in the eighteenth century and the Sears Roebuck catalog to farmers in the United States a hundred years later, tried to win over Mexicans through advertisements in the country's first mass-circulation newspaper, *El Imparcial.* Founded in 1896, it featured ads for domestic producers, such as Carta Blanca beer and Salvatierra crackers, as well as imports like Coca-Cola. The Buen Tono cigarette factory established the best-known brand in Porfirian Mexico through such ingenious promotions as lotteries, balloon ascents, and free motion picture and revista shows. The Revolution of 1910 and the Great Depression delayed the growth of Mexican consumer goods industries, but in the mid-1930s the Cárdenas government sought to stimulate economic recovery by encouraging demand for domestic manufactures. Expanding local markets depended on both providing ordinary people with higher incomes and convincing them that soft drinks, consumer electronics, and automobiles were necessities of modern life, not simply luxuries for the rich. As a symbol of the Mexican pueblo, Cantinflas became a persuasive spokesman for the expansion of consumerism, particularly for foreign corporations seeking to project a local image. At the same time, Mario Moreno acquired a new, more marketable image.

Publicidad Organizada, S.A., the full name of Moreno's production company, Posa Films, revealed the importance of advertising work, both to promote consumer goods and to establish Cantinflas as a brand name in its own right. The inspiration came from Santiago Reachi, a revolutionary veteran with advertising experience and endless ambition. For his first film company, Superproducciones Mexicanas, S.A., in 1938, Reachi concocted an elaborate plan to lure Dolores del Río back from Hollywood to work with director Fernando de Fuentes on a film entitled *Captain Lentils*.[3] This grandiose scheme may have confirmed the actress's opinion of Mexican cinema as amateurish compared with studios in the United States, but Mario Moreno was captivated by the promoter's vision and signed with his production company in 1939. The third partner in Posa Films was Jacques Gelman, a Russian distributor of French films who arrived in Mexico to find himself stranded by the outbreak of World War II. His filmmaking experience, although limited primarily to working as a "still" photographer in European studios during the 1920s, made him an expert compared to Reachi and Moreno. Moreover, his continental background added a cosmopolitan air to the nascent production company.[4]

In the first year of its existence, Posa made five shorts of about fifteen minutes each, directed by Fernando A. Rivero and Carlos Toussaint and based on scripts by Shilinsky. Three were original stories written as advertisements for consumer products, whereas the other two repeated familiar carpa skits. The first, a promotion for Eveready batteries entitled *Siempre listo en tinieblas* ("Always ready in the dark" or "Always smart in the confusion," 1939), transformed Cantinflas into a bourgeois defending his home from robbery, an ironic twist for a character known as a vagabond and thief. Although playing the proud owner of a house full of the tacky knickknacks so beloved of the Mexican middle class, Cantinflas made a connection with his pelado past by pulling his gabardine scarf over a long nightshirt to investigate the strange noises coming from the living room. But when a gust of wind blew out his candle, the macho facade crumbled and he plunged, terrified, back under the bed sheets. At this point his wife took charge, pulling out a flashlight with Eveready batteries conveniently nearby, and sent Cantinflas out to confront the intruder. Peeking cautiously into the living room, Cantinflas asked, "Who's there?" The robber replied, "Nobody," and lifted another bauble from the mantle while Cantinflas returned to bed. After several timid confrontations, Cantinflas finally captured the burglar, becoming a hero, and for a final punch line, demonstrated his marksmanship by shooting a hole in his ceiling.

The next short, *Jengibre contra dinamita* (Ginger ale versus dynamite, 1939), likewise raised the pelado to middle-class respectability when he apprehended a dangerous criminal. Cantinflas won a barroom brawl because he drank Canada Dry ginger ale while the gun-toting outlaw dimmed his reflexes with hard liquor—another bizarre testimonial from Mexico's favorite alcoholic character. Cantinflas once again unsettled masculine behavior by dancing with more feminine grace than his partner, Gloria Marín. Moreover, when the desperado tried to cut in, she pulled away, leaving the pelado dancing with the thug. A pantomime fight ensued in which Cantinflas kept ducking away, at one point crawling between the big man's legs. In all the prancing about, he grabbed the outlaw's pistol, just as the police arrived. Once the brute was safely handcuffed, the emboldened Cantinflas thrashed him soundly with his hat, a cowardly act perhaps, but the detective insisted that the pelado was a "real macho." The film's resolution took place at several levels, prominently emphasizing the sponsor. Cantinflas used his $5,000 reward to buy ginger ale for everyone in the bar, carefully pronouncing the brand name but denying any knowledge of English, thus reaffirming his nationality while spoofing arriviste Mexican nabobs with affected North American accents. The narrative also reached a proper bourgeois conclusion by having Cantinflas marry Gloria Marín. The lesson was clear: The proper consumer lifestyle guaranteed wealth, success with women, and triumph over adversity.

General Motors hired Cantinflas to promote these consumer ideals, along with the 1940 model Chevrolet, in *Cantinflas ruletero* (Cantinflas, cabby, 1940). The short film opened with a scene familiar to all residents of Mexico City: a taxi driver snoozing in an old clunker. Awakened by a customer, Cantinflas could not get the motor started and made the client get out and push. When the exhausted "passenger" finally reached his destination, an automobile dealership, Cantinflas argued with him over the fare. Just then an attractive young woman walked up, and the cabby offered a piropo, "Nice lines." She shot back a dirty look, and he quickly explained that he meant the new model car. He followed her inside but failed either to join her for a test drive or to sneak off with spare parts for his rusted cab. Nevertheless, Cantinflas had a chance to redeem himself when the young woman was attacked by a group of men outside the dealership. He cranked the ignition, causing a tremendous backfire that scared the assailants. She got into the car and they made their getaway, this time with Cantinflas pushing. When they reached her house, she invited him inside to meet her many sisters, and soon the pelado achieved his dream: the Cantinflas taxi company, with a row of shining new Chevrolets each attended by one of the beautiful sisters. But at least the film admitted it was a dream from which the poor cabby awoke at a nudge from his next fare.

These films sought to achieve a double purpose: selling the ideal of consumption to the common people while selling Cantinflas, and by extension the harmless peladito image, to the Mexican bourgeoisie. As entertainment they were hugely successful, and theater owners actually paid for the right to show them, reversing the more usual arrangement of advertisers paying to announce their products. A host of promotional offers followed, including a radio special announcing the grand opening of a department store called Distribuidores 1.2.3, a regular program on XEW sponsored by Coca-Cola, and countless press ads for razor blades, cigarettes, tailor shops, and the like. Reachi obtained a contract to publicize GM car shows by explaining that "Cantinflas was truly the incarnation of the Mexican 'peladito,' festive, happy, a smooth talker, and therefore a great attraction for the humble people."[5] Of course, anyone too humble to possess a driver's license was denied entrance, but the huge demand for Moreno's publicity work provided an eloquent testimonial to his success in selling the consumer dream.

Ahí está el detalle

When Jesús Grovas ordered his director to write a script for Cantinflas, Juan Bustillo Oro naturally suggested Lizardi's *Itching Parrot,* in part for the prestige of adapting a historical and literary classic. But the producer vetoed the concept for financial reasons; having just paid to film nearly three hours of Porfirian musical comedy, he refused to recreate the City of Palaces

for an extended colonial epic. Grovas and Moreno were growing impatient when Bustillo finally delivered a story based on
his early experience as a lawyer, working pro bono to defend
the inmates at Belén jail. His clients had been real-life versions
of Cantinflas, fast-talking, street-wise denizens of Tepito and
Peralvillo who confounded the judicial system with clever arguments that often buried them even deeper in trouble. The film,
Ahí está el detalle, succeeded by exposing the fault lines in
Mexican society between the catrín and the pelado, and as
Emilio García Riera observed, between the artificial theatrical
humor of Bustillo Oro and the spontaneous unpredictability of
the carpa performer Moreno.[6]

The actual filming took less than three weeks in the summer
of 1940, including a one-day break to allow Carlos Toussaint to
film the short *Cantinflas y su prima* (Cantinflas and his cousin).
Perhaps the greatest difficulty for Bustillo Oro was dealing with
Moreno's improvisations. During their initial meeting backstage
at the Follies, the actor had explained that the reason he improvised was the poor quality of the scripts. "If the dialogue is
really funny, I'll take the trouble to learn it and do what I have
to."[7] In his memoirs, the director conceded that the star showed
remarkable discipline throughout the filming and that when he
did ad-lib, the lines were invariably funny. Bustillo Oro nevertheless insisted on stopping to rewrite the script whenever these
vaciladas wandered away from the story line. This practice
helped maintain the film's coherence but at the cost of many
fine jokes, which not even Moreno could duplicate.

As a comedy of manners, juxtaposing high and low, the film
opened with an encounter between two distinct characters from
the Mexico City underworld, the mobster, Bobby Lechuga, and
the vagabond, Cantinflas. The former was lurking outside the
house of a wealthy industrialist in order to blackmail his former
girlfriend, the businessman's wife. While waiting for a signal
from inside, he pulled a packet of incriminating letters from the
pocket of his double-breasted suit, at the same time dropping
his wallet on the ground. Cantinflas, neither well dressed nor
particularly dangerous, emerged from hiding behind a nearby
tree, snatched the loose billfold, and continued on toward the
same house. The two collided, and Cantinflas exclaimed, "I
swear I didn't do it." The mobster looked at him, baffled, while

he continued, "You know that when I walked by, I didn't even walk by. Somebody else had already walked by, and pocketed it first." Bobby snarled, "I don't know what the hell you're talking about." Cantinflas immediately changed his tone to one of superiority. "Well you should have said that to begin with. What if I keep talking and give myself away?" Bobby, still mystified but not wanting to be outsmarted, told him to watch where he was going, and Cantinflas answered literally that he did. "If not, somebody else would have plucked it." With triumphant flourish, he marched past Bobby into the house.[8]

Having spoofed Mexico City's criminal element, the director Bustillo Oro proceeded to lampoon the lower classes in the next scene by comparing the lazy Cantinflas with his dim-witted girlfriend, Pacita, the housekeeper. Dolores Camarillo played this role, which illustrates both the all-star cast of *Ahí está el detalle* and the incestuous nature of Mexican cinema. Popularly known as Fraustita, the wife of Antonio R. Frausto had not only won honors as best supporting actress for *En tiempos de Don Porfirio,* she was also Mexico's leading makeup artist, having received a grant from the Cárdenas government in 1936 to study with Max Factor in Hollywood. As Cantinflas slipped into the wealthy home to bum his next meal, Pacita berated him for not getting a job so they could get married. Cantinflas observed that he already had a job: stopping by her kitchen three times a day to eat. Besides, he continued, "If work were any good, the rich would have cornered the market in it." But Pacita insisted that before he could eat this time, he first had to shoot a rabid dog, also called Bobby. Cantinflas tried to talk his way out of the job, but rather than lose his meal ticket, he finally took the pistol, went out into the garden, closed his eyes tightly, and began firing randomly.

Some of the stray shots went through an upstairs window, leading the action from low to high, an encounter between the pompous industrialist, Don Cayetano, played by Joaquín Pardavé, and his wayward wife, Dolores, played by Sofía Alvarez. The casting again proved magnificent, for during his years in the revista theater, Pardavé had cultivated the supercilious manner and neatly waxed mustache of the Creole elite, while the tall, haughty Alvarez had gained notoriety for her well-publicized affair with the Raja of India.[9] The struggle between them naturally turned on honor. Don Cayetano, insanely jealous, questioned every movement by Dolores as she glanced furtively out the window for a sign from her former lover. Secretly plotting to catch her in the act of adultery, Don Cayetano made a great production of leaving on a business trip, extravagantly promising not to return that night under any circumstances. Bobby Lechuga took the opportunity to sneak upstairs and confront Dolores, while downstairs a drunken Cantinflas lustfully chased the maid. Suddenly, Don Cayetano reappeared at the front door, with detectives in tow. Pacita frantically locked Cantinflas in the liquor closet then hurried upstairs to hide Bobby from the jealous husband.

The succeeding encounter between Don Cayetano and Cantinflas represented an archetypal struggle of Mexican social extremes, played out in times past by the "Couplets of Don Simón" and the "Discourse of Vale Coyote," and most recently, the sly revolutionary mestizo and the pompous Porfirian Creole. Cantinflas gave away his hiding place by sampling one of the fine cigars in the liquor closet. Don Cayetano, assuming Cantinflas to be his wife's lover, threw open the closet door, gun at the ready. The pelado ignored the threat and proceeded to disarm his opponent through his genial, and completely inappropriate, politesse. He cordially invited the businessman to have a drink of his own alcohol, causing Don Cayetano to hesitate for a moment before remembering his purpose and ordering the intruder out. Still playing the polite host, Cantinflas answered, "I'm fine in here, thank you. Why don't you come in? There are cookies, brandy, cigars. . . ." Again the unexpected response beguiled the Creole, who demurred, "Thank you, I just ate," before repeating his order to get out. The pelado thereupon agreed that it was late and headed for the door. This time Don Cayetano ordered him to halt there, which caused more confusion as Cantinflas took the command literally and tried to determine precisely *where* he was supposed to stand. When the industrialist finally got past that debate and demanded to know why he was there, Cantinflas inevitably answered, "Well, you told me to stand right here." He then proceeded to ask the same question of Don Cayetano, who replied angrily, "Don't you know that I'm the husband?" The jealous Creole assumed the vagabond to be his wife's lover, but Cantinflas knew nothing of this family matter and inquired, "Whose husband?" Don Cayetano answered with a pronoun of indeterminate gender, "Su marido," which Cantinflas misinterpreted as: "My husband? *¡Ay chirrión!* Listen here. Don't say that. People might overhear. And my reputation!"[10]

Unable to understand the fast-talking vagabond, let alone extract a confession, Don Cayetano left him with the detectives and went upstairs to confront his wife. Thinking that Bobby had been caught, Dolores invented an explanation that he was her long-lost brother, Leonardo del Paso, whose return the couple had been awaiting in order to claim her inheritance. In keeping with Mexican stereotypes of the Creole, Don Cayetano's jealousy was surpassed only by his greed, and the thought of an inheritance instantly transformed him. With a saccharine grin, he descended the stairs to embrace Cantinflas, who prudently held back until Don Cayetano promised not to shoot him. Then the policemen objected to this contrived family reunion, having been promised a chance to see the businessman's statuesque wife in flagrante delicto. Bustillo Oro's camera thus continued

The pelado Cantinflas outwits the jealous Creole played by Joaquín Pardavé. Ahí está el detalle, *production still. Courtesy: Cineteca Nacional.*

its sardonic sweep of Mexican society by portraying the vice squad as a collection of Peeping Toms with badges.

The second part of the movie portrayed Cantinflas's brief flirtation with the Mexican bourgeoisie. Life as Don Cayetano's brother-in-law seemed heaven at first, with no job beyond lounging about in a bathrobe, cuddling his "sister," Dolores, and ordering around the maid, Pacita, to the obvious displeasure of both women. But he soon found himself entangled in the responsibilities of middle-class life because of the arrival of Leonardo del Paso's common law wife, Clothilde, and her eight delinquent children. Sara García, the grandmother of Mexican cinema, revived the role of the lower-class woman earlier made famous by Amelia Wilhelmy. As the picaro's nemesis, every bit as quick-witted as Cantinflas, Clothilde immediately sized up the situation and told the children that if they wanted to eat regular meals they should call Cantinflas "father." Don Cayetano then insisted that "Leonardo" fulfill his familial responsibilities by marrying the woman. Nothing could have been worse for Cantinflas than a wife and children, but unfortunately the civil judge could not hear the nimble words he used while trying to talk his way out of the ceremony. Worse still, the clerk, played by Shilinsky, translated his rambling equivocal responses into unambiguous one-word answers. A moment before the judge pronounced them married, police arrived to arrest Leondardo del Paso for the murder of Bobby Lechuga. Considering incarceration preferable to marriage, the vagabond continued with the false identity. The police searched him, found the victim's wallet, and carried him off to jail.

This confusion of words and identities culminated in the courtroom scene, which Emilio García Riera has described as "one of the most entertaining in the entire history of Mexican cinema."[11] The humor arose from a misunderstanding between the authorities putting Cantinflas on trial for the murder of Bobby Lechuga and the defendant, who answered their questions assuming that Bobby was the rabid dog he had killed in the opening scene. Cantinflas unsettled the courtroom proceedings by misinterpreting the language of authority, just as he had confounded Don Cayetano in an earlier scene. When the clerk tried to take his sworn testimony, using the legal formula that translated literally as, "Do you protest?" Cantinflas answered,

"Certainly, I protest. Why wouldn't I protest when you make such a fuss over my having killed a dog?" The prosecutor jumped on the remark as evidence of his disdain for the murder victim: "Aha. I ask the gentlemen of the jury to take note of the accused's insistence on treating his victim as a dog."

Cantinflas, still oblivious to the murder charges, compounded his apparent guilt through misunderstanding and distrust of his own lawyer. Rather than viewing the public defender as an ally, the pelado considered him as just another authority figure out to get him. The lawyer tried leading him into a plea of self-defense by stating, "Your life was in danger when you met him." But Cantinflas responded truthfully, "No, not really. He only wagged his tail." The defense attorney then switched tactics to an insanity plea, describing the pelado's words as "the typical responses of an idiot . . . the typical interruptions of a mental retard." This only provoked Cantinflas to defend his self-respect by adding "the typical Lerdo de Tejada." His remark parroted the lawyer with an albur sounding like slow (*lerdo*) brained (*techado,* literally "roof"), but redirected back at the legal expert with references to an ineffectual nineteenth-century president, Sebastián Lerdo de Tejada, and a popular but eccentric band leader, Miguel, who played Sunday afternoons in Chapultepec Park. Cantinflas then asked the judge to order the defense attorney to stop insulting him. By this point the verdict seemed a foregone conclusion, and the courtroom reporters spoke for the public in describing the defendant as "hateful" and "cold-blooded." After the litany of disrespectful and self-incriminating statements, the jury did not even bother to deliberate and announced his guilt as self-evident. The judge agreed, invoking the death penalty.

But Cantinflas subverted the moment of truth by infecting the room with his chaotic insanity until the court officials turned against one another. When Leonardo del Paso's family, Dolores, Pacita, and Clothilde, stepped forward to insist that Cantinflas was innocent, the judge assumed it to be another of the defense attorney's tricks and fined the attorney for contempt of court. Then the real Leonardo del Paso revealed himself and confessed to having killed Bobby Lechuga in defense of his own life and his sister's honor. The already overdetermined identities spun completely out of control, leaving the confused officials speaking in cantinflismos. The defense attorney announced, "Ahí está el detalle . . . the dog, the cat . . . Leonardo is innocent . . . the other Leonardo is innocent too . . . or not?" The prosecutor concurred, "Ahí está el detalle . . . totally . . . you, me, all of us . . . just self-defense." Finally, the judge accepted their arguments, "Oh, look . . . ahí está el detalle, really . . . why no . . . why yes . . . why didn't you say so before . . . ? All is explained." Cantinflas crossed his arms and concluded smugly, "Ahí está el detalle. The people understand when we speak among *cristianos*." "Christians" was a common term of the sixteenth century to distinguish the *gente de razón* (people of reason), who spoke Spanish, from Native Americans. By applying it to his own confused language, Cantinflas not only questioned the Mexican government, he turned the clock back on the entire Spanish conquest, more than four centuries of European domination.

Cantinflas Undercover

Mario Moreno continued to gain fame in 1941 with two more universally acclaimed films, *Ni sangre, ni arena* (Neither blood nor sand) and *El gendarme desconocido* (The unknown policeman). Both were produced by Posa Films, which guaranteed him financial and artistic independence; nevertheless, fame had its effects on the character of Cantinflas. The pelado began to assume new roles, first a bullfighter and then a policeman, allowing Moreno to examine critically the Mexican social hierarchy and also beginning an upward mobility that would take the character away from its lower-class roots. At the same time, these films fixed Cantinflas in a new masculine role, thereby putting an end to all but the briefest vaciladas of gender.

Financial success allowed Moreno to build a personal team of filmmakers willing to respect his improvisational acting style. He had been prepared at first to sign an exclusive contract with Jesús Grovas, but the producer refused his demand of $15,000 per film, a small fraction of what he later earned, and Moreno therefore continued with Posa. Reachi immediately proved his worth as a producer by suggesting their first feature-length film, a parody of Rouben Mamulien's production of the Vicente Blasco Ibáñez novel, *Blood and Sand* (1940), thus allowing Cantinflas a free ride on Hollywood publicity. Reachi also helped finance the film through product placements, reportedly charging a Mexican brewing company $10,000 for an extended shot of Cantinflas performing his pelado act framed by an advertising poster.[12] In filming this picture, Moreno acquired a regular screenwriter, Jaime Salvador, a fellow bullfighting aficionado from Barcelona who had come to Mexico, like Gelman, as a film distributor. Salvador was censured more than once for stealing ideas, but Moreno cared little about original scripts, preferring instead to trust his improvisational skills. This tendency to ad-lib quickly brought the former carpa star into conflict with director Alejandro Galindo. He became violently angry, according to Reachi, shouting "cut" and calling Moreno a "*pendejo*" (ass), but the renowned filmmaker simply attributed the differences to the theater, where "actors acquire certain habits . . . well it's difficult to eradicate them."[13] In any event, Galindo walked off the set of *Ni sangre, ni arena* to be replaced by his assistant, Miguel M. Delgado, who had worked in Hollywood in the 1920s and with Fernando de Fuentes a decade later. Delgado possessed both technical skill and infinite patience, allowing him to serve as Moreno's regular director for the rest of his career.

In *Ni sangre, ni arena,* Moreno initiated what would become a regular plot device: questioning the social hierarchy by playing two roles—this time, Cantinflas the pelado and Manolete the bullfighter. The film opened with Cantinflas outside the *plaza de toros* (bullfighting arena), frustrated by his inability to see Manolete perform. When a policeman tried to chase him off for loitering, the pelado taunted him with a matador's technique, swaying back and forth to incite the cop to charge like a bull, then skipping away to safety—a novel use for his macho posturing. Having imitated the bullfighter, Cantinflas then exchanged places with him simply by putting on his flamenco jacket and hat, thereby demonstrating the emptiness of a social hierarchy that ranked people solely on their clothes. The role reversal took place on a train to Pedregal in which Manolete rode first class and Cantinflas stowed away with the baggage. The conductor, who had been chasing Cantinflas, suddenly became respectful when the pelado disguised himself in the flamenco costume, while the bullfighter, having taken off his jacket in the bathroom, was thrown in jail. At a party that evening at a great hacienda, the hosts overlooked the pelado's lack of social graces with the comment, "He's a genius, and like all geniuses, something of an eccentric." Trading places with the bullfighter also allowed Cantinflas to demonstrate the superiority of Mexican culture. At the party, he performed a parody of a Spanish folk song, warbling like a wounded bird and dancing the "flamenco of Ixtacalco." Pedro Armendáriz, a transnational actor with experience in Hollywood, provided another foil for Mexican culture as an Americanized dandy, Frank, who was courting Manolete's girlfriend without success.

The film also showcased Moreno's genuine talent as a comic bullfighter, although he later maintained that "to really know the bulls should be an exclusive privilege of the cows."[14] Manolete had not revealed the mistaken identity because he wished to retire, and therefore he instructed his team of picadors and banderilleros to send Cantinflas into the arena of Pedregal for this final performance. Seeing the terrified pelado desperately trying to avoid entering the arena, Manolete had a change of heart and

Cantinflas modernizes Mexico through a comic bullfight. Courtesy: Archivo General de la Nación.

informed the police chief of the mistake. But when the cop came down to prevent the fight, Cantinflas thought that he was about to be arrested and decided it was safer to confront the bull. The first act involved the banderillas, barbed shafts decorated with colored streamers, which were stabbed into the bull's neck to weaken his muscles and lower his head, thereby allowing the final sword thrust to be made over his horns. Cantinflas's approach could be called "stealth" bullfighting, sidling up to the animal with exaggerated casualness, like an amateur pickpocket approaching a mark on the street, the banderillas hidden behind his back, until suddenly he plunged them in and sprinted to safety. Cantinflas followed that act with a number of graceful cape passes but never actually killed an animal, either on camera or in his numerous benefit performances. He toured frequently for more than two decades, often with "Donky," the world's only *burro bravo* (fighting mule), to the applause of crowds throughout Mexico, Venezuela, and Peru, the principal bullfighting centers of Latin America.

Cantinflas once again subverted Mexican authorities in *El gendarme desconocido,* which featured the pelado transformed, through a series of accidents, into patrolman 777. His badge number became a lifelong talisman, and he also personalized the uniform to his unique sartorial standards by adding a scarf and letting the pants droop. When the inspecting sergeant asked him what happened to the regulation shirt and tie, the new police officer explained that they had been stolen. The sergeant then demanded to see his service pistol and berated him for swapping the standard issue .45 automatic for a .38 revolver. Cantinflas shoved the pistol back inside his pants and jumped from the cold metal. The sergeant bellowed, "No holster?" Cantinflas answered, "No underwear." Agent 777 then displayed his marching technique, swinging his hips back and forth in an effeminate manner, making the whole force out to be a collection of sissies. The sergeant called out "right face," but he turned left instead, disrupting the entire column. When sent to the chief's office, he answered the phone and chatted familiarly with the caller, to the point of cuddling up on the desk. The commandant looked bemused at the obvious affection and finally asked Agent 777 who was speaking. Cantinflas passed him the phone with the words, "Your wife."

The two films also settled Cantinflas into a new form of masculine behavior in which he became the object of a rivalry between girlfriends, allowing him to subvert macho posturing but without the threatening transgressions of his performances with Manuel Medel. In *Ni sangre, ni arena,* the pelado's working-class girlfriend saw his picture in the newspaper with the bull-fighter's wealthy lover and jealously chased him all the way to Pedregal. But in perhaps the most romantic conclusion of any Cantinflas film, she broke out in tears when he emerged from the arena unharmed, and he tenderly comforted her. The romantic triangle of *El gendarme desconocido* included two of the most prominent actresses in Hispanic cinema, Moreno's long-time friend from the carpa, Gloria Marín, as Agent 777's girl-friend, and the cherubic Puerto Rican starlet, Mapy Cortés, as a gangster's moll. Cantinflas joined the police force after capturing a group of bank robbers in the coffee shop owned by Marín's mother. The chaotic brawl comprised two separate fights, with Cantinflas trying mainly to avoid the older woman's wrath and only incidentally subduing the crooks. Later, as an undercover agent, he reverted to adolescent shyness when confronted by the seductive charms of Cortés. In the end, it was the mother who captured the criminal ringleader.[15]

Each new Cantinflas film smashed the box office records of the previous one, and the critics gushed their approval. This cinematic success proved a fatal blow to the carpa theater, iron-ically since *El gendarme desconocido* had been filmed from a collection of theatrical skits; indeed, a scandal arose when the author, Alfredo Robledo, having sold the story to Moreno for $500, claimed that he still retained the movie rights.[16] Moreno returned to the Follies stage at the end of his triumphant year with *Se fue el 41* (There goes '41), which was lambasted by crit-ics for its raunchy albures. He clearly loved the interaction with live audiences, but his inspiration was gone, and the public could sense it. A successful show playing the secretary general of an asylum helped him recover briefly in January, but when the show closed at the end of the winter season, he broke with his theatrical partner, Manolo Ferrándiz. Moreno made one last carpa appearance in 1943, accepting an unbelievable $6,000 a night to help save the failing show of ventriloquist Paco Miller. Nostalgic fans mobbed the theater, leading Miller to call him "the cheapest actor around," but Moreno never again returned to the Follies stage.[17]

Exporting the Pelado

At the height of his Mexican popularity, Mario Moreno began casting about for a universal theme to extend his fame throughout the world. Hollywood executives, impressed by his ticket sales if not by his jokes, tried to lure him north with promises of more proficient studios and broader distribution networks. Meanwhile, his partners in Posa Films, Santiago Reachi and Jacques Gelman, hoped to use the revenues from Cantinflas films to build a Mexican studio capable of competing with RKO, MGM, or Columbia. The years 1942 and 1943 were crucial for his career as Moreno took on the Hollywood giants directly by producing Mexican pictures for the United States market. Expectations ran high among Mexicans who staked their national self-image on the global reception of their beloved peladito. Cantinflas smashed box office records throughout the Hispanic world, assuring regional supremacy for the Mexican film industry. But that success proved small consolation when his films failed to gain favor in the United States. Having made Moreno a symbol for all things Mexican, disappointed critics turned on him with a vengeance, an ironic twist given that his poor reception north of the border resulted in large part from his loyalty to Mexican audiences.

Moreno entered discussions with Hollywood producers following the runaway success of *Ahí está el detalle.* Columbia Pictures had turned down the distribution rights, considering it a provincial film with little attraction beyond Mexico City, and Grovas contracted it out successfully with local distributors throughout the region. Studio bosses finally took notice at the Hollywood premiere of *Ni sangre, ni arena,* when no less a figure than Charlie Chaplin declared Moreno to be the leading comic of the day. In early December 1941, executives from RKO Pictures came to Mexico for a private screening of *El gendarme desconocido,* prompting frantic speculation that Moreno would leave for Hollywood and thereby begin an exodus of talent that would gut the national film industry. But the attack on Pearl

Harbor diverted studio attention away from Latin America to the production of propaganda and newsreels for the war effort.[18]

Far from leaving Mexico, Moreno led the national cinema industry into a golden age of growing domestic markets, reaching annual sales of 100 million tickets by 1947. Although a substantial portion of that total went to imported Hollywood features, as early as 1939 the Cárdenas government had required every movie theater in the country to show at least one Mexican film per month. Moreover, the industry's decision to subtitle rather than dub foreign-language films assured a preference for domestic production among the large numbers of moviegoers with weak reading skills. The formation of the Banco Cinematográfico in 1942 helped guarantee financing for Mexican filmmakers, but the biggest boon to the national cinema industry came from World War II, which diverted United States exports away from Latin America, allowing Mexican filmmakers to fill the gap. Producer Salvador Elizondo recalled that "during the war years it was hard to find a film that didn't cover its costs."[19]

To take advantage of these favorable conditions, Mexican producers tried to emulate Hollywood's studio system and sign stars to exclusive contracts. Jesús Grovas, having failed to obtain such a contract with Moreno, produced the first film starring María Félix, who became Mexico's most popular actress. Grovas was a founding board member of the Banco Cinematográfico but nevertheless fell into financial trouble and resigned from his production company at the end of 1942, before he could capitalize on her rising fame. Félix went on to star in Fernando de Fuentes's *Doña Bárbara* (1943), which established her in the role of *la devoradora,* the devourer of men. The only male competition for Moreno's domination of the industry came from the singing *charro,* Jorge Negrete, a baritone of great range who made his name in *¡Ay, Jalisco, no te rajes!* (Oh, Jalisco, don't back down! 1941). Negrete appropriated the silver-buckled, tight pants and jacket from elite rural dandies and made them into a macho national symbol, thereby guaranteeing the success of the mariachi industry and his own status as a popular idol.

Santiago Reachi hoped to use Posa Films and its exclusive artist, Moreno, as the foundation for a studio capable of competing with Hollywood. When Reachi replaced Grovas as head of the Producers' Association in 1943, he gave frequent interviews lamenting the undercapitalization of domestic studios and described his plans to overcome that problem. Inspiration for an actor-based studio came from United Artists, founded by the three biggest movie stars of the 1920s, Charlie Chaplin, Douglas Fairbanks, and Mary Pickford, in their quest for artistic independence from studio moguls. In 1942, while preparing the next Cantinflas feature, Reachi entered negotiations with a number of actors. Based on Moreno's experience in the theater, he sought out old-time revista performers, a mistake perhaps, for the future of cinema lay with new discoveries, such as María Félix. Posa signed an exclusive contract with Angel Garasa, a stage actor from Barcelona who had fled to Mexico following the Spanish Civil War. Although the cinema press reported that Posa had also signed Delia Magaña, who had performed with Moreno in the carpa, she did not appear in one of his films for another decade. But the biggest star, Joaquín Pardavé, had ambitions of directing his own films and declined an offer from Posa. Without Pardavé to recreate the magic of *Ahí está el detalle,* Garasa became Moreno's regular straight man, and Reachi shelved his plans of building a Cantinflas studio.[20]

Jacques Gelman, the most cosmopolitan member of the Posa board of directors, took the lead in suggesting foreign classics as a vehicle for expanding Moreno's fame beyond Latin America. Moreno had already considered filming *The Two Musketeers* with his former partner, Manuel Medel, and Arcady Boytler directing, but the project never panned out. This time, to fit the Mexican pelado into seventeenth-century France, screenwriter Jaime Salvador resorted to the well-worn device of a dream sequence. Cantinflas and three friends from the barrio returned a stolen necklace to an actress, who invited them to be extras at CLASA studios, where the pelado dreamed of fighting to save the honor of Queen Anne. *Los tres mosqueteros* was produced in June 1942 and opened that August, with Garasa costarring in the dual role of film director and Cardinal Richelieu. No such artifice was needed for the next movie, *El circo,* a tribute to Charlie Chaplin, which was filmed at the end of 1942 and premiered the following spring. Cantinflas fit right into the role of the tramp who joined the circus and fell in love with the owner's daughter. Finally, in May 1943, Moreno made the parody *Romeo y Julieta.* The *versión festiva* by Jaime Salvador carried the multiplicity of identities to new extremes, with Cantinflas as a cabbie drafted by Angel Garasa into giving an intentionally bumbling impersonation of a famous European actor playing the star-crossed lover. The film was released in Mexico City in September and subtitled for the United States the following spring.

The splendid production values achieved by Posa Films in these three features raised Mexican cinematography to new levels. Many producers saw filmmaking as a quick source of profits and refused to invest more than the bare minimum needed to finish a film. Moreno, by contrast, had both the inclination, based on his theatrical training, and the income, from his earlier hits, to produce spectacular films of a technical quality seldom seen in Mexico. Posa commissioned the Catalan designer Manolo Fontanals to recreate the court of Louis XIII and imported costumes from Hollywood. The company also contracted the world-renowned Ballet Theatre for a magnificent ballroom scene. To film *El circo*, Posa raised a big top forty-five meters long and twenty-five high, providing ample space for the trapeze work of its exclusive artist. And even these splendid sets paled in comparison with the medieval Verona constructed for *Romeo y Julieta* on the banks of the Churubusco River at a cost of $68,000, more than the entire budget of many films. Pride rather than mere publicity inspired Moreno's statement to reporters that his greatest ambition was "to contribute with my modest work to the consolidation of the artistic film industry of my *patria* [fatherland]."[21]

The Mexican patria truly pervaded these films, notwithstanding their foreign story lines. The plumed hats and wigs of *Los tres mosqueteros* may have been imported from Hollywood, but the patched and drooping pants came straight from Tepito. Moreno also added a local touch to his sword fights by dispatching Richelieu's guards with moves from *lucha libre*, the hokey professional wrestling so popular in working-class barrios. For *El circo*, he devised a uniquely national approach to animal hygiene, using a feather duster, ubiquitous among Mexican housekeepers, to clean the circus elephant. Moreno also added a personal twist to the classic Chaplin ending by setting off down the road with the elephant, doing business as the "Gran Zapatería: El Chanclazo Ambulante" (Great Cobbler Shop: The Ambulatory Old Shoe). The festive version of Shakespeare's play included Romeo serenading Juliet with mariachi music, which elicited an annoyed remark from the Capulet patriarch that complained about foreigners in Verona. Although hilarious to Mexican audiences, local gestures, colloquialisms, and anachronisms did not travel well. Emilio García Riera ventured: "One could frankly say that the comic had not read *The Three Musketeers,* and that, without a clear idea of what he should be parodying, resorted to [jokes] of sure effect."[22]

Flirting with gender boundaries constituted one endless source of humor for Moreno. By this point in his career, the homosexual allusion amounted to little more than a crude albur, one of the many tricks used by Cantinflas to humiliate opponents. For example, when Richelieu indirectly questioned Queen Anne's loyalty by pronouncing a eulogy to love, D'Artagnan subverted the ploy by resting his head on the Cardinal's chest. Moreno also retained his penchant for cross-dressing, although likewise toned down in *El circo* to an outdated women's bathing suit, complete with frilly leggings, that he wore while auditioning for the circus act of a high dive into an empty water barrel. The most outrageous of these allusions, and the most offensive to critics, were paradoxically the most understated. Moreno demonstrated his ambivalent masculinity simply by overacting the romantic lead of Romeo. In the wedding scene he appeared far more interested in drinking his chocolate than in kissing Juliet, and he stuttered through the wedding vows with a hesitant "no . . . er . . . yes." The dual suicide, also played to kitsch extremes, ended not in a benediction but a brawl when Cantinflas's jealous film girlfriend assaulted the actress playing Juliet on stage. Moreno thus continued his nontraditional position as the object of romance, a timid youth fought over by brazen women instead of the macho subject portrayed by his charro rival, Jorge Negrete. And here he incurred the wrath of critics expecting timeless romance from Shakespeare.

On his first international venture, *Los tres mosqueteros,* Moreno received unanimous applause in Mexico from both critics and the public alike. As part of the publicity campaign, Posa Films coyly apologized to the reportedly three thousand people waiting outside the box office who could not get tickets for the opening night but promised that the film would continue to play as long as people demanded to see Cantinflas. The only

Cantinflas Mexicanizes the classics. (Top) *Cantinflas grooms an elephant with the ubiquitous Mexican feather duster to the dismay of strongman Rafael Burguete.* El circo, *production still. Courtesy: Dirección General de Actividades Cinematográficas de la UNAM.* (Bottom) *Romeo from Tepito, complete with drooping pants.* Romeo y Julieta, *production still. Courtesy: Dirección General de Actividades Cinematográficas de la UNAM.*

complaint voiced by one reviewer was the inability to hear the jokes because of the audience's nonstop laughter. Critics lamented the absence of a worthy costar and noted that Moreno was the entire picture. The conservative paper *La Nación* considered the film to be Moreno's best work ever, raising the pelado from a social critic to a noble figure in the positive service of the queen's honor and the king's power. "With this new Cantinflas, which is the true and desired one, the people will no longer cry from laughter. Instead, they will think. And feel and be moved deeply."[23]

Mexican critics used the premiere of *El circo* to venture comparisons between Moreno and Charlie Chaplin. The English actor inspired such discussions with his often-repeated designation of Moreno as the most notable comic of the times. One writer respectfully expressed the desire not to rank order the two comedians but rather to contrast their fundamental characteristics. Nevertheless, he went on to slant the comparison in favor of the local star, describing Cantinflas as hero, not victim; theater, not circus; and picaro by choice, not by circumstance. Critics invariably remarked on the obvious difference between the silent humor of the tramp and the endless blather of the pelado, but Moreno loyalists considered their hero equal to Chaplin even in body language. Mexican writers attached great significance to the fact that Chaplin, on the one hand, had no roots and belonged to all of humanity, with the unstated implication that he was not a creature of Hollywood. Cantinflas, on the other hand, emerged from a distinctive patria and barrio. Even the distinguished critic Xavier Villaurrutia, who was above such puerile comparisons, noted in reviewing *El circo* that while Moreno was "naturally Chaplinesque on occasion . . . the Mexican actor imprints his own unique seal . . . a character that corresponds to an ambient human reality."[24]

At the height of Moreno's fame, Cantinflas provided Mexicans with a vehicle for talking about themselves, and the praise of Chaplin allowed them to bask in international recognition. Theater critic Humberto Olguin Hermida wrote that "the basic force of his personality as a comic resides in the fact that he is the representative of Mexican comedy. . . . He condenses all of the matrices of the Mexican joke. And the result cannot be other than a complete triumph."[25] Critics had internalized his success to such a degree that they took it upon themselves to coach the national cinema champion. Eusebio Lambarri warned Moreno of the danger of making too many movies, observing that he had a patriotic duty not to squander his talent. The actor encouraged this nationalist identification through well-publicized appearances, such as a pilgrimage to the basilica of the Virgin of Guadalupe, where he impressed reporters with his exemplary respect for the national shrine.[26]

The repository of national virtue was transformed into a symbol of public vice when Moreno's films lost their critical approval in 1943. *El circo* received mixed reviews, but the abuse reached a crescendo with *Romeo y Julieta*. Critics were outraged by the "festive" script, which added albures to Shakespeare and which featured Juliet calling out, "Romeo, Romeo, where for art thou . . ." and then dropping a flowerpot on his head. Worst of all was the battle scene between Capulets and Montegues that led to Mercurio's death and Romeo's exile, which began with a food fight. Edmundo Báez declared Cantinflas to have been counterfeited, and *Novelas de la Pantalla* deplored the film's bad taste, "which damages the ears and the hearts of those spectators who oppose vulgarity."[27] Duende Filme, writing in *El Universal,* found only three good things in the entire movie: the scenery, the wardrobe, and the advertising posters. The public laughed, he admitted, but it was therefore "a film for a public of limited mentality. It owes its box office success to the popularity of Cantinflas and the masses that cannot distinguish if the actor is a fine clown or a buffoon. The film is appropriate for a gross public that can appreciate its gross jokes."[28]

Romeo y Julieta bombed in the United States primarily because Anglo audiences did not understand those gross jokes, an ironic twist given the Mexican critics' simultaneous desire for foreign approval and haughty disdain for popular culture. Moreno first traveled to the United States in 1939 for the New York premiere of *Así es mi tierra,* which was screened for its folkloric content as a spin-off of the hugely successful *Allá en el Rancho Grande.* He received a brief, and misspelled, notice in the *New York Times* for the "funny burlesque of a novillera with the popular comics Mario Marena [sic] and Manuel Medel as bullfighters."[29] Nevertheless, he remained unknown except for his reputation as a star in Latin America and for Chaplin's favorable appraisal. In 1943, *El Cine Gráfico* took offense when the *Times* criticized one of his shorts, but the paper expressed confidence about the future success of his feature films.[30] The optimism proved premature, for when *Romeo y Julieta* finally appeared with subtitles in the summer of 1944, Moreno failed to live up to his reputation. Part of the problem derived from mistaken expectations; a review by Latin American correspondent Paul Kennedy perceptively compared Moreno to nut comic Joe E. Brown, a star of early sound comedy, rather than to the silent film star, Chaplin. And Moreno's carpa aesthetic resembled the improvised jokes of vaudeville more than the painstaking rehearsal of Chaplin's mature films. Unfortunately, viewers in the United States had been led to expect pantomime; indeed, the distributors had not even tried to translate and subtitle Cantinflas's nonsense speeches. As a result, Kennedy considered it "doubtful if more than 2 percent of his antics would leave North American audiences with anything but nostalgia for good old Mack Sennett's gang." This reference to Keystone comics of the silent era, when pantomime was essential, indicated an appreciation for vaudeville's Shakespearean satire; Kennedy certainly did not expect Laurence Olivier. Contrary to Mexican critics, who denounced Moreno's disrespect for the Bard of Avon, Kennedy had liked most the irreverent food fight and death scenes.[31]

Despite the lack of appreciation by English speakers, Moreno won a dedicated Hispanic following that helped Mexico become the film capital of Latin America. Each new movie smashed box office records throughout the region, despite the differences in dialect between the various countries. Even the Brazilians laughed at *El gendarme desconocido,* demonstrating that one could still find humor in his nonsense speech with limited command of the Spanish language. His reception varied in some respects; for example, smaller countries without media industries often showed greater interest than countries with established stars. On his way to a South American tour in 1943, a forced landing in Managua, Nicaragua, turned into a triumphant parade of ecstatic fans, yet once in Argentina, Moreno succeeded only with the endorsement of his local counterpart, Luis Sandrini. Cubans greeted Moreno warmly a year later on a tour of the Caribbean, but with nothing like the enthusiasm shown in neighboring Puerto Rico. Even before he arrived in San Juan, a newspaper editorial cartoon predicted the comedian's bemused expression to find the entire island already speaking in cantinflismos.[32]

Business details were never far from Moreno's mind on these trips. In addition to promoting his movies, he earned top dollar for stage and radio appearances. A 1941 visit to Central America prompted newspapers to speculate on Cantinflas's skills as an ambassador for Mexican capitalism, opening Guatemala to Mexican exports. During a brief stop in Havana in 1944, he produced advertisements for a Cuban brand of cigarettes, a menswear firm, and the local radio station. Moreno also opened a foothold in the Spanish market, which had formerly resisted Mexican cinema. Although *Allá en el Rancho Grande* had made a big impression on its arrival in Spain, it did not pass into the second-run theaters, and promoters had no luck at all with *María Candelaria* (1943) or *Doña Bárbara* (1943), until a Cantinflas film arrived, almost by accident. The comedian caused such a sensation that to satisfy demand, Mexican distributors shipped copies of what they considered to be his inferior earlier films *Aguila o sol, Así es mi tierra,* and *El signo de la muerte.*[33]

Back to the Barrio

If Moreno felt any regrets about his poor reception in the United States, he did not share them with the press. In 1944 he filmed *Gran Hotel,* based loosely on the Greta Garbo film of the 1930s but nevertheless clearly returning Cantinflas to his Mexican roots. The movie depicted for the first time the pelado's progress from the countryside and his picaresque adventures trying to make a living in the big city. As a bellboy in the capital's most luxurious hotel, Cantinflas performed a devastating critique of arriviste members of the Mexican bourgeoisie. Although reviewers joyfully welcomed Cantinflas home to Mexico City after his ill-fated adventures with European literature, the newly rich Moreno may have felt a twinge of irony at his alter ego's satire.

With *Gran Hotel,* Moreno addressed one of the primary social concerns of the 1940s, the massive migration of people to the city. Revolutionary reforms had finally achieved a dramatic lowering of the infant mortality rate, launching Mexico on a sustained period of population growth in the postwar era. Unable to support themselves, even after Cardenista agrarian reform, young people left the land in search of factory work, helping Mexico City to double in size during the decade, from 1.6 to 3.2 million people. Studies have shown that the migrants tended to come from relatively affluent and educated families.[34] Moreno depicted a less common but more nostalgic view of being forced from his pueblo by circumstance rather than leaving voluntarily in search of opportunity. As the town drunk, Cantinflas was about to be thrown out in the street by the boarding house manager for not paying the rent when he preemptively evicted himself, refused to stay a minute longer, and then proceeded to describe in lurid detail his pathetic future as a vagabond. The beguiled landlady pleaded with him not to leave and even offered him a job collecting rent from the other tenants. He used the money to treat his buddy at the cantina, and after a long binge, they staggered into the town fiesta, where a piñata dangled above the merry crowd. Taking up the stick, Cantinflas proceeded to smash the owner of boarding house over the head.

After arriving in Mexico City, Cantinflas found employment as a waiter in a fancy French restaurant. With pants drooping from under his tuxedo, he mocked the sophisticated airs of the Mexican elite, speaking to patrons in pidgin French and drinking champagne out of their glasses. The pelado also spoofed the French pimps, known as Apaches in the Barrio Latino, with a misogynist Apache dance, tossing his Parisian partner about in the rough style of a Harlem nightclub jitterbug. But unlike his African American counterparts, Cantinflas neglected to catch the poor woman. The dance quickly degenerated into a lucha libre, in which she pulled his pants down, and he sent her flying into the audience. As a bellboy, Cantinflas showed a similar lack of respect for hotel guests by making them carry their own luggage up to their rooms.

The abuse Cantinflas heaped upon the Mexican bourgeoisie seemed all the more ironic given Mario Moreno's personal efforts to live up to their expectations. After a decade of marriage and a breathtaking rise to wealth, he and Valentina remained happy together with only one regret, their inability to have children. In the early 1940s, the couple tried twice to adopt a child from the streets, as if trying to combine cinema fantasy with real life in creating an heir worthy of both Mario Moreno and Cantinflas simultaneously. The urchins who waited for him to hand out a few coins each night after performing at the Follies Bergère were some of his most loyal fans, but the conflicting demands of Moreno's dual identity proved too much for their young minds to handle. When taken into the actor's mansion, the two boys acted like Cantinflas in *Ahí está el detalle,* loafing in luxury and refusing to do homework. One even became overly familiar in caressing his adopted mother, just as the pelado had on screen with his supposed sister, Dolores. Consequently, Moreno took the role of Don Cayetano and ordered them out of the house, delaying for two decades his dreams of fatherhood.[35]

The Predicament of Stardom

In the early 1940s, Mario Moreno brought fame to Mexico. His films achieved international recognition and catapulted the national film industry to the forefront of the Spanish-speaking world. But he changed Mexican society even more profoundly by creating stardom as a form of universal recognition. Before Cantinflas, such renown had crowned only a few politicians and generals, such as Benito Juárez and Pancho Villa. While radio brought celebrity to the voice of the musical poet Agustín Lara in the 1920s, his gaunt frame and scarred face remained enigmatic and slightly sinister. By contrast, the inquisitive eyes and animated mustache of Mario Moreno caught the imagination of the Mexican people, and for a few brief years, they could think of little else. Huge crowds formed whenever he appeared in movies, theater, comic bullfights, or just on the street. Intellectuals used Cantinflas as a means for discussing Mexican society and its place in the world. He even shaped news coverage beyond the gossip columns. *Todo* ran an editorial cover critical of bullfighting shortly before the premiere of *Ni sangre, ni arena,* and later, while Moreno was filming *El gendarme desconocido,* the magazine published a series of exposés on the Mexico City police.[36] His international success seemed to unify the nation and to vindicate the revolutionary ideology of the mestizo, bringing pride to both the popular masses he represented and to a newly ascendant bourgeoisie who profited from him.

Although everyone saw something to admire in Cantinflas, not everyone saw the same thing. The elite imagined the pelado as a poster child for their revolutionary program of social engineering, a member of the lower classes who had been cleaned up and seated at their exclusive banquet table. One illustrated magazine published a photo of the comic star standing next to Governor Bonifacio Salinas Leal at a dinner of the Monterrey bankers' association.[37] Financiers held Moreno as an exemplar of success through hard work, a new Horatio Alger figure more appropriate to industrial society than the boxers and bullfighters acclaimed by the popular masses. Working-class kids in the old barrios of Tepito and Peralvillo, as well as in the growing industrial suburbs such as Cuauhtitlán, did indeed dream of becoming as rich as Moreno. Nevertheless, to them he symbolized not hard work and stodgy manners but wealth acquired through street smarts and spent with Bohemian delight. After one banquet, Moreno pulled a $1,000 bill out of his wallet and exclaimed, "Tonight we'll finish this off, and then we'll see how we're finished off."[38]

The popular view of Cantinflas as a lazy pelado who lived by his wits, outsmarting pompous Creoles, in no way reflected the hard work Mario Moreno invested in constructing his public image. During the early years of his stardom, he traveled widely in Latin America and the United States to satisfy his fans and to win over new audiences. His talented partners, Santiago Reachi and Jacques Gelman, spread his recognition even further through lucrative promotional deals, such as the product placements in *Ni sangre, ni arena*.[39] The production company Posa Films never became an independent studio, but it did employ a team dedicated to Moreno's fame, including director Miguel Delgado, scriptwriters Jaime Salvador and Alfredo Robledo, straight man Angel Garasa, and Moreno's younger brother and indispensable right-hand man, Eduardo Moreno. Such behind-the-scenes work was essential for his success, but that situation does not support the extreme views of mass culture that depict the media industry as nothing but artificial propaganda foisted on an undiscerning population. Moreno had proved his popularity before businessmen ever noticed him, and without his genial personality, the advertising would have been wasted.

In retrospect, the years 1942 and 1943 marked a turning point in Moreno's career. His failure to conquer Hollywood from outside by adding Mexican touches to foreign themes showed that even Cantinflas had limits. The wrath of critics soon descended, made all the worse by their sense of betrayal that Moreno had not single-handedly transformed Coyoacán into a rival of Hollywood. Reachi later blamed Gelman for the failure, arguing that Cantinflas should never have strayed from his pelado roots, but at the time their decisions seemed imminently sensible. The boom years of World War II brought tremendous gains to the entire Mexican film industry, and Cantinflas in particular seemed unstoppable. In such circumstances, Moreno would have been negligent not to try opening up markets in the United States for Mexican cinema. But success in that endeavor could only come by sacrificing those peculiar qualities that so endeared Cantinflas to Mexican audiences. Having fought so long to gain artistic independence, Moreno refused to sell out to Hollywood. Thus, while critics such as Duende Filme decried him for pandering to the gross taste of the Mexican masses, the people themselves rewarded him with their loyalty.

Nevertheless, Moreno had to defend this newly won artistic freedom against union machinations that had long been brewing within the cinema industry. The responsibilities of fame came forward in 1944, and having spoofed politicians for a decade, Moreno had to become one to continue his career. He entered the battle against corrupt union officials with widespread popular support that few bureaucrats could match. But the actor found a potentially far more dangerous foe in his own character, Cantinflas, who threatened to sabotage the fame of Mario Moreno.

4

SYNDICALISM AND STARDOM

The revista show at the Esperanza Iris Theater opened on Friday nights to a mixed audience of stylish young catrines, working-class families, and more than a few drunks. But the premiere of a Spanish folk dancer on March 8, 1946, attracted a particularly unusual crowd of police *granaderos* with tear gas and riot armor and union thugs, also heavily armed, albeit more discretely. Both sides expected violence; Fidel Velázquez, national leader of the official union, the CTM, had staged the performance as a scab action against a union of independent actors who had been locked out of the theater. The actors had been fighting for years to break away from the CTM-affiliated cinema union, the Sindicato de Trabajadores de la Industria Cinematográfica (STIC), amid charges of corruption and incidents of violence. Into this lions' den walked the president of the nascent actors' guild, Mario Moreno. Getting a ticket had not been easy, but once he showed it, STIC *pistoleros* allowed the comedian to pass. Miguel de Molina, the star of the show, had sleepy eyes and hair full of Vaseline, and the government of Juan Perón had expelled him from Argentina for lewd behavior. Moreno had warned him earlier not to play a theater barred to the independent Mexican actors, and as Molina broke into a gypsy number, "Avellanero," the comedian strode down the aisle, stopped in front of the stage, and shouted, "Traitor!" STIC workers jumped from their seats throughout the theater and converged on the famous interloper, who escaped only with police protection. The show went on, as did the union battle, but Moreno had made his point, defying the powerful head of the national union.

That confrontation actually took place, but it might very well have come from a Cantinflas movie. His humor of endless, meaningless chatter portrayed the tragic bravado of the Mexican underdog, bullied in the streets but determined to keep his dignity. Virtually every movie he ever made contained at least one scene in which he talked himself into trouble only to slink coyly away. The conflation of the movie character Cantinflas with the real-life union battles of Mario Moreno provides a revealing early example of the ways in which politics and the media have become indistinguishable in the modern world.

The battle with Fidel Velázquez from 1944 to 1946 came at a crucial moment in Mexican history. World War II provided a great stimulus to the national economy, primarily in the form of raw material exports for the Allied war effort, but domestic consumer products manufacturers also benefited from the absence of competition from the United States. As the war came to an end, Mexican industry had to mature and establish itself in the international marketplace. Labor relations played an important role in this transition. A unity pact had limited strikes that might have damaged wartime production, but the pact took a heavy toll on the working classes, whose wages fell far behind the rising cost of living. Fidel Velázquez and the CTM leadership were determined to maintain union discipline to help local manufacturers compete for postwar markets. But the union rank and file no longer felt any patriotic pressure to suffer inflation gladly and demanded a more militant stance against capital. The highly popular screen actors' guild championed the cause of workers in a struggle to determine the course of Mexican industry.

The struggle between Moreno and Velázquez was far from a straightforward battle between corrupt leaders and union democracy, and it revealed the growing chaos within Mexico's industrial structure. Rather than open class conflict of labor against capital, the cinema struggle of the 1940s entailed jurisdictional disputes between rival unions of a kind unanticipated by Mexican labor law. Moreover, the actors held an ambiguous position within the industry as both workers in front of the camera and as managers of production companies, such as Posa Films, of which Cantinflas was the exclusive artist and Mario Moreno a major partner. Nor were the actors alone; union leaders held seats on company boards either as union representatives or on their own account, with wealth diverted from union dues. Finally, the union struggle revolved around inflated egos as much as economic realities, with some of the most popular and powerful figures contending for supremacy, both on screen and off.

1944: The Regime of Enrique Solís

The Mexican army traditionally marched on Revolution Day to commemorate the anniversary of Francisco I. Madero's call to arms on November 20, 1910, but the parade acquired special significance in 1942 as Mexico mobilized for war against the Axis powers. Multitudes of people lined the streets of Mexico City to applaud as soldiers marched smartly past. Workers in military uniforms, organized by unions, also received warm ovations in recognition that Mexico would contribute to Allied victory primarily through economic means. But the crowds cheered loudest for the theatrical union when they recognized—despite his sergeant's stripes and serious demeanor—Cantinflas. This odd juxtaposition of patriotism, syndicalism, and stardom extended beyond a single parade to shape the development of the cinema industry, first in the glory days of World War II and later as it confronted the challenges of international competition.

That Moreno marched with the theater actors despite his cinematic fame highlighted the complexity of union jurisdictions in the film industry and the economy in general. Early filmmakers throughout the world borrowed talent and genres from the popular theater, but in Mexico such crossovers took place within a particularly contentious labor environment. Syndicalism, the movement to take over the means of production by organizing syndicates of workers from each industry, thrived in the revolutionary climate of the 1920s. Within the entertainment industry, various craft guilds united to form the National Federation of Theater and Public Spectacle Unions. This syndicate acquired a notorious reputation for both militancy and corruption, even by the high standards of Luis N. Morones's CROM. Stagehands, movie projectionists, musicians, and ushers divided up their jurisdictions meticulously, for example, allowing theaters to show either movies or operas but not both, and bankrupting impresarios who crossed their lines. Yet arbitrary decisions and harsh discipline could also provoke resentment within the rank and file, as happened one Sunday afternoon in 1927 when the Chapultepec Park Orchestra happened to include on its program a song by Ignacio Fernández Esperón. The band leader, Miguel Lerdo de Tejada, spotted the famous composer in the audience and invited him up to conduct the piece to the acclaim of all, except Federation bosses, who fined the entire orchestra even though "Tata Nacho" belonged to the authors' union, another CROM affiliate.[1]

In 1934 the cinema industry organized itself, still rather haphazardly, into three basic, although not mutually exclusive, associations. First, the Association of Mexican Film Producers and Distributors (Asociación de Productores y Distribuidores de Películas Mexicanas) represented management in contract negotiations, even though much of the industry's capital lay in separately owned studios. Second, diverse actors' guilds from throughout the country organized themselves into the National Association of Actors (Asociación Nacional de Actores, ANDA). Finally, the Union of Cinema Studio Workers (Unión de los Trabajadores de Estudios Cinematográficos, UTEC) brought together cinematographers and other studio technicians, whose various craft unions dated back to 1919.

Jurisdictional problems between ANDA and UTEC arose during the national power struggle between President Lázaro Cárdenas and the jefe máximo, Plutarco Elías Calles, in 1936. The actors' association was part of the National Theater Federation and therefore an affiliate of Luis Morones's CROM, whereas the cinematographers became founding members of the CTM in February 1936. When Vicente Lombardo Toledano helped Cárdenas drive Calles and Morones into exile in April, the resulting enmity between CROM and the CTM, together with closed-shop contracts, created an impossible situation in which ANDA actors and UTEC cinematographers could not work in the same film studio. But impossible situations arose all the time within the Mexican labor bureaucracy, and union leaders simply became accustomed to negotiating informal working agreements called *acuerdos*. In this case, ANDA head Angel T. Sala met with UTEC boss Enrique Solís to arrange an agreement. Because the CTM held greater political clout, the film actors found themselves drafted against their will into the technical workers' union.[2]

While ANDA accepted membership in the Cardenista labor confederation, they struggled for years to gain autonomy from UTEC. Nevertheless, the actors faced an uphill battle against the CTM program of consolidating control over the entire cinema industry. After numerous petitions, in 1938 the National Executive Board of the CTM finally encouraged the actors to "form special organizations to defend their own interests."[3] But when they attempted to do just that, the CTM blocked their registration with the Labor Arbitration Board, which effectively denied them the legal authority to negotiate contracts. The actors welcomed the formation of STIC in December 1939 as an opportunity to gain independence as section 7 of the National Federation of Cinema Workers. Yet once again they reckoned without the power of Enrique Solís, who made arrangements with the executive board to relegate the actors into a special artistic branch of UTEC's section 2. His determination to retain control over the actors grew out of his dream of parlaying the union position into a personal motion picture empire. The handsome young Solís had already acquired the flashy suits of a Hollywood mogul in addition to a business renting film equipment—a highly profitable sideline because of his threat to strike any producer who did not pay him personally for lights and cameras.[4]

The actors' desire for independence, even from such a corrupt leader, ran counter to the national trend toward concentrating workers in industrywide syndicates controlled by the CTM bureaucracy. Emphasis on union discipline had already begun during the final years of Cárdenas's administration, precisely because of the success in asserting state control over the means of production. The nationalization of oil companies and railroads had transformed revolutionary politicians into capitalist managers, concerned with production schedules as well as social reforms. In 1939 the president's mentor, Francisco Múgica, observed that union leaders "used to preaching the religion of their rights . . . do not know how to preach the religion of duty."[5] Efforts to curtail strikes accelerated during the presidency of General Manuel Avila Camacho (1940–1946). Although a former schoolmate of Vicente Lombardo Toledano, the conservative president forced the committed Marxist to step down from the CTM leadership at the union congress in February 1941.

Fidel Velázquez, a former milkman from Azcapotzalco and the new secretary general, first gained national attention in 1929 when CROM boss Luis Morones called him an "earthworm." This insult referred to the manner in which Velázquez and his four partners within the Mexico City Federation of Worker Syndicates were undermining the national union. Another dissident leader, Luis Araiza, came to their defense, informing Morones that instead of earthworms, they were "five little wolves [*lobitos*], who soon, very soon, will gobble down all the hens in your corral."[6] The prediction proved apt, for Velázquez showed himself more interested in achieving power than in reforming the corrupt CROM. He gained a seat on the CTM executive board in 1936 by threatening to withdraw Mexico City workers from the new confederation if Miguel Angel Velasco, a communist elected to the board, did not resign. As organizational secretary for the CTM, Velázquez became quite skilled at manipulating the union bureaucracy and eventually maneuvered to succeed Lombardo when he lost the support of Avila Camacho. Nevertheless, the majority of workers still remained either unorganized in marginal industries or members of independent unions, limiting the power of the five lobitos over the hen house of Mexican labor.[7]

The Avila Camacho administration joined the CTM's conservative new leadership in working to extend government control over the entire Mexican workforce. Shortly after taking office, the president proposed reforms to the Federal Labor Law increasing government power to arbitrate labor disputes. The CTM delegation in Congress approved this law without protest in March 1941 on the grounds that at least it preserved the right of workers to strike. Nevertheless, the change represented a major concession by giving both the secretary of labor authority to declare strikes illegal and business owners the right to fire wildcat strikers. Mexico's entry into World War II provided a pretext for further government control over unions when Fidel Velázquez unilaterally disarmed the CTM in its class warfare by renouncing the right to strike for the duration of the conflict, while asking for management concessions in return. The administration formalized this arrangement by helping to negotiate a "pact of unity" to assure uninterrupted production. The number of strikes actually increased in response to wartime inflation.

Nevertheless, an attempt to challenge Velázquez's conservative leadership in 1943, led by Vidal Díaz Muñoz of the sugarcane workers, was crushed with the support Lombardo Toledano. Even after losing his position as secretary general, the CTM founder remained convinced of the need for rigid discipline within the CTM. The author of *Union Liberty in Mexico* had therefore come a long way from his former belief that workers must force both capitalists and the state to grant their rights.[8]

Union democracy, the rights of workers to negotiate their own contracts and to strike if dissatisfied with those arrangements, suffered serious reverses in the early years of the Avila Camacho government, not least for the screen actors' guild. The STIC executive board had still not acted on their request for autonomy when Mario Moreno took over as president of ANDA in March 1942. A year later Fidel Velázquez personally assured the actors he would look into the conflict as soon as possible—the same promise that STIC leaders had been making for the past three years. But if the CTM turned a deaf ear to their pleas, the actors could count on the attention of other powerful Mexicans, most notably, General Maximino Avila Camacho, the president's older brother. The siblings shared a conservative outlook, but whereas the stolid Manuel became known as the "Gentleman President," the extravagant Maximino was notorious for hiring gangsters to intimidate or murder his many enemies. He acquired a fortune as governor of the state of Puebla from 1937 to 1941, then as secretary of public works in his brother's cabinet; and he served as patron for two future media barons: theater owner William O. Jenkins and newspaper and television tycoon Rómulo O'Farrill. Maximino also favored the company of media stars; he publicly flaunted his affairs with movie actresses and became a close friend of fellow bullfighter Mario Moreno.

With the assistance of such a powerful figure, the actors' guild finally received a favorable decision from the CTM. On March 30, 1944, more than a thousand members of ANDA gathered at the Ideal Theater to celebrate the recognition of their autonomy within section 7. Jorge Negrete, the incoming secretary general, charro singer, movie star, and the biggest sex-symbol-without-a-chin in Mexico, read the official judgment to general applause. Mario Moreno then stood up to reflect on the long struggle, but as he did so, the image of Cantinflas intervened, if not to the entire audience then at least to one reporter who wrote that he spoke "seriously, gravely, syndically . . . until he seriously made them laugh."[9] But Enrique Solís, for one, did not see the humor and ordered STIC section 2 out on strike to protest the dismemberment of his union. It was a risky move, for UTEC's economic conflict lay not with management, the classic justification for a strike to be declared legal, but rather in a jurisdictional dispute with another union. Nevertheless, he was determined to close down the studios until the actors recognized his leadership.

The walkout raised the long-running internal dispute between UTEC and ANDA to a new level, and all attention turned to the president in his role as economic arbitrator. The actors assembled again on April 10 and listed their grievances, most importantly, the inability to negotiate contracts or to discuss any business at all without submitting it to the UTEC general assembly. Dues constituted another sore spot—5 percent of the actors' salaries, some 178,000 pesos a month, gone without any benefits in return. While STIC maintained a hospital, the actors could not get treatment there, nor did they receive life insurance. Worse still, Solís collected a day's salary from workers on the pretext of paying a bribe to the Treasury to avoid paying taxes on the union office, a luxurious building on the Paseo de la Reforma. Solís responded in the meeting by disclaiming responsibility for the walkout and by assuring the president of UTEC's willingness to resolve the struggle fraternally by allowing greater autonomy to the actors' branch of section 2. The union boss also warned that the actions of a mere craft guild, the ANDA, in dividing an entire industrial syndicate set a nefarious precedent that endangered the entire Mexican labor regime.[10]

The walkout did not affect Mario Moreno directly because he had just finished filming *Gran Hotel* and was scheduled to begin a theatrical tour of the Caribbean and South America. On April 10, immediately following the actors' assembly and without even stopping to sign the petition, he boarded a plane for Cuba. Then, after a triumphal visit to Puerto Rico, he returned to Mexico to find that studio work had resumed, at least temporarily. A month later he flew off again, bound for Argentina and a fateful meeting with the Spanish folkloric dancer Miguel de Molina.

During his visit in Havana, Moreno had noticed that the comic persona of Cantinflas made the press reluctant to take him seriously as a union leader. His description of the union conflict sounded to Cuban reporters like one of Cantinflas's nonsense discourses, and they printed just his summary conclusion: "Well, it's like this, the actors want to 'administer' themselves."[11] This pattern of hearing only a semantic joke and not the content of his message continued to subvert Moreno's political forays throughout his long career.

Meanwhile, Enrique Solís, having been cast out of favor by the CTM executive board, discovered new faith in the principles of union democracy. Declaring his resolve to lead UTEC to the promised land—and to drag the actors kicking and screaming along—on July 20 he announced another strike against the studios. Thus, after years of neglect, ANDA finally gained the support of the STIC national leadership. Secretary General Salvador Carrillo, a short, round-faced man with slicked-back hair, called on the vast resources of the cinema workers' national bureaucracy to crush this challenge to his leadership. STIC employees from throughout the country flooded the president with telegraphs condemning the separatist movement. The actors also did their part to publicize the struggle; for example, comedian Jesús Martínez "Palillo" (Toothpick) declared himself on hunger strike on the steps of the Palace of Fine Arts, where passersby must have feared his imminent demise.

Behind the scenes, Moreno, Negrete, and Carrillo met with the secretary of labor in an attempt to ease Solís out of power and to reorganize section 2. But when UTEC assembled on August 4, the studio workers stood firmly behind their leader, rejecting his offer to resign and vowing to continue the struggle. Moreover, the conflict threatened to spread, as STIC section 8, studio musicians, denounced corruption on the part of Salvador Carrillo and demanded their own independence. The cinema technicians disclaimed any intention of leaving the CTM, despite its egregious jurisdictional ruling in the spring, and insisted that all citizens had the right to defend their liberty. But the president disagreed, and on August 8, he ordered police to break the picket lines outside the film studios. Federal agents also surrounded UTEC headquarters, where Solís barricaded himself for a few hours, threatening violence, before finally surrendering.[12]

The union struggle had apparently been resolved following this dramatic showdown. UTEC regained its autonomy as section 2 of STIC under a new secretary general, the respected cinematographer Gabriel Figueroa, while Solís appeared before a Federal judge to account for $316,000 of union dues. Carrillo cranked up the STIC bureaucracy and ordered another wave of telegraphs to thank the president for his righteous intervention to assure the film syndicate's integrity. Moreno paid off his political debts by publicly joining the president's literacy campaign and taking personal responsibility for the reading skills of children living near his ranch in Pujal, San Luis Potosí. And a week later, on August 18, *Gran Hotel* premiered to critical acclaim, helping to recover Cantinflas's reputation after the harsh criticism of *Romeo y Julieta* the previous year.

1945: Salvador Carrillo versus "Fortress Cantinflas"

The cinema workers had freed themselves from the corrupt leadership of Enrique Solís, but gangster activity still pervaded section 2, as Gabriel Figueroa soon discovered. One day in the winter of 1945, while Figueroa was working at the UTEC office building on the fashionable Paseo de la Reforma, a lawyer arrived with a large briefcase and an urgent need to see him alone. The lawyer announced that the filmmakers would have to vacate the building because it had just been sold. "Just so there are no problems at all," he continued, opening the briefcase full of pesos, "This is yours, no receipts, nothing, you just have to move."[13] Figueroa replied by throwing the lawyer and his pesos out of the office, but it soon became clear that although union funds had paid for the building, Solís held the title personally. This latest financial scandal united the former antagonists of UTEC and ANDA in an attempt to break completely away from STIC. And in doing so, the film stars became champions of a movement for union democracy that threatened to undermine CTM control of Mexican industry.

Nevertheless, at the beginning of 1945, the most likely union struggle seemed to be an internecine one within the actors' section 7. A long-simmering rivalry between Moreno and Negrete burst into the open and threatened the gains they had made the previous year. During a union assembly in early February, Moreno accused the new secretary general of vanity, self-centeredness, and tyranny. He then resigned his position as the union's interior secretary to avoid being associated with a "miniature Germany."[14] The ploy failed when Negrete emphatically refused to resign and instead condemned the political intrigues being plotted against him. The assembly pleaded for reconciliation, but Moreno refused to give a fraternal hug to his rival. As the actors filed out of the auditorium, they had already begun taking sides in an impending power struggle. Duende Filme, the critic for *El Universal* who had savaged *Romeo y Julieta,* blamed the outburst on personal rivalries over who had done the most for the actors' guild and who was the biggest star in Mexico. As if to answer the latter question, that Friday night, February 9, a rival newspaper, *Excelsior,* sponsored a reception at the swanky Patio restaurant honoring Moreno as the most popular male celebrity in the Spanish-speaking world, while María Félix received the complementary award for an actress.

As egos stewed over the weekend, Enrique Solís sent a moving crew on Sunday night to clean out the UTEC offices, down to the last filing cabinet. The police became suspicious when they saw movers carting off furniture in the middle of the night, but Figueroa arrived on the scene with his cousin, a young labor lawyer named Adolfo López Mateos, to find a seeming fait accompli. The police chief explained that the former labor leader had showed the legal documents needed to empty the building and refused to order his arrest. López Mateos then pointed out that the thorough Solís had bundled off not only the desks and files but the telephone as well, which really was a federal offense. Cutting the telephone cable constituted an attack on the national communication lines, and the police promptly arrested Solís, together with his lawyer Humberto Ferral Hernández.

Having arranged for the return of the furniture, Figueroa concluded the episode by sending an open letter to the Mexico City press denouncing union corruption and gangster tactics. Although the announcement named no names, Fidel Velázquez interpreted it as an attack on the entire CTM. He therefore called Figueroa in for a meeting on the evening of February 14 with STIC and CTM leaders. "Compañero Figueroa, you're new at this," Velázquez began. "I just want to tell you that, generally, the dirty laundry gets washed at home." The cinematographer replied, "In your home, because in mine we hang them out to dry." Carrillo then insisted on knowing just who were the accomplices of Solís referred to in the newspapers. Figueroa answered, "You want names? Well you're at the head of the list."[15] Carrillo sprang from his seat in a rage, and when Figueroa rose to meet him, the burly labor leader punched him in the face. The slim cameraman dropped to the floor, his cheek broken by a heavy ring, which had been fashionable in Mexican union circles since the days of Luis Morones.

Whatever personal satisfaction Carrillo might have received from showing the self-righteous little artiste who the real union boss was soon vanished. Figueroa did not get up and had to be carried to the hospital, where he became a temporary martyr, uniting the entire studio labor movement. Moreno and Negrete forgot their earlier quarrel and rushed to his bedside. Studio workers, who had just begun production of the new Cantinflas film, walked off the job in protest of the STIC leader's violence. The next day, Alejandro Galindo called a meeting of the directors' guild, section 47, and formally withdrew recognition from Carrillo. The STIC bureaucracy, well-oiled from the previous year's conflicts, responded almost mechanically with a flood of telegrams to President Avila Camacho condemning the "frank rebellion of section 2 headed by Gabriel Figueroa for calumnious declarations in the press [against] the clearly irreproachable moral conduct of our union leaders."[16] Carrillo tried to downplay the situation, informing reporters almost flippantly, "We had some words, we lost our tempers and quarreled. There were blows back and forth."[17] But such statements only compounded the cinematographers' resentment of union practices and their personal acrimony against Carrillo.

Meanwhile, Fidel Velázquez must have regretted ever meeting Figueroa, because the cinema union's disintegration could not have happened at a worse time. Congressman Pedro Téllez Vargas, secretary general of STIC section 1, the Mexico City cinema projectionists, had just been arrested, along with Carlos Madrazo and Sacramento Joffre, for selling falsified tickets allowing Mexican workers to enter the United States. Legitimate tickets were used by Mexican workers in the bracero program, which had been established in 1943 to replace U.S. agricultural and railroad workers who had entered military service during World War II. This scandal discredited the entire labor movement at a critical moment in the selection of a presidential candidate for 1946. Moreover, the producers had petitioned the government to end the union dispute that paralyzed the industry. Rather than risk outside intervention, Velázquez acted quickly to try to resolve the conflict. On February 23 the CTM executive committee granted section 2 autonomy within the STIC, allowing the cinematographers freedom to register with the Ministry of Labor and to negotiate union contracts without interference from the STIC leadership.[18] When that failed to satisfy the dissident filmmakers, on February 26 Carrillo offered what he probably considered to be a public apology. He lamented that Figueroa's precarious health had complicated his recovery, then added that the blow had been an "instinctive reaction against an injury that no man could tolerate."[19] Carrillo also reminded the newspapers that no court had indicted him as an accomplice to Solís, and he threatened to sue anybody who slandered him.

The filmmakers were not impressed with his show of contrition and broke definitively from STIC. The declaration of independence came on March 2 at an assembly in the Virginia Fabregas Theater, where more than two thousand cinema workers from STIC sections 2, 7, 45, and 47, representing technicians, actors, writers, and directors, formed the Union of Cinema Production Workers (Sindicato de Trabajadores de la Producción Cinematográfica, STPC). Roberto Gavaldón christened the new organization when he referred to the patriotic importance of their action in forming an autonomous union for national production. Mario Moreno, elected secretary general of the new union, immediately went to work filing for legal registration with the secretary of labor. Jesús Martínez, wearing an outrageous purple tie, declared himself ready to defend the cause at any moment by going back on hunger strike.[20]

CTM leaders portrayed the STPC as an attack on Mexican labor unity and therefore a counterrevolutionary threat to the nation. Fidel Velázquez circulated an urgent petition among the nation's top union officials, obtaining signatures from all the prominent unions except, significantly, the electricians and telephone operators, who had their own disagreements with the CTM leadership. The letter condemned the separatist movement and urged the president not to allow registration of the new union. STIC constituted the sole legal representative of cinema industry workers, and the STPC was merely a revival of Solís's separatist movement of 1944, which placed personal interests above the union organization and the Fatherland. Indeed, the letter argued that the STPC constituted the seed of labor fragmentation that could tear apart the entire union movement, causing industrial anarchy and endangering the social peace.[21]

While the president pondered that weighty thought, the CTM opened a second front against the STPC in the popular press by accusing Mario Moreno of being a fascist. Not that Moreno had embraced the ideology of Adolf Hitler, who with less than two months to live was then hiding in a Berlin bunker. Nevertheless, the charge had some validity to the extent that many twentieth-century authoritarian regimes, of both left and right, had been organized along the principles of syndicalism. Benito Mussolini began his political career as a revolutionary socialist about 1912, and the idea of organizing entire industries under worker control later provided the inspiration for Italian fascist society. His system of corporatism entailed a vertical organization of society to counter the Marxist threat of class conflict. He formed the Italian economy into twenty-two corporate entities representing various industries in the hopes of making capitalists and laborers work together for national glory. Meanwhile in Argentina, Juan Perón was following fascist principles and constructing an authoritarian regime based on an uneasy alliance between the military and state-controlled labor unions. The Mexican ruling party, organized functionally according to social sectors, likewise resembled a corporatist system, notwithstanding the exclusion of capitalists from direct participation in the government. On a personal scale, the fact that Mario Moreno was both a capitalist, as partner in Posa films, and a worker, as the screen actor Cantinflas, provided the factual basis for the STIC's tortured logic of accusing him of corporatism and hence fascism.

"Nazi" made a useful insult for STIC orators, but the public relations campaign did not achieve widespread acceptance. The newsmagazine *Hoy* spoofed the STIC argument with genuine cantinflair, "We see . . . this Mr. Moreno has not joined the circle . . . and that is . . . an artist . . . well yes . . . but you don't understand . . . things are clear . . . they become weighty . . . as you see . . . he's a fascist . . . that's it . . . a fascist."[22] Moreno, for his own part, put a novel spin on the cryptic motto given by José Vasconcelos to Mexico's National University, "Por mi raza hablará el espíritu" (The spirit will speak for my race). Adding a reference to Cantinflas's signature gabardine, Moreno announced, "My spirit and my clothes will speak for me."[23] To the more serious charge of dividing the country's unions, he responded that the STPC wanted to be seen as a purifying movement, a battle to clean up the country's unions rather than to splinter them.[24]

As the public relations battle raged in the press, both sides worked to consolidate their organizations. The STPC assembled again on March 8 at the Virginia Fabregas Theater to elect a national council, headed by Mario Moreno as secretary general, Jorge Negrete as secretary of conflicts, and Gabriel Figueroa, having recovered from his injuries, as secretary of labor. The new union also encouraged remaining STIC members to join their organization, an invitation accepted by the musicians of section 8, the composers of section 9, and many of the laboratory workers from section 50. Carrillo countered with a vain call for deserters from the STPC to meet on March 12 and 13 to reconstitute the rebellious sections 2, 7, 45, and 47. But the chief priority for leaders on both sides was lobbying the government concerning the new union's legal registration, and after a couple of weeks the actors appeared to be winning.

The filmmakers filed into the Fronton México (Jai Alai Palace) on March 14 fully expecting to celebrate their victory over the STIC. Mario Moreno had already grown his whiskers in preparation for returning to work on his new movie, but he appeared on stage with a solemn look that belied the Cantinflas image. The decision was still pending, he informed the assembly. "Nevertheless, compañeros, we know that recognition has to arrive. . . . It should be here any minute." He spoke for a while about the justice of their cause, then concluded, "I believe . . . I believe that it isn't just for our compañeros the musicians to stay quiet."[25] A band started playing "The Virgin of the Macarena," while Moreno slipped out of the auditorium in search of an answer. He was gone for five hours, but the auditorium was full of out-of-work entertainers, eager to show off their talents. Finally, at eleven o'clock, after the musicians had played the themes from countless movies, Moreno returned and took the stage. The dry legal text registering the STPC as a Federal Industrial Organization, read in complete deadpan, received a greater ovation than "Como México no hay dos" (There's no place like Mexico).

The victorious actors wisely sought reconciliation with the labor establishment by publishing an open letter describing their registration with the secretary of labor as a triumph of justice rather than an attack on the CTM. Moreno expressed the STPC's desire to remain within the national confederation, then concluded with thanks to the public, the president, the secretary of labor, the press, and honest workers for their support in the struggle. Moreover, he told reporters that he did not want the new union to serve simply as a bureaucratic machine. Instead the cinema workers had projects and initiatives for improving production. But the STIC, gutted by the loss of its artists, was not in a conciliatory mood. Carrillo roared with threats to shut down the national cinema industry in protest, but at the last minute, he delayed the walkout and limited himself to a protest before the Federal Arbitration Board. Moreno then took the opportunity to return to work, while he still could, on the long-delayed film entitled—ironically after his run-in with Fidel Velázquez—*Seis días con el diablo* (Six days with the devil).

But Moreno was mistaken if he thought he had escaped from the hell of union war. Secession from the CTM had already begun to spread in late March as the powerful Mexico City electricians' union (Sindicato Mexicano de Electricistas, SME) petitioned the secretary of labor to form a National Confederation of Electricians (Confederación Nacional de Electricistas, CNE) as an alternative to the CTM-controlled National Federation of Electrical Industry Workers (Federación Nacional de Trabajadores de la Industria Eléctrica, FNTIE). Fidel Velázquez was therefore determined to crush the highly visible cinema union as an example to other potential challengers. He had already specifically rejected the STPC's request for inclusion within the national confederation. Now the renegade film artists had to choose between the carrot and the stick. If they returned to the STIC fold, he offered to purge the union's leadership. If not, they could prepare for an extended war of attrition against the CTM, with all its strong-arm tactics.

Aware of the danger, Moreno sought to cultivate allies for the STPC even as he rushed to finish production of his latest film before the STIC made good on its promised strike. The new union cemented relations with management by signing contracts with the three major studios, CLASA, Azteca, and Stahl. The actors also threw a banquet for the Mexico City garrison to win friends in the army. Jorge Negrete, a graduate of the military academy, toasted the soldiers while Mario Moreno and Andrés Soler served as waiters. Not surprisingly, the biggest hit among the young conscripts was La Doña, María Félix, who chose a low-cut dress for the occasion. Moreno also worked to gain supporters within the labor movement. On June 8, he joined the electricians for a march through Mexico City in support of their struggle to form an independent national confederation.

When the STIC finally struck, it did so not at the Mexico City studios but in provincial cinemas and against the filmmakers' allies on stage. Projectionists in Monterrey began sabotaging films

Mario Moreno marches with workers from the independent Confederación Nacional de Electricistas on June 8, 1945, to gain union allies. The electricians were crucial for the STPC's endgame against the STIC and the CTM. Courtesy: Archivo General de la Nación.

in early April to protest the "Cantinflas union," an act made all the more sinister because it undercut national production in its competition with Hollywood imports. By the end of the month, armed STIC hoodlums in Torreón had become more brazen, busting up a performance by Palillo, a loyal member of the STPC. The outspoken comedian fled the theater in search of the mayor, only to find him in cahoots with the STIC. Even Roberto "El Panzón" Soto, the godfather of Mexican political comedy, who had stared down Luis Morones fifteen years earlier, was roughed up by Carrillo followers in Orizaba. On the Cinco de Mayo holiday, CTM workers refused to raise the curtain at the Esperanza Iris Theater when Jorge Negrete was scheduled to appear with the ventriloquist Paco Miller. With this last incident, the jurisdictional struggle of the cinema industry crossed over to the stage, where actors protested STIC machinations by going on strike, shutting down all the theaters in Mexico City.[26]

Theaters remained open in the provinces, but they were subject to struggles between the rival unions, such as the violence that interrupted a performance by Horacio Ugalde's theater company in Torreón. Perhaps remembering that STIC activists had roughed up Palillo there a few weeks before, Ugalde had renounced his affiliation with the actors' union headed by Moreno and reached an accord with STIC. Nevertheless, the comedian Antonio Cortés "Bobito" remained loyal to Moreno and refused to work for the apostate company. He did take the opportunity to go on stage, explain the actors' position, and tell a few jokes to placate the spectators. Even this brief appearance was too much for a STIC worker, who snatched the microphone away from Cortés, manhandling him in the process. The manager tried to calm things down by proceeding immediately to a dance marathon scheduled for later in the evening. The STIC loyalist thereupon grabbed an actress and dragged her out to join the contest, but they quickly retreated when the crowd expressed their annoyance by throwing bottles. Although the dancing stagehand claimed union leaders had put him up to it, back in Mexico City, Carrillo dismissed the troubles both at the Iris Theater and throughout the country as purely local conflicts and denied all charges of industrial sabotage. In a joint assembly of stage and screen actors, Moreno pledged his personal fortune to assure the success of their common cause while accusing the

STIC of "doing what any common thief would when caught with his hands in the pie, 'Now that's *suave* . . . !'"[27]

Emboldened by these successes and using the few remaining loyal laboratory workers of section 50 as a pretext, the STIC threatened to hang the red and black strike flag on the studio doors. When the actors learned that Carrillo was recruiting shock troops, they fell back on an old movie trick and circled the wagons, barricading themselves inside the CLASA and Azteca studios, armed with an assortment of pistols, rifles, and shotguns. Even the cherub-faced starlet Mapy Cortés took up a club to defend her workplace. They filmed during the day and drank cognac at night, with sentries standing guard at all times. Tensions grew on the morning of July 16 as the filmmakers braced themselves for an STIC assault. Moreno, looking martial in a leather jacket and dark sunglasses, prowled about the CLASA grounds inspecting the defenses while Negrete held the command post in the studio manager's office, coordinating with the other studios by telephone. A shock went through the ranks when the young Ricardo Montalbán appeared covered with blood, but he turned out to have been filming a movie scene. Precisely at noon the phone rang, and an excited caller informed Negrete of an attack on Azteca. But that too turned out to be a false alarm, either a prank call or an STIC provocation. When the actors learned that Carrillo had already left town with Fidel Velázquez, they gradually relaxed, although they still kept guards posted outside the studios.

The war of nerves continued through the summer as Moreno sought the media high ground, going on national radio to plead the STPC cause. The actors cultivated presidential favor by offering to produce shorts in support of the national literacy campaign, but at the same time they held out the threat of leaving the country to produce films unhindered by STIC interference. Carrillo sneered that his union had no cannons, tanks, or airplanes to attack "Fortress Cantinflas," as the studios had become, and he assured reporters that federal mediators would provide justice for the laboratory workers driven out by "cantinflista" elements. Moreover, he pressured the CTM-affiliated Union of Radio Musicians to pull the plug on the actors' propaganda.[28]

President Avila Camacho finally decreed an end to the conflict on September 3, by awarding a complete victory to the

STPC. The executive decision terminated the jurisdictional battles by assigning control over all feature-length films to the production workers. This left the STIC with the right to make and
distribute only newsreels and short educational films, the least
profitable works. Moreover, to forestall any future disputes between the two unions, he ordered any jurisdictional questions
to be referred directly to the secretary of labor for arbitration.
Stunned by the decision, Carrillo sent a desperate plea to the
president asking him to reconsider his opinion or at least concede the STIC leaders an audience. The actors once again used
their victory to try to ingratiate themselves within the CTM but
received a brisk dismissal from Velázquez. They returned the
favor when the CTM boss, acting on behalf of the STIC, tried to
negotiate some measure of control over feature film production.
In a letter dated September 6, the STPC executive board answered that the "terms of the presidential decree are absolutely
clear, detailed, and easy to apply, without the slightest need for
arrangement."[29] When Velázquez continued to dispute the issue,
the STPC called a protest march on the Zócalo for Monday, September 10. Some five thousand union members and sympathizers gathered in the Plaza of the Revolution, and by the time
they reached the National Palace, at least two thousand more
had joined the cinema stars. The president invited Moreno, Negrete, Figueroa, and María Félix up to his balcony to receive the
ovations of the crowds. As the actors were leaving, Avila Camacho said, "I never imagined you had so many members."[30] The
next day the president's secretary, Jesús González Gallo, wrote
a sharp letter to Velázquez reminding him that the "social util-
ity and respectability of labor leaders reside in their proper orientation and discipline."[31]

With the STIC defeated, at least temporarily, preparations
began for the opening of the latest Cantinflas movie, produced
in the spring between the various studio closures. The film represented Moreno's contribution to the war effort, with Cantinflas
mistaken for a deserter and drafted into the army. Despite a series of misadventures, such as driving a tank through army HQ,
he rose to sergeant and was shipped off to fight the Japanese.
The movie borrowed liberally from Chaplin's *Shoulder Arms*
(1918), as Cantinflas bungled a dangerous mission and fell into
enemy hands, only to capture war plans and prisoners by

mistake. The film then took a distinctive Cantinflas turn as the hero fell to a Japanese sniper, which launched him on a Mexican version of the Divine Comedy. He rose first to the pearly gates, where Saint Peter set him to work shining angel wings, then descended to the infernal region for a heartfelt cry with the devil, and finally returned to his bunk to discover that it had all been a dream. A last-minute title change, from "six days with the devil" to "one," prompted Duende Filme to suggest other improvements, such as completely reshooting the second half of the film. But Moreno had already left the country, headed for San Antonio to pay a political debt by raising money for the upcoming presidential campaign of the official party candidate, Miguel Alemán.[32]

1946: The Showdown with Fidel Velázquez

In January 1946, Pedro Téllez Vargas, back in charge of STIC section 1 after his release from jail the previous October, appeared at the Chinese Palace Theater to inform the people of Mexico City that they would not be seeing Jorge Negrete spank Lilia Michel in *No basta ser charro* (It's not enough to be a charro, 1945). The projectionists had long held back their ultimate weapon, a boycott of STPC films, but after failing to negotiate around the presidential decree, they had nothing left to lose. Fidel Velázquez personally orchestrated the STIC national conference in Monterrey to assure Salvador Carrillo's reelection as secretary general. With the rank and file securely behind them, Velázquez and Carrillo prepared for their final showdown with Moreno and the STPC, a battle not only for control of the union leadership but for the future of the national film industry.

Like all of Mexico, the actors had begun the year preoccupied with thoughts of the national elections scheduled for July. Hoping to gain as much favor from the incoming president as they had received from Avila Camacho, they formed a chapter of "Friends of Licenciado Alemán" and worked to raise money for the candidate. With all their recent political activity, they even aspired to elect a congressman of their own, a possibility at least given the CTM's regular allotment of representatives, such as Téllez Vargas. When the National Association of Actors endorsed Jorge Negrete for Congress, the official party did not add him to the ticket. Nevertheless, an organizing committee for the Federal District selected Moreno as their congressional candidate, while Palillo received the nomination for the suburb of Tacubaya. One journalist even touted the presidential qualities of Moreno, although serious citizens decried all this as a mockery of the Mexican political system, and none of the actors made it onto the final slate.[33]

Meanwhile, the CTM was determined that Cantinflas would never again appear on screen, let alone on the official party ticket. On January 19, STIC workers refused to allow the comedian on stage at the Arbeu Theater, even to help celebrate the hundredth performance of Roberto Ratti's show "Rhythms and Songs." Then the film boycott took effect, forcing distributors to shelve Jorge Negrete's new charro film, along with *El socio* (The associate, 1945), directed by STPC activist Roberto Gavaldón. In their places appeared Hollywood productions, such as *Mildred Pierce* (1945), starring Joan Crawford. The STPC executive board reportedly met with theater owners to discuss "energetic" measures against the boycott, not through the courts but of a "more practical" nature.[34] Nevertheless, when the whole union assembled at the Ideal Theater on February 11, they remained confident of the government's favor and chose to respond with words rather than violence, drafting a memo to the president accusing the STIC of industrial espionage against national filmmakers and in favor of foreigners.[35]

Even as the actors sought legal protection against the boycott, the STIC attempted to undermine public support for the Mexican actors by bringing in the Spanish dancer Miguel de Molina. He had entered Mexico under the auspices of the STPC, which had posted bond with the secretary of government to assure his good conduct. This standard procedure required foreign workers to affiliate themselves with Mexican unions. Although the Sevillian dancer with a gypsy air had a checkered past, he was an internationally known artist, having toured Paris and London before the war, and his company of eighty dancers and musicians promised a gala spectacle of authentic Spanish folklore. Unfortunately, the Esperanza Iris, the only theater in Mexico City that could do it justice, was still embroiled in union warfare, with CTM workers refusing to allow STPC actors or their stage allies to perform.

Either from self-confidence or egotism, Molina simply could not imagine anyone caring about politics in the presence of his artistry. Salvador Novo overheard him lament that the premature death of Federico García Lorca at the hands of Spanish fascists had tragically deprived the playwright "'of seeing him, Miguel de Molina, in the plentitude of his folkloric art.' As if that had been the only tragedy in Federico's death."[36] Moreno tried to explain personally that Carrillo and Velázquez were using Molina as a scab against Mexican actors who had been locked out of the Iris Theater. The STPC even offered to compensate him for the costs of changing the venue, but the dancer ignored their pleas. Finally, a day before the premiere, Moreno gave up on him and appealed to the public. A full-page newspaper ad paid for by the STPC denounced Molina as a "farcical dancer shamefully expelled from the Argentine Republic who now seeks to trample the sacred rights of authentic Mexican workers, cowardly betraying and mocking them by performing his hybrid art on a stage picketed by artists who have not made common cause with nefarious leaders."[37]

On May 8, while Miguel de Molina waited for the curtain to rise, malevolent forces gathered outside the Iris Theater. Fidel Velázquez, delighted to have an international artist dancing for the Mexican national union, was determined to allow nothing to disrupt the premiere. The STIC replaced the usual doormen with union enforcers, and distributed free tickets to CTM butchers, long considered the most sinister of all tradesmen. Meanwhile, STPC ally Tomás Palomino Rojas, leader of a breakaway or "purified" CTM, formed rival worker brigades to break up the performance. Manuel Avila Camacho asked both sides to maintain the peace and, just to be sure, ordered the district governor, Javier Rojo Gómez, to fill the streets outside the theater with police. The STPC executive board agreed to the president's request to avoid violence but sent an open letter to the newspapers repeating their desire for a permanent end to the union conflict. That evening the filmmakers gathered in their office, fuming about the foreign scab, when more unwelcome news arrived. The producers' association had knuckled under to the STIC boycott and decided to suspend all production until the unions had resolved their dispute. Although stars, such as Moreno and Negrete, had the financial resources to outlast another shutdown, extras and studio hands did not, which further threatened unity within the STPC. Moreno knew the union could not allow an STIC victory, and without explaining his intentions, he slipped out of the building to do something about it.

Numerous conflicting versions make it impossible to reconstruct exactly what happened in the Iris Theater on the night of March 8, 1946. Nevertheless, comparisons between the various reports reveal much about political, ethnic, and gender discourses in Mexico at midcentury. The basic outline of the night's events remained relatively consistent throughout the accounts. Molina was performing his second act when Moreno presented his ticket to the STIC doormen. They could not have failed to recognize the celebrity but expected to confront whole brigades of STPC thugs; the very audacity in coming alone, or perhaps with one companion, got Moreno past the front gate. Once inside the darkened theater, he made his way down the central aisle to the orchestra seats and shouted, "traitor," twice. He then tried to make a speech denouncing the show, but spectators booed him, pelted him with projectiles, and attempted to throw him out of the theater. Before they could grab him, however, the police arrived and escorted him safely back to STPC headquarters while Molina resumed his performance.

An anonymous theater critic, reviewing the premiere for *Excelsior,* portrayed the event as an artistic duel in which the Spanish dancer had triumphed over the Mexican comedian. Molina came across to readers as a genial artist in a magnificent spectacle—the finest theatrical presentation of the times—and a brilliant social event. This image contrasted sharply with Cantinflas, as he was called, who had appeared pallid and emaciated while denouncing the show. When the crowds failed to respond, "his face acquired an infinitely bitter expression, he raised his eyes to the galleries, and with a weak voice, making a dramatic gesture that will never be forgotten by those of us who were within three or four meters of him, repeated the harsh description, 'traitor.'" He tried once again to win the audience over, but they shouted him down. "For the first time in his magnificent career, the public did not respond.

Morally beaten, pale, and looking sad, Cantinflas abandoned the Iris."[38]

Moreno rightly questioned such theatrical metaphors for what he considered to be a political struggle. In response to the critic, he admitted having appeared pale and emaciated, but when surrounded by hundreds of STIC thugs, baying for his blood, who would expect him to be rosy? Although he had looked up to the balcony, it was not in search of applause but rather to see who was throwing things at him. And far from a disappointment, he described that night as one of the greatest triumphs of his life because it was real. "Now [there is] no more playacting [teatro]," he told reporters after returning from the Iris. "Today [there are] only deeds."[39] But regardless of the real physical danger, his deeds were a form of theater, intended to gain the approval of the Mexican public and their political leaders.

As a result, the question of just who attended the Iris Theater on March 8 gained real significance. Moreno and the STPC had launched a massive public relations campaign against Molina, so those who showed up had essentially repudiated the actors and their struggle against the STIC. The rude reception given to Moreno—telling him to shut up and get out—had compounded the insult. The comedian denied that they constituted "the public" and insisted that the only people there were STIC thugs and other CTM workers sent by Fidel Velázquez to fill the seats, a captive audience common to political rallies staged by the Mexican ruling party. But that seems implausible given the well-known fact that negative publicity draws crowds more surely than positive advertising. The critic for *Excélsior* described the usual mixed theater crowd, ranging across Mexican society, from wealthy Bohemians to the working class. He noted large numbers of pistol-toting STIC thugs but also many Spanish refugees nostalgic for the folklore of their homeland, currently under the dictatorship of Francisco Franco. The STPC's public statements before the performance had specifically called upon Spaniards to repudiate the scab dancer, and Moreno insisted that the crowd contained "undesirable individuals," not legitimate refugees.[40]

Even if Molina had triumphed before a crowd of Spanish refugees, as the newspaper reported, Moreno remained a heavy favorite in the theater of Mexican public opinion. After two years of union struggles and many more of political satire, the comedian had his script down pat. To convince the public, and more importantly the president, of the justice of his cause, Moreno played upon profound fears of foreign intervention, social unrest, and gender transgression. Nevertheless, these very themes threatened to boomerang and undermine the comedian's popularity. The STPC therefore took care in formulating its position in a special assembly held on Monday, March 11, at the Fronton. After a vote of confidence for Moreno, who still looked pale and tired after the previous Friday's confrontation, the actors agreed on three basic points. First, they called for an executive order expelling Molina from the country, under Article 33 of the Constitution of 1917, which gave the president the power to deport foreigners who threatened Mexican society. Next, they resolved to preempt the studio shutdown by walking out, even as the producers suspended work. Finally, the STPC sought political alliances with the administration and independent unions to bring an end to the STIC boycott and implement the presidential decree of the previous September 3.

Less than a decade after President Lázaro Cárdenas had declared Mexico's economic independence through the expropriation of foreign oil companies, economic nationalism still appealed to the masses. Nevertheless, the foreign card was not as straightforward as it had been in 1938. Mexico and the United States had become formal allies, for the first time ever, in World War II. While the actors condemned the STIC as an agent of foreign filmmakers, Hollywood films were actually quite popular in Mexico. Moreover, the portrayal of Molina as a foreign contamination was also problematic. Colonial stereotypes of Spaniards as price-gouging merchants had persisted long after independence, but this image changed dramatically after the fascist General Francisco Franco overthrew the Spanish Republic and large numbers of Spaniards arrived as refugees instead of as conquistadors.

To avoid any appearance of attacking the refugees and thus recalling the fascist label pinned to him by the CTM, Moreno went to great pains to emphasize his sympathy with the refugees' cause. And to redirect attention from the Spaniards' artistic and intellectual contributions, he emphasized Molina's meddling in the economy, the special preserve of Mexican nationals. That Molina had arrived under the auspices of the STPC only compounded the sense of betrayal, and the actors' guild withdrew the bond they had placed for him with the secretary of government. But even this argument played into the hands of STIC leaders, who accused the actors of divisive tactics, dividing the Mexican labor movement and encouraging social unrest, which could only harm the working classes and benefit rapacious capitalists.

The morality question had similar repercussions in the political discourse. Molina had gained antifascist credentials simply by having been run out of Argentina, which was governed by a military regime that had remained neutral throughout World War II. Rumors that Molina had fled under similar circumstances from Portugal, another fascist country, not to mention Franco's Spain, reinforced this image. Newspapers favorable to Molina spoke highly of his antifascist position. The actors carefully distinguished Molina's supposed immorality from political protest, but by attacking the refugee dancer, Moreno nevertheless risked reviving the CTM's charges of fascism.

Immorality was really just shorthand for effeminacy, and that trait alone constituted a prima facie case for Molina's conviction before the court of public opinion. *El Universal,* which generally took a favorable stance toward Moreno, notwithstanding the critiques of Duende Filme, reported that Moreno had yelled not "traitor" but "*maricón*" (passive homosexual) and that the audience had taken up the chant. Another strong supporter of Moreno, or rather critic of the CTM, the conservative *La Nación,* added that the Spanish dancer was known throughout Argentina by the feminine form *la Miguela.* This effeminate reputation earned him nothing but contempt within the culture of machismo, which nevertheless considered the active partner, who dominated both men and women, to be respectable. Other papers also favorable to Moreno referred vaguely to the dancer's "antecedents" and his "shameful expulsion from Argentina." The comedian himself apparently never publicly used albures questioning Molina's masculinity, although cinematographer Gabriel Figueroa could scarcely mention the man without some reference to his lack of manhood. Salvador Novo avoided the polemic entirely by taking a nationalistic stance, denouncing Molina for his failure to appreciate Mexican culture but refusing to endorse the filmmakers' attacks.

The possible stumbling blocks for Moreno's public relations campaign, however, were nothing compared with the troubles Molina had gaining popular support. In addition, Molina did not help his cause with the unconvincing claim that on stage he could not see what had happened, and that if he had known, he would have invited Moreno up to explain his position. He gave an equally lame response to the charges of immorality by claiming that he had not been physically thrown out of Argentina, just asked to leave. Finally, he published a forlorn letter in *Excélsior* insisting that he had no political agenda and wanted only to gratify Mexicans with the joys of Spanish art. But the Mexican people, already annoyed by the film boycott that kept them from seeing Jorge Negrete's latest charro film, rallied behind the national film industry. When the actors revived the previous year's threat to make films abroad, announcing "he goes or we go," the cry went up for Molina's expulsion. The president received petitions from bakers, sugar cane workers, and other unions requesting Article 33 treatment for the Spanish dancer. Nevertheless, crowds continued filling the Iris Theater to see the notorious act.

The actors found their most powerful union ally among Mexico City's independent electricians, who were seeking to create a national confederation outside the CTM. The previous summer, Moreno had marched in support of their goal, and the electricians returned the favor by offering a mutual defense pact. The STPC quickly accepted, and on March 13 the electricians succeeded where the actors could not, in pulling the plug on Miguel de Molina. At 6:30 P.M., when the box office had sold the last ticket, the theater lights gradually dimmed, then flickered out completely. CTM loyalists from the National Syndicate of Federal Electricians anticipated such a move and stood ready to restore power, ultimately resorting to an illegal connection with the building next door, which happened to contain the offices of the Secretary of Health and Welfare. But making the actual repairs was only the first step in the complex bureaucratic maze that had taken over the Mexican labor movement. As electricians reset their switches, CTM official Maximino Medina filled out the paperwork registering the power outage with the proper authorities as an act of economic sabotage. A notary public, Carlos Diego, also arrived to affix the proper seals. Meanwhile,

STIC orators filled time denouncing the rival union. Pedro Téllez Vargas announced that Mexico would never again see the films of Cantinflas or Negrete. After two hours of wiring, scribbling, and haranguing, the lights finally came back, to cheers of "¡Arriba el STIC!" (Hooray for STIC!). The audience took the stoppage stoically and most accepted rain checks for the next day's show. Nevertheless, theater officials worried about bad publicity, and with good reason, for the next day the Cantinflas electricians again pulled the plug on Molina.[41]

The struggle between the rival cinema unions became ever more bitter. Public opinion grew increasingly hostile toward Molina, who missed performances and was even rumored to have fled the country. Negotiations between the STPC and STIC proceeded under the supervision of the secretary of labor, but Moreno also visited the attorney general to press charges against Pedro Téllez Vargas personally for the boycott of *No basta ser charro.* Juan José Rivera Rojas, head of the electricians' union, meanwhile increased pressure on the government by shutting off power to the entire Federal District for fifteen minutes beginning at ten o'clock on May 15, with promises of nightly blackouts until a favorable settlement was reached.[42]

Once again the issue was decided by executive action, and once again the presidential favor fell to the STPC. The electricians called off the blackouts on March 19, and work resumed at the film studios the following day. The rival unions performed one last time their tired lines, with Moreno declaring neither winners nor losers and Carrillo protesting the cancellation of the long-departed aesthetic sections of cinematographers, actors, musicians, writers, and directors. The STIC tried one more time to renew the boycott, but without the legal approval of the secretary of labor, theater owners promised to cancel their contracts, and the threat of a strike evaporated.[43]

Moreno celebrated the victory with a comic bullfight against Stiquito, a bull from the personal ranch of Fidel Velázquez, according to an "exclusive graphic history of inter-union conflict" featured in *La Nación.* Cantinflas easily mastered the bull, leading it through an extended *veronica* (pass), despite the boycott, as well as a *manoletina,* a maneuver perfected by the renowned Spanish bullfighter Manolete, and even an extravagant *miguelina,* a reference to the notorious Spanish dancer. Finally, "to popular acclaim, the matador received both ears, the tail, registration, presidential decrees, judicial protection, a victory parade around the ring, and was carried out on the people's shoulders."[44]

Afterword

The two-year struggle for control of the cinema industry left an unclear legacy. The final resolution of the conflict—dividing film production arbitrarily between two rival unions—reflected political expedience rather than economic logic. That both unions remained within the CTM reduced union democracy to a hollow slogan adopted by the losers in any given power struggle. On a personal level, Salvador Carrillo was frustrated in his ambitions to become a media tycoon. Although he gained a special exemption from Mexican courts in 1947 to make a long reel film called *No te dejaré nunca* (I'll never leave you), it proved a financial bust. Nevertheless, he retained an iron grip over the remaining sections of STIC. Fidel Velázquez resigned his position of CTM secretary general in 1947 but only to hand over power to an old crony and fellow lobito, Fernando Amilpa.

Nationalist language became as convoluted as union democracy within the dispute. Carrillo's boycotts struck a terrific blow against domestic movie producers and actors to the benefit of Hollywood imports, prompting the STPC to call for his criminal prosecution on charges of economic espionage. The actors also condemned the actions of Miguel de Molina as a foreign interloper meddling in a national labor dispute and therefore liable for expulsion under Article 33 of the Constitution. Conversely, one of Hollywood's biggest partners in Mexico was Posa Films, which had signed an exclusive distribution agreement with Columbia Pictures for all Cantinflas films. The STIC therefore rightly accused the rival union leader of being a champion of U.S. distributors. Moreover, when Carrillo called his boycotts, the Mexican actors responded by threatening to leave the country and make films in Hollywood.[45] But in the end, Cantinflas remained secure in the public mind as the prototypical Mexican, a fact that became apparent in the public relations war with Molina.

The combination of politics and stardom likewise produced mixed results. Moreno's massive exposure in the news media, particularly the popular support for his protest at the Esperanza Iris Theater, added new energy to his film career. CTM accusations of fascism did not generally stick, even among many workers who mechanically telegraphed such charges to the president. Critics rightly questioned whether union activities distracted him from artistic production, but one can scarcely imagine him making better movies in an industry dominated by Salvador Carrillo or, worse still, Enrique Solís. Union activity also raised the comedian to new political heights as presidential candidate Miguel Alemán discovered the favorable publicity he could gain by appearing with Moreno.

However accustomed he had grown to popular adulation, Moreno must have been stunned by the almost Faustian bargain to become a spokesman for the Mexican government. The possibilities for helping the people seemed endless, but the media's refusal to take him seriously during the union struggle may have reminded him of the limits of political involvement. The warning came even more clearly at a dinner party in 1945 given by Maximino Avila Camacho shortly before his death. When the conversation turned to the upcoming presidential election, Moreno attempted to talk seriously about politics. Everybody at the table laughed, taking his statements as simply a Cantinflas joke, except for Gonzalo Santos, the powerful boss of San Luis Potosí, who cut him off abruptly: "Shut up and stick to your own language, you know nothing of the people, all you know is the public."[46]

5

THE MAGICIAN

By midcentury, Moreno had become so well known and his scripts so repetitive, that filmgoers could predict the contents of his movies based on the title alone. In *El mago* (The magician, 1948), for example, the pelado was mistaken for a fortuneteller—a fake of a fake—in keeping with his penchant for confused identity. The crystal ball and oriental turban provided material for familiar gags; when an attractive young woman arrived for a consultation, Cantinflas twitched his eyebrows, polished the glass, and pretended to see her husband being unfaithful in order to make a date with her. As a pretext for assuming the identity of a magician, Cantinflas worked as a messenger boy for Su Otro Yo (Your Other Self), a company that offered identical substitutes to professionals, allowing vacation time for busy lawyers, doctors, and even magicians. Although an imaginary company, SOY (I Am) resonated with the Mexican penchant for masks, particularly at a time when the government was updating its public face. A new generation of university-trained professionals was replacing the revolutionary generals who had dominated Mexican politics since the 1920s and was largely responsible for the government's new image.

This shift in governmental leadership was exemplified by the election of Miguel Alemán as president in 1946, the first time a civilian had been elected to the post since Francisco Madero in 1911. Just as Moreno institutionalized and commercialized his mistaken identity in *El mago,* Alemán and his fellows transformed the corporatist party that Cárdenas built, renaming it the Institutional Revolutionary Party (Partido Revolucionario Institucional, PRI) and harnessing it to the single-minded pursuit of economic development. They achieved stunning results in terms of rapid economic growth, political stability, and social peace, but the question remained whether the government's statistical measures reflected genuine improvements for the Mexican people or simply a magician's sleight of hand.

Numbers alone gave Mexico an international reputation as an economic "miracle." For three decades beginning in the late 1930s, the economy grew at an average annual rate of 6 percent, faster than all but a few Asian countries in the postwar era, such as Japan and South Korea. Even allowing for rapid population growth, per capita figures indicated a solid 3 percent growth that could have improved living standards for all citizens. Unfortunately, the so-called institutional revolution redirected national income away from those who needed it most. The extended boom had begun under Cárdenas with Keynesian-style policies intended to provide workers with enough income to consume Mexican manufactured goods, thereby overcoming the fundamental dilemma of Porfirian development, the lack of a domestic market. But the 1940s marked a profound shift away from

Cantinflas attempts to hypnotize the Mexican people. El mago, *production still. Courtesy: Archivo General de la Nación.*

demand-led development toward a supply-side program focused on capital accumulation. Alemán employed banks, taxes,
and tariffs to direct income toward investment in the belief that
by forgoing mass consumption for a generation, Mexico could
build the industrial base needed for a modern economy. The
plan seemed to work for a few export-oriented Asian economies,
but Mexican businesses remained largely content with domestic
monopolies and never developed the competitive edge needed
to break into international markets. Consequently, the postwar
generation of Mexican workers suffered declining standards of
living in order to finance not the construction of self-sustaining
industry but rather the conspicuous consumption of a handful
of newly rich financiers.

Maintaining the government's legitimacy as heir to the Revolution of 1910 while showing such favoritism to big business required still further sleight of hand. The ruling party's goal was to
modernize the authoritarian system to achieve the appearance of
a democratic society while in fact tightening its grip on power.
The Alemán administration proved extremely adept at co-opting
working class leaders by offering them power and privilege
within the official party in exchange for restraining the wage demands of the union rank and file. Those who sought independence from the PRI were cast out into the political wilderness,
losing access to government patronage and risking violent repression if they pursued their demands too forcefully. Although
labor and the peasantry composed the vast majority of the party's
membership, the middle sectors came increasingly to dominate its
leadership. These politicians went through the motions of con-
sulting the popular will, either directly through national elections
or behind the scenes in discussions with Cárdenas and other
populist leaders. Nevertheless, the policies that resulted showed
an unmistakable conservative bent. Nationalism, for example,
which had meant bold defiance of the domination of foreign oil
companies in the late thirties evolved into anticommunism and an
alliance with the United States during the Cold War.

Mario Moreno followed the PRI down its increasingly conservative path while his movies grew ever more formulaic. The
playful gender transgression he had engaged in for the first
decade of his film career gave way to the conventional story line
of boy meets girl—a different, beautiful, often foreign, actress for

each movie. With a few exceptions, Cantinflas and the girl married in the end. The pelado thereby exchanged his earlier footloose existence for the happy ending of bourgeois family life demanded by middle-class audiences. His verbal sparring partners also declined in quality from the level of Medel and Pardavé, reducing the unique chaos of his wordplay to rather unimaginative puns. Even his film production became institutionalized in a pattern of a single movie a year, timed for release to maximize profits from the holiday crowds on the Cinco de Mayo, Independence Day, or Christmas. He made two attempts at reviving the moribund revista theater by staging lavish spectacles, but lost money on both occasions and never again returned to the stage. Although Cantinflas assumed some of the less savory aspects of the Alemanista new rich, Moreno remained the most popular star in Mexico, in part because the studio system, like the PRI, closed out possible alternatives. In their constant search for profits, producers tried to force potential rivals, including the brilliant actor Germán Valdés "Tin Tan," into an artistically stagnant mold as Cantinflas imitators.

Cantinflas at Cannes

Cantinflas began to acquire magical new powers in his first film after the resolution of the union crisis. *Soy un prófugo* (I'm a fugitive, 1946) opened with an unusual image of the pelado as a banker directing large sums of money on the telephone. The camera then panned back to reveal his true identity as a janitor, illustrating once again the lack of real distinction between rich and poor. As the plot developed, Cantinflas was accused of robbing the bank, and he became a fugitive trying to clear his name. He developed the power of hypnotism (deus ex machina) and brought the real gang of thieves to justice. In the end the real hypnotist turned out to be his old girlfriend, a faithful shop clerk.

Mexicans hoped that this spell would also extend to Europe, because Moreno received an invitation to show *Los tres mosqueteros* at the Cannes Film Festival. Charlie Chaplin's endorsement had earned him a billing on September 21, 1946, the opening day of the first festival since the liberation of Europe.

Shortly before he departed for France, Moreno had a close call in the plaza de toros when a bull's horn nicked him in the drooping seat of his pants, but that was a minor indignity compared to the savagery of the French film critics. *Le Figaro* began its coverage of the festival with the headline: "Cantinflas, new comic star, not very funny." The reviewer expected great things, having heard Chaplin's description of him as the greatest comedian of the age, but "the disappointment was total." It did not help that the two-hour-and-twenty-minute film played at the end of a very long day, concluding shortly before midnight. The critic for *Le Monde,* bored with the sagging trousers, described it as "an interminable *pantalonnade.*"[1]

The Mexican press, left speechless by the French drubbing of their national champion, soon recovered its voice to trumpet the success of another local filmmaker, Gabriel Figueroa, who won the best cinematography award for *María Candelaria* (1943). One bold commentator, Luis Garrido, ventured to discuss the significance of Moreno's fate. Although none could doubt the artist's talent, Garrido believed that success had come too easily. Moreno squandered his filmmaking energies on union struggles, radio shows and newspaper columns, public discourses, and even politics. The entire nation must learn from his misfortune, Garrido concluded, and direct its energies to achieving works of lasting merit and artistry. The hopes pinned on Moreno by the Mexican public also became apparent when Mexican journalists reported on his reception in Spain using the religious language of nationalist discourse: that he had converted the masses.[2] Moreover, despite the dismissive words of Parisian critics, Moreno gained great popularity among ordinary French people, who saw in him a New World version of their folksy comedian Fernandel.

Moreno's growing fascination with foreign culture also extended to his costars. In 1947, he chose the Czech beauty Miroslava Sternova, known simply by her first name in Mexico, for the film *¡A volar joven!* (Fly boy). Miroslava played an ugly duckling, ordered to marry by doctor's prescription, whose parents convinced an air force recruit, Cantinflas, to go through with the wedding in return for a dinner of *mole poblano* (turkey in chile pepper sauce). The bride removed her glasses after the ceremony, revealing her beauty, but Cantinflas had to become a pilot hero before they could share their honeymoon. The aeronautical twist notwithstanding, this film marked an important shift in Cantinflas's character, the domestication of the pelado to middle-class standards of family life. This change followed in part from a campaign by the Catholic Church to impose morality upon a film industry that was turning increasingly toward the theme of prostitution in cabaret films starring such actresses as the sultry Cuban dancer Ninón Sevilla. Moreno told the Catholic journal *La Nación* that the national cinema needed a proper orientation and that he welcomed censorship intended to create standards "according to our personality, as a country, and as Mexicans."3 The acceptance of family values marked an important step in taking Cantinflas away from his carefree pelado origins and toward the bourgeoisie.

The Economic Miracle

Although critics seemed at a loss to explain Cantinflas's magical ability to please filmgoers, Mario Moreno always insisted that his character needed to evolve to hold the public's attention. From the pelado of the thirties, he had become a union leader in the midforties, and toward the end of the decade, to fit with the Alemán generation, he reinvented himself once again, this time as a businessman. In November 1949, Moreno used this executive persona to entertain reporters in his suite on the thirty-third floor of the Hampshire House in Manhattan. He promised the journalists a detailed account of his business interests, only to give them the Cantinflas treatment of a meaningless discourse on lana, a slang term for money. But when the telephone rang, he fulfilled his promise, albeit indirectly. "Hello," he answered in English, before exclaiming in Spanish, "Your Excellency the Ambassador . . . ? Get out of here . . . ! Pardon me, it wasn't my idea to insult my dignity . . . I mean yours . . ."4 This typical Cantinflas speech, alternating respect for authority with excessive familiarity, really was the detalle of doing business in the era of Miguel Alemán. Industrial fortunes awaited those with the political connections to speak with both respect and familiarity to the nation's economic planners, thereby ensuring the success of their personal investments.

The state assumed a dominant role in directing the economy during the so-called miracle by guiding investment toward select industries and by assuring the supremacy of capital in labor negotiations. The federal investment bank, Nacional Financiera, founded in 1934, provided credit for public works and private investment, including hydroelectric dams and road construction. State control of the economy also helped restrain wage demands from labor unions, further contributing to business profits. The Alemán generation carried on the economic nationalism of Lázaro Cárdenas, at least in rhetoric. A decree of 1944 required Mexican ownership of at least 51 percent of all firms in strategic industries, and a tariff law of 1947 raised duties from 15 to 100 percent on a wide range of consumer goods. When middle- and upper-class consumers still showed a preference for foreign goods, upsetting the balance of payments, the government devalued the peso by 40 percent in 1948, limiting imports and protecting currency reserves but at the expense of even greater inflation.[5]

Moreno became a spokesman for Mexican economic nationalism in a 1948 feature film, *El supersabio* (The egghead), about the malevolent multinational Petroleum Trust, which sought to suppress a Mexican scientist's discovery of a synthetic gasoline. Cantinflas appeared as a lab assistant more interested in using graduated cylinders to mix martinis than in rendering the petroleum industry obsolete. Nevertheless, when the old scientist died of a heart attack, the pelado had to flee from assassins hired by the Petroleum Trust in the belief that he had learned the secret formula. A reporter, played by the Cuban actress Perla Aguiar, came to his defense, publicizing the foreign company's machinations and inciting crowds to demand Cantinflas's safety. Rather than risk the public wrath, the trust president decided to bribe Cantinflas with a check for a million pesos not to reveal the secret formula, which of course he never had. They appeared together on a balcony, and Cantinflas parodied Evita Perón, then at the height of her popularity in Argentina, by waving to the frenzied crowds and announcing, "Citizens of this city, I am not dead! I look pretty bad, but I'm not dead!" The film ended with Cantinflas and the reporter falling in love and the foreign capitalist looking ridiculous for having paid a million pesos to suppress a nonexistent formula.

Such populist images of an enraged pueblo humiliating the representatives of foreign capital delighted Mexican filmgoers with nationalist memories of the triumphant oil expropriation of 1938, but those memories bore no relation to the current economic reality. In fact, United States corporations used their very technical superiority to gain access to Mexican markets, abrogating legal restrictions in the process. They evaded the 51 percent ownership requirement through the use of *prestanombres* (borrowed names) from local politicians who received fat salaries for sitting on boards of directors. Moreover, many of the factories that opened in the postwar era to build automobiles, appliances, and other consumer goods in Mexico merely assembled parts that had been manufactured elsewhere. Even genuinely national firms imported their technology and machinery from the United States and Europe, undermining both the nationalist quest for self-sufficiency and their ability to compete in international markets. After all, Mario Moreno bought the story for *El supersabio* in France, where it had originally been filmed by Fernandel in 1942 with the title *Ne le criez pas sur les toits* (Don't shout it from the roofs).[6]

The government took an active role in the motion picture industry, which ranked as the sixth largest manufacturer in the country. Manuel Avila Camacho exempted filmmakers from income taxes in 1946, and the following year Miguel Alemán nationalized the Banco Cinematográfico, increasing its capital to ten million pesos. The Cinema Law of 1949 increased state participation in the industry by forming a directorate under the Ministry of Gobernación responsible for fomenting the production and authorizing the distribution of films. A subsequent law of 1952 declared motion pictures to be a public good subject to federal regulation and required every theater in the country to devote at least half of its screenings to Mexican films.[7]

The crony capitalism that pervaded so many sections of the economy also characterized the film industry. Abelardo Rodríguez, one of the foremost examples of the revolutionary bourgeoisie, or generals who parlayed their political power into industrial fortunes, had a longtime interest in filmmaking, dating back to his early holdings in CLASA studios. In 1946, he opened Tepeyac studios, at the time the best-equipped facilities in Mexico, and he also diversified into the exhibition end of the business, building the cinema chain Circuito de Cines primarily in the north but with a flagship, the Chapultepec theater, in Mexico City. Meanwhile, the dominant power in motion picture theaters was William O. Jenkins, a businessman from the United States with close connections to the Avila Camacho family and a shady career in revolutionary Mexico. In the 1920s, he had built a fortune from sugar plantations, bootlegging rum to the United States during Prohibition. When Cardenista agrarian reform threatened his landholdings, he began buying up movie houses. By the mid-1940s, he had acquired two separate chains, Operadora de Teatros and Cadena de Oro, controlling all film exhibition in a dozen states in eastern and central Mexico and one fourth of the theaters in the nation's capital.[8]

These distribution networks gave Jenkins enormous power over cinema production. Filmmakers relied on advances from distributors and theater owners to finance their work, and Jenkins used this influence to dictate a series of regulations aimed at standardizing production within a few already established genres. He gained further influence through his investment in Churubusco Studios, built by the American industrialist Harry Wright with the assistance of RKO Pictures and Twentieth Century-Fox. The studio opened in 1944 but grew slowly at first, in part because RKO did not accept Mexican accounting practices, in which "double entry" meant keeping two separate sets of books; instead everything had to be up to the standards of the accounting firm Price, Waterhouse. Mario Moreno, another investor in Churubusco, filmed there for the first time in 1947, with *¡A volar joven!* and it became his preferred studio. By the end of the 1950s, mergers and closures had eliminated CLASA, Azteca, and Tepeyac studios, leaving only Churubusco and Jorge Stahl's San Angel Inn.[9]

The concentration of studios and theaters brought about a decline in both the number and quality of films, effectively ending the "golden age" of Mexican cinema in the late 1940s. As the Jenkins chains began "canning," or withholding from exhibition, large numbers of domestic films in order to screen more Hollywood imports, directors increasingly limited themselves to formulaic and low-budget *churros* (Spanish donuts fried in a distinctive ridged, cigar shape). The growing repetitiveness of Cantinflas scripts brought accusations that even he had lowered himself by making such cheap flicks. Moreno, who had long since stopped listening to domestic critics, responded playfully with an advertisement for *El mago* that showed a cartoon Cantinflas holding a magic wand with the distinctive ridges and promising, for his next trick, to make "a 'churro' into a movie, or vice versa."[10]

With Cantinflas films regularly grossing more than one million pesos on their premiere runs alone, Moreno had the freedom to film whatever he wanted. Posa Films demanded 70 percent of box office revenues, a figure granted only to Hollywood blockbusters and exactly the reverse of the usual 30 percent allocated to domestic producers. Less affluent producers demanded government intervention to break up the Jenkins monopoly. Miguel Contreras Torres, the spokesman for the independents and director of the first Cantinflas film, later speculated that political alliances between Alemán and Avila Camacho had raised Jenkins above the law, making him, in the popular usage, "untouchable." In fact, the administration attempted to negotiate an acuerdo satisfactory to all interest groups by establishing Peliculas Nacionales in 1947 as a domestic counterpart to the foreign distributorship, Peliculas Mexicanas. But the deal failed to satisfy independent filmmakers because Jenkins, acting through the National Cinema Bank, dominated the new company, leaving Abelardo Rodríguez's theater chain as the only domestic exhibitor willing to show the independents' films.[11]

Meanwhile, in 1948, Mario Moreno reportedly used his box office clout to attempt to take control of Peliculas Mexicanas by having its European representative, William Karol, replaced by a nephew of Jacques Gelman. The comedian's rival, Jorge Negrete, was delighted with Karol's work distributing *Historia de un gran amor* (Story of a great love, 1942) and wrote to his wife and costar Gloria Marín complaining about the attempt by Posa to have Karol removed by pulling strings with the Cinema Bank and the Mexican ambassador in Paris. "Mario said that my movies were in the hands of a Jewish thief and that they should be in the hands of Mexicans," Negrete fumed. "Imagine, him talking of Jews and foreign distributors with Gelman, Reachi, and Levy by his side; that's the limit!"[12] And Negrete had not even mentioned Posa's contract with Columbia Pictures for the international distribution of Cantinflas films. In any case, Moreno's attempt to take over PelMex ultimately failed.

Although Moreno plowed more of his box office profits back into film making than did many other Mexican producers, he nevertheless diversified his investments throughout the economy. Tourism emerged as the fastest growing sector of the postwar economy, and as chief executive, Miguel Alemán showed great leadership in promoting this vital industry by buying up beachfront property in Acapulco, then ordering the construction of a superhighway from Mexico City and airport facilities to increase its value. Mario Moreno likewise helped develop the trade by constructing tourist bungalows next to the Hotel Majestic. He also advertised the resort in a number of films, starting with *El mago,* when the overworked fortuneteller took his vacation in Acapulco, lounging in a hammock, while Cantinflas held down the shop.[13]

Mario Moreno also invested in the modernization of Mexican agriculture, another dynamic sector of the postwar economy. Once again he followed presidential leadership, as demonstrated by the Valsequillo Dam, which had been built during World War II with technical assistance from the United States. Given high priority for its contributions to the war effort, the project stimulated regional development in Puebla and irrigated a hundred thousand acres of prime farmland, helping to feed urban consumers with corn and wheat grown on estates owned personally by the president.[14] On a more modest scale, Mario Moreno purchased the latest farm machinery to modernize his cattle ranch, El Detalle, in San Luis Potosí.[15] The technological improvements adopted by progressive farmers, coupled with massive irrigation works, increased agricultural productivity dramatically. This so-called Green Revolution helped to provide cheap food to urban workers, further stimulating economic growth. Another result was that rural incomes plummeted, compelling ever greater numbers of impoverished farmers to leave the land, creating a new generation of Mexican pelados.

Unfortunately, when the displaced rural workers arrived in the city, not enough jobs awaited them. The capital-intensive rather than labor-intensive nature of Mexican industrialization created the paradoxical situation of widespread unemployment

in a rapidly expanding economy. This failure to provide suffi-
cient jobs in turn undermined the entire theory of "trickle
down" development. The mechanisms by which income supposedly "trickled down" simply did not exist in highly polarized
societies. Moreno recognized this fact of Mexican life in his
films, at least implicitly, by not making a counterpart of Chaplin's classic *Modern Times*. Industrial workers in Mexico benefited from the protection of government-sponsored unions,
health insurance, and social security. Cantinflas, like most poor
city dwellers, eked out a subsistence in such low-paying jobs as
barber, window washer, or shoeshine boy. Beneath the illusion
of the economic miracle, underemployment in the service sector
formed the reality of Mexican modernity.

Bonjour, Mexique

While profiting handsomely from his diverse investments, Mario
Moreno had a personal stake in the modernization of one particular sector of the economy, the theater. His cinema conquests
made him one of the country's leading celebrities, but he still
missed the immediate rewards of applause for a live performance. He had dreamed for years of importing the most beautiful European dancers and constructing the most lavish stages
in order to raise the revista theater up to the international standards of New York's Broadway or Paris's Moulin Rouge. On a
trip to the continent in 1948, he signed a contract with a troupe
of French dancers, but his impresario plans to revolutionize
Mexican theater were soon engulfed in a chaos that only Cantinflas could resolve.

Moreno originally planned for *Bonjour, Mexique* to premiere
in time for the independence holidays in September, but the
dancers did not arrive until November, and even that date
proved far too early for the stage work. As a result, Moreno had
to support the fifty-five artists at the luxurious Viceroy Hotel
while preparations continued at the Iris Theater. Union troubles
further hampered the production, because the Agustín Lara orchestra, which he hoped to contract for the show, belonged to
the Union of Musical Workers, a rival of Moreno's own STPC.
He had intervened a year earlier in union affairs to support his

old friend, the flaco de oro, and the syndicate leaders returned the favor by rejecting his offer of an acuerdo. "You may be Cantinflas, but the interests of our organization come first. Discipline yourself."[16]

The production had already cost the astronomical sum of a million and a half pesos before the opening in January 1949. Reviewers noted that while theatrical spectacles had long claimed Parisian origins on only the slightest pretense, Mario Moreno actually had imported everything from France to recreate the stately minuets of Louis XIV's Versailles and the racy cancan of Toulouse Lautrec's dance halls. Unfortunately, the Mexican public, preoccupied with the cinema, showed little interest in the production. One critic recommended that Moreno take his show to New York where audiences appreciated such a spectacle. Instead, he took to the stage personally in February, renaming the show *Cantinflas en Paris*. Crowds suddenly began to fill the theater, but even then the production closed in the red on March 15. The financial picture improved somewhat when President Alemán granted the enterprise a tax rebate, demonstrating once again the government's favoritism toward business.[17]

A Piece of the PRI

The devastating consequences of industrialization for the lower classes posed a dilemma to those with a social conscience among the Mexican elite, including Mario Moreno. Trickle-down economic growth required low industrial wages, and the government restrained worker protests by co-opting the leadership of industrial unions. Policies that so blatantly contradicted popular opinion seriously undermined the ruling party's legitimacy as the rightful representative of the Mexican people. While agreeing on the need for political change, the Alemán generation merely tried to improve the party's image by purging the pistol-toting regional bosses without relinquishing the official party's monopoly on public office. Populist leaders therefore had to choose between working within the system to distribute patronage more equally or to demand genuine democracy from the outside, at the risk of government repression. Although a film celebrity rather than an elected politician, Moreno directed his personal prestige to this midcentury renovation of the Mexican political system. Although he was working in the name of democratic renewal, he actually helped to modernize an authoritarian system that co-opted working-class leadership and replaced old-style political bosses with college-educated bureaucrats.

Since its founding in 1929, the official party had undergone a series of changes that broadened its popular base while concentrating political and economic power. The coalition of revolutionary leaders, established by the jefe máximo Calles, was expanded by Cárdenas to include organized peasants and trade unions. The paternalistic Cárdenas imposed a "functional" democracy that gave popular groups a voice only through the party's bureaucracy of union, peasant, military, and middle-class representatives. Political decisions were negotiated by party leaders, and the choice of presidential succession was determined by executive fiat rather than by popular vote.

Party discipline was tested at the beginning of Alemán's administration, in 1947, when the CTM national congress met to choose a successor for Fidel Velázquez. The old guard supported Fernando Amilpa, another of the "five little wolves," knowing he would continue the conservative policies begun by Velázquez, but declining real wages prompted several important unions to support an opposition candidate, the railroad worker Luis Gómez Z. For personal reasons, Vicente Lombardo Toledano tipped the balance in favor of Amilpa. As a result, dissident unions, including the electricians and the railroad and telephone workers, withdrew to form an independent confederation. With the most radical unions gone, Amilpa purged the CTM of communists, swore unconditional loyalty to the president, and changed the union's motto from the aggressively Marxist demand, "For a society without classes," to a hollow patriotic slogan, "For the emancipation of Mexico."[18]

The political wilderness awaiting those outside the official party became clear with the fate of Vicente Lombardo Toledano. Sensing his own declining influence within the PRI and hoping to create an independent leftist party, he signed a Faustian deal. In exchange for endorsing Amilpa's candidacy to succeed Velázquez, he requested CTM assistance in establishing the Partido Popular. Lombardo may have gained particular pleasure in recruiting as secretary of propaganda for the new party his old antagonist from the Cardenista days, Salvador Novo. But this reconciliation between two of Mexico's leading intellectuals provided little consolation when Amilpa reneged on the deal and ordered the expulsion of any CTM worker who joined the new party, starting with Lombardo himself. When the disciplined union bureaucracy that he had created was turned on him, the CTM founder could only reflect bitterly on the emptiness of "functional" democracy.[19]

This point was not lost on Mario Moreno, a seasoned observer of Lombardo Toledano, and he gave Cantinflas a brief but memorable encounter with the Mexican political system in his next film, *Puerta, joven* (The door, boy, 1949). After a string of mediocre foreign scripts, Cantinflas returned to his roots as the doorman of an urban tenement house in what Emilio García Riera has called "certainly the best film by the comic since *El gendarme desconocido* and, perhaps, the last in which his grace outweighs the prepotency of the magnate."[20] The story recalled Chaplin's *City Lights* (1931), as Cantinflas arranged for an operation to cure an attractive young woman with crippled legs, played by Silvia Pinal, only to lose her to another man. The pelado sang drunken mariachi tunes to befriend a celebrated doctor who conducted the surgery, and he paid for the clinic fees by placing a bet at the races then riding the horse to victory when the regular jockey disappeared. Along the way, he saved the barrio school from being closed through a masterfully confusing discourse with a Department of Education functionary. Cantinflas questioned bureaucratic priorities, with a play on the CTM's former slogan, by suggesting that they were working "for a society without classes, and worse still, without teachers." But in the end only a reference to (imagined) political connections kept the school open.

Meanwhile, Alemán plotted with CTM leaders against the dissident railroad workers union. When Luis Gómez Z. moved to become secretary general of an independent national labor confederation, the government encouraged an internal coup by his replacement at the railroad union, Jesús Díaz de León, who was known as "the Charro" for the flamboyant Mexican cowboy costumes he wore to union rallies. In October 1948, Díaz de León accused his predecessor of fraud for having used union funds first to finance his bid for the CTM presidency a year earlier and then to help establish the independent confederation. In fact, the local sections had approved the expenditures, and when the Charro called for a financial investigation by the federal attorney general, setting a dangerous precedent for government intervention in union activities, the railroad workers' national committee suspended him from office. But Díaz de León regained control of the union with the assistance of federal agents, who arrested Gómez Z. and held him in jail for six months. The Charro changed union rules to deny voting rights to rank and file workers and withdrew the union from Gómez Z.'s independent coalition, causing its collapse. Alemán pushed through a new contract increasing management control over the railroad union, then proceeded to install captive leaders, who came to be known derisively as "charros," in the independent petroleum workers' and miners' unions.

One year later, in 1950, Mario Moreno filmed *El siete machos* (Seven machos), a satire of charro movies at the height of the charro sellout of Mexico's labor unions. Unlike the irrelevant jokes of *Los tres mosqueteros* or *Romeo y Julieta*, Moreno knew exactly what to parody in the Mexican cowboy film, and he did so to brutal effect. The film included a singing bandit who fought like Robin Hood to free the peasants from an abusive landowner, a role that Jorge Negrete established in *¡Ay, Jalisco, no te rajes!* Moreno naturally played double roles: the bandit Siete Machos, with a dubbed baritone singing voice, and the Cantinflas character, a peon on the evil patron's hacienda who actually saved the day. The charro movie formula required the bandit hero not only to free the peasants from the greedy hacendado but also to win the heart of the beautiful young heiress through a moonlight serenade. The carpa star Delia Magaña finally had her chance to appear on film with Moreno, but as Chole, the jealous servant, while Alma Rosa Aguirre played the love interest, Rosario, the patron's niece. In the movie, Cantinflas visited an herbalist to deepen his voice but took the wrong formula by mistake, and so when he crooned to his sweetheart, the words came out in a soprano pitch. The macho challenge between the bandit hero and his rough gang of outlaws, another staple of the charro genre, provided a perfect setting for the pelado's ambivalent macho posturing, this time through an encounter of Russian roulette. Moreno still retained his hilarious facial expressions, running through a range of contorted gestures with each pull of the trigger. A nervous gang member accidentally fired his own gun, and Cantinflas fell to the ground, certain that he was dead. But when he realized that he had won the challenge, he quickly recovered his macho front and proceeded to slap around his insubordinate henchmen. The movie ended on a mixed note, subverting the charro's patriarchal authority—Chole conquered the bandit Siete Machos with her love potions—but reaffirming bourgeois propriety through the marriage of Cantinflas and Rosario.

The spread of charro union leaders represented part of a mounting crisis in the official party's legitimacy as heir to the Revolution of 1910. Alemán had entered office promising to make his number-one priority the improvement of working-class standards of living. He then spent the next six years accumulating one of the largest fortunes in Mexico while real wages fell more than 30 percent. Alemán also amended the constitution to allow landowners to sue in federal courts to block agrarian reform. The final straw came when rumors emerged that the president planned to repudiate the most basic revolutionary principle, "No Reelection," by installing his own cousin, Fernando Casas Alemán, as the official party's presidential candidate for 1952. Disgusted by corruption and betrayal, prominent members of the PRI broke away to form an independent party endorsing the candidacy of agrarian reformer and revolutionary veteran, General Miguel Henríquez Guzmán. The common cause between a middle-class hungry for democracy and workers' demands for land reform and better wages, together with the political clout of the new party's leaders and the public sympathy of General Cárdenas, seemed to herald genuinely free elections.[21]

Mario Moreno was caught up in the excitement and considered it his civic duty to participate in the elections by making the movie *Si yo fuera diputado* (If I were a congressman). He rushed the film through production, canning an earlier effort, *El bombero atómico* (The atomic fireman), and shooting in September 1951 to allow a premiere on January 30, 1952, less than six months before the balloting. The importance Moreno attached to this effort became even more clear in the opening credits, which attributed the screenplay to him personally, albeit with additional lines by his long-time collaborators, Jaime Salvador and Carlos León. This Mexican version of *Mr. Smith Goes to Washington* therefore presented perhaps his closest approach to the personal statement that auteur critics look for in a film.

Following a well-established pattern, Cantinflas appeared as a barber in a working-class neighborhood of Mexico City, but this time he applied his street smarts to learning the law rather than subverting it as in previous films. After proving his legal skills by saving a widow from eviction by a slumlord and flirtatiously defending a femme fatale on trial for murder, he accepted the nomination as the people's candidate for the local congressional seat. The campaign against a corrupt political boss illustrated various aspects of the Mexican political experience, including a raucous debate, the ubiquitous campaign posters, an attempt to steal the ballot box, and finally the candidate's victory speech.

Moreno clearly believed that he was contributing to the growth of democracy by drawing on symbolism from some of the great moments in the history of Mexican politics. The nefarious boss illegally posted campaign slogans that would be attributed to Cantinflas on public walls in order to have him arrested before the election, a clear reference to Francisco I. Madero, the Apostle of Mexican Democracy, jailed in his campaign against the dictator Porfirio Díaz. But in an outpouring of popular support, reminiscent of the oil expropriation of 1938, citizens of the barrio contributed their humble savings to pay the fine. And when the political boss sent his henchmen to steal the box with votes for Cantinflas, the people stood guard over the precinct house with guns and sticks to foil the attempt. Their vigilance recalled another revolutionary tradition, at least in theory, for the Electoral Law of 1918 had entrusted the polling booths to the first voters who arrived to take control of them. Intended to prevent the fraud so common under Díaz, this system created irregularities of its own, not to mention considerable violence as rival parties fought for possession of the ballot boxes, before a 1945 reform centralized control of elections under a federal commission. Nevertheless, it symbolized to many people the revolutionary ideal of effective suffrage.[22]

By presenting anachronistic images of citizenship, *Si yo fuera diputado* may actually have helped legitimize the Alemán project of modernizing an authoritarian political system. The new generation of civilian politicians made their primary concern the centralization of federal authority by weeding out regional strongmen who wielded power through pistoleros and replacing them with university-trained administrators. Although this campaign promised to impose greater government efficiency and to enhance Mexico's international image as a safe destination for tourism and investment, it did nothing to further the cause of Mexican democracy. In defeating such an old-time boss, Cantinflas bestowed his considerable prestige on a legislature still dominated by the PRI and, like so many young lawyers of the Alemán generation, without really answering the question of what he would do if elected. As the critic Hortensia Elizondo observed, "The political discourses that the public avidly awaited were lukewarm comic fare of a kind unlikely to shake up Congress."[23]

Moreno lent further credibility to the political system by serving as president of a local polling station on election day, July 6, 1952. The film character of Cantinflas once again blended with real life, or at least with newspaper reports, of an encounter between Moreno and an unnamed policeman. In a scene recalling *El gendarme desconocido,* a policeman asked for permission to vote without his registration card using the same excuse Cantinflas had given his sergeant, that it had been stolen. But this time Moreno spoke with the voice of authority, saying, "Well, I don't permit you to vote, so you keep a look out for the crooks, boy." He then turned to Alemán's secretary of commerce and industry, Antonio Martínez Báez, who was waiting in line to vote, and said, "That'll teach him."[24] Moreno thus publicly applied the Cantinflas seal of approval to the election, which journalists dutifully proclaimed to be the cleanest in Mexican history.

Savvy observers recognized the 1952 election not as a turning point toward democracy but rather as confirmation of the president's control over succession through a process known as the *dedazo* (the stroke of a finger). By attempting to impose the wrong man, Alemán had threatened the smooth succession of the presidency through the PRI. Cárdenas openly voiced his sympathy for Henríquez as a way of pressuring the president to find a more suitable candidate. The hesitant finger finally pointed to Adolfo Ruiz Cortines, a career civil servant with a reputation for honesty, just what the government needed to restore the appearance of propriety tarnished by corruption within the Alemán administration. Henceforth, with a simple wave of the finger, future presidents revealed *el tapado* (the hidden one), the official party's candidate, and therefore the man destined to govern Mexico for the next six years. Elections became mere formalities as all attention focused on the unveiling of the tapado. Politicians within the PRI inner circle had an enormous stake in guessing correctly, for the first ones to jump on the candidate's bandwagon could expect to gain high office in the forthcoming administration. Those outside the official party who protested electoral fraud, as did the followers of Henríquez, could expect only government repression.[25]

In July 1952, as the disputed election took place, Moreno was in the midst of filming his version of a Cold War thriller, *El señor fotógrafo* (Mr. Photographer). Rodolfo Sánchez Taboada, president of the PRI, had declared in 1947 the government's opposition to communism, and the union crackdown that followed resembled Joseph McCarthy's witch-hunt in the United States. Cantinflas joked, "Stalin rubs me the wrong way," and steadfastly supported the official policy conflating anticommunism with anti-imperialism as a basic tenant of Mexican nationalism. In this movie, he played a photographer caught up in an international conspiracy to kidnap Angel Garasa, creator of the dreaded Z-Bomb. Like *The Mouse that Roared,* later filmed by Peter Sellers, the bomb proved a dud, as Cantinflas discovered when he confused it with a ball, causing it to explode. The film concluded with the police capturing the villains and Cantinflas and Garasa marrying their respective sweethearts.

Just as the Mexican political system closed out alternatives to the PRI, so the movie studios held up Cantinflas as the nation's official comedian and, in their quest for predictable profits, tried to mold other performers in his image. The principal challenge to the Mexico City pelado's representation of the national identity came from the most economically dynamic and culturally elastic region of the country, the border with the United States. Germán Valdés brought the transnational figure of the Mexican-American *pachuco* to the screen under the name of Tin Tan. He spoke a rapid-fire Spanglish dialect that bewildered middle-class Mexico City audiences of the 1940s as much as the

Tepito slang of Cantinflas had a decade earlier. Respectable citizens also felt threatened by his signature zoot suit: a jacket worn down to the knees, bright suspenders holding his trousers up to his armpits, a silk shirt with flowered tie, a pocket watch on a dangling gold chain, and a plumed fedora. Worst of all, this pachuco in a pimp costume speaking broken Spanish attacked corruption in the Alemán administration more openly than Cantinflas had ever dared, at least since his days at the Follies.

Born in Mexico City in 1915, Valdés grew up in the border town of Ciudad Juárez, where he started in radio doing comic imitations of Agustín Lara and other celebrities. He later joined ventriloquist Paco Miller's company and toured Mexico and the southwestern United States. He returned to Mexico City in 1943, whereupon the company nearly went bust until Miller persuaded Moreno to join the show. Valdés got his first starring role in the 1945 film *El hijo desobediente* (The disobedient son) and gave free reign to his border slang and musical imitations, including an irreverent parody of Jorge Negrete as a drunken mariachi. In his most subversive film, *El rey del barrio* (The king of the barrio, 1949), Tin Tan ridiculed government corruption by contrasting an inept small-time thief with the industrialists who made fortunes through their political connections. His linguistic skills and outrageous costumes provided a series of disguises while he tried unsuccessfully to rob from the rich. Starting as a gangster from Chicago, "Illinoise," Tin Tan gathered up his henchmen then cased a wealthy household in the middle of a party by imitating a Spanish flamenco singer, examining the chandelier through a jeweler's glass while dancing on the table. He returned later in the guise of a French interior decorator, ruining the house by splashing paint everywhere, but he left without cracking the safe. As an Italian opera maestro, he finally succeeded in stealing diamonds from an heiress but then decided to go straight and returned the jewels. His sidekick Marcelo Chávez, in the role of a drunken policeman, berated him for giving up the life of crime. "Steal, steal and get rich. Money will make you decent and respectable. That's the way things are here," he insisted. Then, looking into the camera, he added, "Look at all the millionaire crooks running around loose."[26] Tin Tan, also speaking directly to the camera, begged the film audience not to listen to those drunken words, perhaps for fear of reprisals from the Alemán administration.

Tin Tan had already encountered censorship. Shortly after the release of *El hijo desobediente,* the government warned him to stop speaking Spanglish to avoid corrupting the speech of Mexican youth. The studios meanwhile forced him to be more of a Mexico City pelado like Cantinflas than a borderland pachuco. The newspaper *Hoy* welcomed these changes, announcing that "Tin Tan has the privilege of no longer being designated the 'pachuco comic'" and predicting that "this totally different comic will soon be applauded by the people of Mexico [City] and of all the Republic."[27] Nevertheless, critics who liked Cantinflas continued to attack Tin Tan whenever possible; in January 1949, *Cinema Reporter* ranked him as one of the worst-dressed celebrities in Mexico. Cantinflas offered his own rebuke in *Si yo fuera diputado* with a sign on his barbershop window refusing service to pachucos because "they rub me the wrong way."

The only other social criticism in midcentury Mexican cinema came from another outsider, Luis Buñuel. This Spanish filmmaker had achieved notoriety as a leader of the surrealist movement with his film *Un Chien andalou* (An Andalucian dog, 1928), made with the assistance of Salvador Dali. He fled to the United States after the Spanish Civil War, and with his reputation on the decline, he continued on to Mexico following World War II. After a couple of box office failures, in 1950 he filmed the critically acclaimed *Los olvidados* (released in the United States as *The Young and the Damned*). Unlike the tame and romanticized peladito Cantinflas, Buñuel graphically depicted the harsh life in Mexico City barrios, on the outskirts of Alemán's industrialization project. International critics hailed it as a triumph comparable to Italian neorealist film, but Mexican audiences, accustomed to such scenes in their everyday life, shunned it. Buñuel followed *Los olvidados* with a series of critically acclaimed films, including *Nazarín* (Nazarene, 1958) and *El ángel exterminador* (The exterminating angel, 1962), which allowed him to return to France, where he capped his career with *Belle de jour* (1966) and *The Discreet Charm of the Bourgeoisie* (1974). Unlike Sergei Eisenstein, who left a tremendous impression on Mexican filmmakers, Buñuel had little contemporary influence despite his international prestige. Mexican cinema had hardened around a nationalist shell impervious to foreign influences, whether the pachuco lunacy of Tin Tan, the ironic wit of Buñuel, or any other subversive idea that might arise from the Cold War.

Trapitos al sol

In the age of Porfirio Díaz, Reforma Avenue had reshaped the urban geography of Mexico City as the newly rich moved west from the crumbing palaces of the city center, past a parade of civic statues, to the affluent suburbs near Chapultepec Park. Half a century later, population growth and automobiles had congested the central streets once again, and the opening of Insurgentes Avenue effected a similar exodus to the south by the Alemán generation. The president bequeathed the first great monument on this new thoroughfare: a modern campus for his alma mater, the National University. Although he neglected to buy books to put inside the library, its magnificent exterior murals came to symbolize Mexico's progress. Meanwhile, the architect Luis Barragán scored one of the real estate bonanzas of the century by convincing the newly rich that it was chic to build mansions on the barren volcanic rock of the nearby Pedregal. Finally, the self-styled Lorenzo d'Medici of the revolution, José María Dávila, constructed the Insurgentes Theater, which provided both the last stage appearance of Mario Moreno and a lasting public tribute to the comic.

Dávila commissioned the controversial muralist Diego Rivera to decorate the facade with a visual history of Mexican theater. The artist placed Cantinflas at the center of his design, in the form of a Robin Hood taking money from the rich and distributing it to the poor. The millionaires stood on bars of gold with the legend $1,000,000 \times 9,000$, while the indigents numbered $20,000,000 = 000$. Rivera aroused controversy not by graphically displaying Mexico's distribution of wealth but rather by his plan to adorn the pelado's gabardine with the Virgin of Guadalupe. In his memoirs, he explained that "there was nothing contradictory between Cantinflas and the Virgin of Guadalupe. Cantinflas was an artist who symbolized the people of Mexico and the Virgin was the banner of their faith."[28] Moreno reassured reporters by posing with his own medallion of the Virgin, which he wore all the time, but ultimately the aging Rivera followed a prudent course and neglected to paint in the saint's image.

Cantinflas not only decorated the new theater but also inaugurated it with a musical revista entitled *Yo, Colón* (I, Columbus). The idea of having the statue of Christopher Columbus step down from its pedestal on Reforma Avenue and "discover" the absurdities of contemporary Mexico had been a theatrical commonplace in the 1910s and 1920s. The script by Alfredo Robledo and Carlos León contained no novelties, just old jokes reworked around current headlines. Scenes included Columbus in Porfirian and modern Mexico, a *pachanga* (slang for dance) in the court of Isabel and Ferdinand, the Empire of the Monopolies (a reference to the high cost of living), and for the grand finale, an homage to *la raza huehuenche*. The modernist stage and costume designs were impressive, particularly the nighttime scene of the three caravels crossing the Atlantic. The long-time revista critic Armando de María y Campos grumbled that the cast contained neither actresses nor dancers, just "all the pretty girls in Mexico willing to strip in public."[29] But in fact the island women who greeted Columbus wore flowered bikinis modest enough for all but the most old-fashioned tastes.

Advertisements for the show promised "trapitos al sol" (cleaning the dirty laundry in public), a staple of the lively political theater in the twenties. The curtain rose on a scene titled "the rites of spring"—election season—to reveal Columbus's pedestal festooned with posters, the most prominent of which said, "Vote for the PRI." Columbus stepped down as a gringo wandered by asking for directions to the street of the Moneda (literally "money," the mint in colonial times, located on the north side of the National Palace). "Follow the Avenue Casas Alemán," Columbus began, with a reference to the former president's cousin. "From there take another called Miguel Alemán, then over the bridge Miguel Alemán, next a traffic circle Miguel Alemán, after that you have to pass through the Amargura [affliction] to reach the Sonrisal [Alemán's nickname, also slang for a purgative cure], where you'll find the money." The bewildered gringo said he would rather not have an affliction, and Columbus replied, "Well, what do you think we've been suffering for the past six years?"[30]

These jokes, the only ones surviving from the show, were recorded along with the audience's laughter by Salvador de la

Cantinflas at the pachanga *of Isabel and Ferdinand in* Yo, Colón. *Courtesy: Archivo General de la Nación.*

Cruz García, a reviewer for the opposition party newspaper *La Nación*. A less appreciative view came from Armando de María y Campos, who found the jokes "inexplicable in the mouth of Mario Moreno because when they did not drip aggression, venom, and rancor, they were bitter fruit [chabacanos] and revealed ingratitude and cowardice." The distinguished theater historian sacrificed his claim to impartiality by publishing the review in *Novedades,* a newspaper run by Alemán's business partner, Rómulo O'Farrill. The theater owner Dávila, another associate of the former president, published a statement explicitly disclaiming the jokes. Moreno expressed his surprise at the bitter response through a circuitous, Cantinflas-style letter to the editor of *Mañana* that denounced attacks from "individuals without individuality" working for "interested interests" who deserved "far more blame from knowing all that could have been said."[31]

This public exchange, seemingly revealing in its veiled allusions, in fact amounted to more sleight of hand; charges of corruption aimed at the former administration had already become the ruling party's new claim to legitimacy. Tin Tan had showed genuine courage in making a film that denounced millionaire crooks at the height of Alemán's power. Palillo had even served time in jail in 1950 for jokes on stage about government corruption. Mario Moreno, by contrast, waited until after Ruiz Contines's Law of Public Responsibility had supposedly cleaned up the government before airing criticisms. And the lower classes could not listen to the jokes anyway because Dávila had installed no cheap balcony seats in his deluxe theater. All tickets sold for 25 pesos, four days' pay at the minimum wage most workers received. Even the middle class had trouble getting to the theater, for the producers had neglected at first to provide bus service that far out of the city. This assumption, that everybody who was anybody owned a car, revealed Moreno's growing distance from his popular origins at the Follies Bergère far more clearly than did any wisecracks about a former president.

Yo, Colón ran for 160 showings then closed in July, with a reportedly unfavorable balance sheet. Rumors circulated that the company would tour the provinces, but Moreno ultimately decided against it and instead recouped his losses the following year by filming *Abajo el telón* (Down curtain). This tale of Cantinflas's adventures in the theater was also the first Mexican movie by the French actress Christiane Martell, winner of the Miss Universe pageant in 1953. Moreno introduced her to her future husband, Miguel Alemán Jr., showing that there were no hard feelings within the revolutionary family. But this last stage appearance by Cantinflas demonstrated just how far the pelado had traveled from the barrio of Tepito.

Midcentury Views of the Millionaire Pelado

The shift from Cárdenas's social revolution to Alemán's institutional one entailed a reexamination of the question, posed earlier by Samuel Ramos, of the meaning of Mexican identity. The pelado remained the center of attention for writers of the Hiperión group, influenced by Octavio Paz's celebrated essay, *The Labyrinth of Solitude* (1950). And the foremost pelado, Cantinflas, seemed to encapsulate the supposed Mexican genius for chaos (*relajo*), which both promised artistic success and frustrated material accomplishment. But true to the spirit of chaos, Moreno had come to represent precisely the opposite, bad movies that nevertheless attracted huge crowds and earned fortunes. Intellectuals therefore sought to unlock the contradictions of Mexican society through an examination of its leading celebrity.

Film critics had long been amazed by the comedian's ability to turn a bad script into a popular movie. "Cantinflas saves the film," had become a stock line in reviews both positive and negative. One writer suggested that people would fill the theaters to see nothing more than Cantinflas standing in front of a camera for an hour and a half in his gabardine telling jokes, and some of his colleagues wondered if the prediction had already come true. A review of *El mago,* for example, described the "bitter taste remaining in the mouth" from the film's "unpardonable defects." The distinguished Cuban critic Walfredo Piñero speculated that Moreno filmed such "horrendous scripts" precisely to achieve "the miracle of converting a shoddy [*chapucera*] movie into a spectacle that inspires a single expression from the public at the cinema exit: Great!"[32]

One explanation for his popular success, in Mexico if not Cuba, derived from the nationalist content of his movies. In *El mago,* Cantinflas showed that he preferred being a Mexican pelado to an Oriental sultan. Seated on a cushion in the midst of his harem, he could only complain about the odalisques' inability to prepare decent *chicharrones* (pork cracklings). And when the time came to select new women for the harem, he treated the misogynist exercise like a matador judging bulls, according to their weight and fighting potential. Even on vacation, Moreno never missed an opportunity to enhance his nationalist credentials. On a visit to the "Museum of Alcohol" at the Madrid nightclub of Perico Chicote, rather than sample the selection of fine sherry or cognac, he demonstrated the proper technique for drinking a shot of tequila.[33]

Moreno also acquired a reputation for philanthropy, causing lines of people to wait outside his office in the hope of receiving charity. His public service became prominent in the mid-1940s with highly publicized campaigns in support of education. He also staged charity bullfights for flood victims and other needy causes, doing "everything possible to replace the replaceable, save the savable, and fix the broken. To stop such a desire is gacho, boy. Or not?"[34] In 1951, he was elected president of the elite Variety Club, where he worked to provide schools for the blind and homes and medical service for the poor. His movies also served to publicize his charitable spirit; *Puerta, joven* showed him obtaining surgery for a crippled woman and a school for the barrio children, and in *El bombero atómico* he saved an orphan.

Critics viewed these philanthropic endeavors as simply another reflection of his affiliation with the new rich. José Alvarado conceded that Moreno had one of the "cleanest fortunes of any Mexican millionaire," acquired through hard work rather than the sale of adulterated milk, union racketeering, or the friendship of politicians. Nevertheless, the critic wondered why Cantinflas affiliated with such "individuals of bastard fortunes" in his 1953 movie, *Un caballero a la medida* (A gentleman made to measure). Cantinflas played a tailor who befriended a millionaire and convinced him to support charity. But the theory that the hunger of poor children will be resolved through philanthropy, Alvarado continued, was the excuse of the wives of those millionaires who accumulated their fortunes through the sale of adulterated foods then handed out stale bread in the nearest poor neighborhood.[35]

In addition, Moreno showed other traits of the new rich, most notably a taste for conspicuous consumption. During the filming of *¡A volar joven!* he learned to fly and soon began piloting his own DC-3, *El Detalle,* to Acapulco. While staying in his beach house, he was not content with playing tennis and instead installed a Jai Alai court. He then reputedly bought the fastest launch in Mexico, dubbed the *777,* and began water skiing. His partners in Posa Films meanwhile acquired expensive artistic tastes. Diego Rivera decorated the home of Santiago Reachi with murals of children breaking a piñata and celebrating Christmas, and he painted a portrait of Jacques Gelman's wife Natasha. The Russian also collected exotic pre-Hispanic art, even as studio workers complained about producers' penny-pinching habits. Yet those extravagant tastes were precisely what the lower classes may have enjoyed for themselves if they had the money, and thus they accepted and even expected it from Moreno.

Perhaps more compromising to the pelado image was the European cultural baggage that accompanied Moreno's wealth. Cantinflas began to display an arriviste sophistication in his attempts to speak French and English in a number of films, but a neo-Porfirian savoir faire blossomed fully in *Si yo fuera diputado.* In campaigning for office, he covered his shabby pants with a perfectly tailored glen plaid jacket. Worse still, he developed a taste for opera and invited the Mexican singer Emperatriz Carvajal to give a guest performance. In a scene recalling the Marx Brothers' *A Night at the Opera* (1935), Cantinflas ran around backstage, chased by the police, and finally took cover as the orchestra director. But instead of subverting the stuffy high culture in the manner of Groucho, Cantinflas conducted Franz Liszt's "Hungarian Rhapsody" to the applause of the rich.

Although film critics accused Moreno of losing touch with his origins, the comedian retained his enormous popularity with the lower classes. His comic bullfighting demonstrations regularly filled the greatest arenas in Mexico, and crowds even waited for him at airports and outside his hotel rooms when he traveled through the provinces. In Mexico City, he regularly visited poor neighborhoods for charity or to promote cultural projects, such as popular art exhibitions. One poignant expression of popular affection for Cantinflas came in the form of a tribute sponsored by the capital's paperboys. They waited for him out-side Churubusco Studios until he finished filming for the day, then escorted him across town to their union hall in Colonia Guerrero. The whole affair took on the aura of a religious pro-cession, with Moreno riding a police motorcycle and the news vendors peddling alongside, torches attached to their bicycles. After a banquet and speeches, they spent the evening watching boxing matches.[36]

The paperboys left no record of exactly what they saw in Moreno, whether a pelado who still represented the common people, a local boy who had risen from Colonia Guerrero to fame and fortune, a patron who might prove useful in the po-litical arena, or simply an excuse to throw a party. It seems likely, though, that great numbers of Mexicans still perceived themselves and their aspirations in the image of Cantinflas. Evi-dence for this conclusion can be found in the multitude of scripts written for Cantinflas and filed with the Mexican copy-right office. Although Moreno ignored these screenplays in favor of stories by his longtime and unimaginative collaborator, Jaime Salvador, aspiring authors nevertheless continued sending him scripts for at least two decades. This fact is unremarkable of it-self, but the diversity of characterizations for Cantinflas within these scripts is revealing. In one proposed screenplay he ap-peared as a kindly policeman who helped out small children lost in the city, whereas another portrayed him as a hard-boiled detective, almost in the tradition of Dashiell Hammett. The au-thor of "Cantinflas in the Land of Fairies" described him as "a tax collector, lazy, grouchy, and rude with the public. At times a poet." Conversely, the script for "Cantinflas, Sailor" gave him cantinfladas with an intellectual tone and pedantic references. In their hopes of making it big, these authors may have projected their own personality onto the image of Cantinflas, demonstrat-ing once again the malleability of the character to Mexican au-diences.[37] Although critics blasted Cantinflas for having lost his sense of humor and sold out to the bourgeoisie, the Argentine guerrilla commander, Ernesto "Che" Guevara, saw *Abajo el telón* while training with Cuban revolutionaries in Mexico and laughed himself silly.[38]

Moreno's combination of populism and charity was shared by another charismatic Latin American film star of the 1940s,

Evita Perón. Snubbed by the Argentine elite upon becoming first lady, she had taken over the charitable Milk Fund and made it an extension of her husband's corporatist government. The lotterylike dream of receiving charity from the Eva Perón Foundation added the support and loyalty from those at the very bottom of Argentine society to the institutional foundations of the Perón regime in organized labor and the military. Moreno's philanthropic activities contributed in a similar fashion to perpetuate the myth of a now-institutionalized revolution among the marginal sectors of Mexican society.[39] Although historians differ about whether Evita was the mastermind of Juan Perón's rise to power, there can be little doubting her complicity in the authoritarian government of Argentina. Likewise, in an incident immediately following the Alemán administration, Mario Moreno actively adopted the PRI's manipulative tactics, thus indicating that he was not simply a naive democrat who had embraced corrupt politicians.

The Palma Affair

With a pack of men in hot pursuit, Leticia Palma came running out of a downtown office building on January 2, 1953. The terrified young actress begged the assistance of a passing army officer, Major Manuel González, who was shocked to confront the leader of her assailants, a fellow graduate of the military academy, the singing charro himself, Jorge Negrete. González nevertheless halted the pursuers and assisted Palma into a taxi bound for police headquarters. When she pressed formal assault charges against Negrete, many considered the incident to be part of a plot by Mario Moreno to gain control of the National Association of Actors. The comedian was therefore embroiled in an affair of honor that threatened to destroy all of their careers.

The disagreement between Negrete and Palma had begun the previous summer with a near collision on Reforma Avenue. "He thinks he owns the entire street," she told reporters. "That's why he drives like his car is the only thing in the city." Palma also accused Negrete of trying to sabotage her career, which had taken off with the hit film *En la palma de tu mano* (In the palm of your hand, 1950), by pushing the union to sanction her.

"What a crazy woman!" Negrete responded, denying involvement in the traffic incident and insisting that he just happened to be nearby at the time. He attributed the union sanctions to her contract violations with the producers Felipe Mier and Oscar Brooks and to her lack of camaraderie at the studios. The ANDA president also pointed out, in an incriminating manner, that the Tabascan actress was married to a millionaire from the United States.[40]

This personal dispute became conflated with the ongoing political struggle between Negrete and Moreno for control of the actors' association. Palma had gone through the theaters, radio stations, and cinema studios collecting signatures in support of Moreno's candidacy for head of the union. In addition to gathering signatures from such stalwart Moreno partisans as Agustín Lara, she had even charmed one from Pedro Infante, although he actually supported his fellow charro Negrete. The personal acrimony between the two leading male stars of the Mexican cinema became even more intense with the highly publicized, studio-arranged marriage of Jorge Negrete to María Félix. The charro had left his former wife, Gloria Marín, and La Doña had divorced Agustín Lara. Moreno was involved in both of these bitter breakups because of his friendships with Marín and Lara; indeed, the musical poet had cried on Cantinflas's shoulder. Supporters of Negrete charged that Palma had stolen documents proving her guilt and that the ANDA administration had been chasing her the previous Friday afternoon trying to recover them. Actress Maruja Grifell asserted that Palma had to be lying because Negrete was such a gentleman that he could never have shown disrespect to a woman. But in fact the charro singer had made an entire career out of precisely such domineering conduct toward women, for example, spanking Lilia Michel in *No basta ser charro*. Meanwhile, Moreno avoided the press, saying only how unfortunate it was that the affair had gone public and affirming that "the dirty laundry [trapos] should be washed at home."[41]

The political implications of the struggle, together with the gravity of the accusations, prompted a special assembly of ANDA on the evening of January 10, 1953, at the Esperanza Iris Theater to decide on Palma's guilt, where Moreno had challenged Miguel de Molina and the STIC almost seven years earlier. When

Moreno spoke in Palma's defense, Negrete supporters shouted at him like a gang of CTM thugs. At one point, he threatened to walk out if they did not keep their peace. While conceding that Palma was guilty of stealing the documents, Moreno tried to arrange a settlement, noting that the traffic incident had been resolved with the payment of a 30 peso fine. But Negrete remained intransigent, declaring that it was a matter of prestige and honor. Palma refused to retract the charges of assault—which were probably true, like virtually all of the accusations in this sordid affair. A number of actresses fled the room before the final vote of 232 to 1 in favor of Palma's expulsion. The crowd called for a final gesture of reconciliation, and Negrete and Moreno exchanged a fraternal hug.

The resolution showed little credit to the Mexican motion picture industry. Moreno withdrew from the leadership contest as a show of solidarity, although opponents claimed he was just disappointed by his failure to persuade the guild. Jesús Martínez "Palillo" tried to appeal the sentence, only to be threatened with expulsion by Negrete. Palma's career ended, thus depriving the Mexican cinema, in the words of Emilio García Riera, "of one of its most interesting feminine presences."[42] Within a year, Negrete had died, to be replaced as head of ANDA by the lawyer and sometime actor Rodolfo Landa, who went on to direct the National Cinema Bank under his real name, Rodolfo Echeverría, between 1970 and 1976 during the presidential administration of his brother Luis.

The Palma Affair illustrated some of the fundamental themes of the Mexican political system at midcentury. The actors' association, like the PRI in general, bestowed wealth and prestige on loyal followers but systematically excluded all who challenged its authority. Moreover, leadership of the association bureaucracy was passing from the flamboyant, popular Negrete and Moreno, who had led the union struggle of the Avila Camacho years, to such functionaries as Rodolfo Echeverría, a law school graduate with more political connections than acting ability. Finally, effective suffrage and the open discussion of grievances had given way, in the name of unity, to backroom politics. An era had truly ended when Cantinflas turned his nimble hands to concealing such machinations rather than to exposing trapitos al sol.

6

AROUND THE WORLD
OR JUST THE STUDIO

Mario Moreno reached the peak of his international career in the fall of 1955 in the wicker basket of a balloon suspended from a crane 180 feet above Universal Studios in Hollywood. He clambered into the rigging for some of the most memorable shots of the comic blockbuster *Around the World in 80 Days,* while his costar, David Niven, struggled not to throw up from fear of heights. The extravagant producer Michael Todd meanwhile calmed their nerves with a steady supply of imported champagne, a gesture typical of the movie's entire production.[1] The balloon scene, although absent from the 1873 novel, became the defining symbol of the movie, lofting Cantinflas around the world to rapturous applause. Moreno thus seemed to have achieved his long-standing goal of captivating North American audiences through the innate charisma of his pelado character. But he had reckoned without the power of Hollywood to seduce outsiders, and soon the king of Mexican cinema found himself drawn inexorably under the control of the studio bosses, who reduced the trickster Cantinflas to the level of a childlike puppet.

Ultimately, Moreno was responsible for his own artistic downfall through his uncertainty about how best to capitalize on the opportunity presented by *Around the World in 80 Days.* Having tasted the fruit of international fame, he returned to Mexican filmmaking only with great reluctance. Domestic producers hoped to capitalize on his global celebrity status to revitalize the moribund Mexican cinema industry, but he concentrated instead on developing foreign projects. Worse still, local audiences could

Cantinflas's balloon ride to global fame. Newspaper ad for the Latin American premiere of Around the World in 80 Days *in Caracas, Venezuela— "uncensored" by the military dictatorship.* El Nacional, *June 25, 1957. Courtesy: Library of Congress.*

not even share their hero's triumph in *Around the World* because a dispute with the distributors delayed its Mexican premiere. Moreno's ties to Columbia Pictures further alienated the national film establishment as well as his longtime business partners. Finally, in 1960, having burned bridges at home, he made his second Hollywood picture, *Pepe*—a terrible mistake. The screenwriters did not even bother trying to translate the character of Cantinflas for audiences in the United States and resorted instead to the crude exploitation of racist stereotypes. Critics in Mexico had long complained that Moreno had sacrificed artistry for box office receipts, but *Pepe* was not even a financial success. Although Columbia executives continued to profit by distributing Moreno's Mexican films, they never again trusted Cantinflas in one of their own, thus ending a Hollywood career that had begun with such promise five years earlier.

Passepartout

Mario Moreno had received a succession of Hollywood movie offers through the years and turned down every one of them, refusing to compromise the Mexican character of Cantinflas to studio moguls. His patience finally paid off when an industry outsider, Michael Todd, asked him to play the role of Passepartout, the valet who accompanied Phileas Fogg on his global voyage. In a cast of nearly fifty international stars, Moreno once again found a suitable challenge for his acting skills, so long taken for granted in the Mexican cinema. Particularly fortuitous was the casting of David Niven in the role of Fogg, a stuffy English version of the Creole straight men who had inspired such hilarious comedy from Cantinflas in *Ahí está el detalle*. Although the Mexican actor could not make use of his distinctive Spanish doubletalk, he fit perfectly into the Passepartout character with his physical comedy, outlandish gestures, and personal charm. Moreover, the carpa aesthetic that Moreno retained throughout his career proved ideal for a film that resembled a theatrical spectacle, a series of episodes unified loosely by a few central characters and the concept of traveling around the world to win a bet.

Hollywood insiders found the filming of *Around the World* remarkably similar to the original novel and considered the producer, Michael Todd, to be an incarnation of the gambler Phileas Fogg. Where Jules Verne kept the Englishman one step ahead of the sinister detective, Mr. Fix, Todd filmed the movie completely on credit and was constantly in search of his next payroll. But through ingenuity and improvisation, both Fogg and Todd won their bets and married beautiful princesses, for the former, the Hindu Aouda, and for the latter, Hollywood's foremost starlet, Elizabeth Taylor. In making the film, Todd invented what later became a standard motion picture device, the cameo, a term referring to a small, gemlike portrait. He signed the biggest names of classical cinema and theater to play these brief roles, including the likes of Noel Coward, Sir John Gielgud, Marlene Dietrich, and Buster Keaton. Even more important than the parade of stars was the huge screen on which they appeared. *Around the World* was shot on 70-mm film using an improved, single-camera version of Cinerama named Todd-AO after the producer and his development partners, the American Optical Company. This wide-screen technology simulated a three-dimensional effect for viewers without having to wear colored glasses, and Todd made the most of it by filming everything possible on location, from Fogg's balloon rising past the gargoyles of Notre Dame and over Loire Valley châteaux to the magnificent landscapes of the Rocky Mountains and the Far East.[2]

In keeping with his impresario past, Todd used spectacle and pageantry to fill in for the lack of literary drama in Verne's novel. The motion picture opened with primitive black-and-white scenes from another fantastic voyage, *A Trip to the Moon,* filmed by Georges Méliès in 1902; then the scene expanded out to fill the huge curved Todd-AO screen with brilliant color footage of a ballistic missile launch. Following the prologue, a shot of the changing of the guard at Buckingham Palace symbolized the precision and formality of British imperialism embodied in the character of Phileas Fogg. By contrast, the rambunctious Passepartout entered the film on a high-wheeled bicycle careening through the streets of London. Once Fogg had made his bet at the Reform Club and the pair set off around the world, an elaborate fanfare introduced each passing scene. In Paris, the comic actor Fernandel carried them on a coach ride into the magnificent Place Vendôme; in Spain, Passepartout joined in a colorful flamenco dance and bullfight; in India, he saved the princess Aouda, played by Shirley MacLaine, from human sacrifice in a torch-lit religious ritual; and finally in San Francisco, Fogg fought a duel with a local dandy while framed by a backdrop of fireworks and political rallies from a local election.[3]

David Niven and Mario Moreno gave inspired performances of the fin de siècle imperial dialogue between the imperturbable colonial master, Fogg, and the supposedly inconstant servant, Passepartout. Niven played the quintessential English gentleman determined to colonize the planet by forcing the natives to accept his metropolitan lifestyle. He completed the mad dash around the globe at a stately pace, never hurried, but with one eye on the clock, and always confident of the scientific regularity of English train and steamer schedules. He refused to vary his English diet from the customary roast beef and treacle pudding, even under the tropical Indian sun. While sailing over the Alps in a balloon, he instructed Passepartout to grab snow off the mountaintop to chill his champagne. The magnificent landscapes of the Ganges Valley and the Rocky Mountains, which enthralled the valet, passed unnoticed by Fogg, who preferred a game of whist with a fellow Englishman to sightseeing. Niven played the character more rigidly than even Verne had intended; when he seemed to have lost the bet at the last moment because of his false arrest by Fix, rather than punching the detective, he observed dryly, "I have never really enjoyed your company, and furthermore you play an abominable game of whist." Meanwhile, Moreno brought an element of Sancho Panza to the character of Passepartout: loyal to his master but distracted by the demands of his stomach and libido. In Paris, he chased after Martine Carol, receiving a slap in the face for his trouble, and in San Francisco he risked even greater injury from Red Skelton after propositioning Marlene Dietrich.[4]

This promiscuous colonial stereotype notwithstanding, Moreno appropriated Verne's resourceful French valet and blended it with the character of Cantinflas. This Hispanic element was exemplified by the magnificent bullfighting scene, filmed in Chichón, a small town outside Madrid that resembled provincial Spain in 1872. When the balloon was blown off course, landing in Spain by mistake, Passepartout performed in the plaza de toros to win the favor of a local potentate and gain the use of his yacht to reach Marseilles and the next steamer bound for Suez. The Mexican comic also used his bullfighting skills to personalize the Bombay pagoda scene later in the movie. In the book, Passepartout had mistakenly wandered into the Malebar Hill temple, prompting crowds of outraged Hindus to chase him onto a departing train. Moreno created a more compelling visual scene by performing a matador's pass with his jacket at a sacred Brahma bull, thus provoking the riot. Moreover, although Verne's novel was set at the height of European imperialism, the movie gave consideration to the decolonization underway in Africa and Asia in the 1950s. For example, the final scene featured the Hispanic valet and the Indian princess bursting into the exclusively Anglo male Reform Club, causing one shocked member to exclaim, "This is the end!"

Moreno even served, at times, as a real life Passepartout to Michael Todd's Fogg during the film's production, which balanced equal parts of financial desperation and publicity bravado. Todd began work by convincing NBC to pay $20,000 for the rights to broadcast live a comic bullfight by Cantinflas from Tijuana, Mexico. The event on June 30, 1955, was attended by such celebrities as Humphrey Bogart, Rita Moreno, and David Niven. Once in Spain to begin the actual shooting, Moreno personally recruited two of the first cameos, the flamenco dancer José Greco and the bullfighter Luis Miguel Dominguín. Local aficionados were disappointed when the work was finished in just two days, allowing no time for Cantinflas to perform in the Madrid arena. The crew moved immediately to London for the Reform Club scene and then on to Paris for the balloon ascent. For the latter scene, Todd cleared the Place Vendôme by towing all the parked cars, including one belonging to a former cabinet member. The chief of police arrived personally to round up the production crew, but only after the wily producer had escaped with his film on a plane to London. One of the film's recurring financial crises struck during the filming of the Malebar Hill pagoda scene in Hollywood. The director had finished work in the early evening, but Todd ordered him to just keep shooting, then vanished mysteriously from the set. The payroll finally arrived at ten o'clock that night, to the relief of the director, who later explained, "If they had known what was going on, I would have had a *really* angry crowd chasing Mario."[5] The Mexican comic later traveled to Asia with a location crew for shots in front of the Great Buddha in the ancient imperial capital of Kamakura and at the Meiji Palace in the modern city of Tokyo—displaying the same blissful disregard for geography that had piloted a balloon over the Alps to Spain. He also saw Durango, Colorado, where they filmed Fogg's transcontinental railroad trip from San Francisco to New York, including the Sioux Indian attack in which Passepartout was nearly burned at the stake.

The filming finally ended in December 1955, allowing an exhausted Mario Moreno, who was used to finishing movies in under a month, to return home to Mexico after the most arduous acting role of his career. Because of the haphazard schedule, he was called back to the United States several times during the lengthy postproduction process to film additional scenes. This last-minute work proved enormously expensive, but Michael Todd paid without hesitation to assure that everything about the movie looked authentic. His most extravagant fine-tuning came in discarding a quarter-million-dollar scene of the *Henrietta,* the ship on which Fogg made his last dash across the Atlantic. The intrepid voyager had disassembled the ship's deck and superstructure to burn as fuel when the coal ran out. At first Todd filmed a miniature version of the ship—convincing by Hollywood standards—but which nevertheless looked out of place at the end of an otherwise realistic movie. Therefore he went back and spent another half million to refit an old yacht with a paddlewheel in order to tear it apart and burn it at sea. The expensive episode at least paid dividends in publicity from the crowd of reporters he invited to witness the maritime filming.

Another of these postproduction adventures, this time in Mexico with the inadvertent assistance of Mario Moreno, allowed Todd to win the affections of Elizabeth Taylor. While Marlene Dietrich had been chasing the producer around Hollywood ever since he charmed her into appearing in a cameo as a San Francisco showgirl, Todd was determined to marry Taylor, who had not yet divorced the British actor Michael Wilding. Complicating the scene still further, her current lover was none other than Todd's assistant producer. When the latter suggested some close-up shots to provide a dramatic conclusion to the bullfight scene, Todd jumped at the chance to get his unwitting rival out of the country. Moreno was equally delighted at the prospect of an exciting finish, although Gelman was less than thrilled about having his famous partner kneel inches from the horns of a bull, forcing the comic to find an excuse to get him out of town. As soon as the shooting was finished, Todd left his assistant behind in Mexico City to wrap up the details and flew directly to New York to meet with Taylor. She accepted his marriage proposal almost immediately, explaining later that "Mike's courtship was like being hit by a tornado."[6]

Todd negotiated the film's distribution with the same flair for showmanship that characterized its production. Before releasing the film for mass exhibition at ordinary theaters, he demanded a theatrical road show of 125 engagements in cities throughout the world. Despite this unusual demand, all the big studios were eager to bid for the rights. Todd showed the film first to Harry Cohn of Columbia Pictures, out of deference to his relationship with Moreno, but ultimately signed with United Artists. To further heighten interest in the gala premiere, which took place in New York on October 17, 1956, Todd made it his first public appearance with Elizabeth Taylor. Moreno arrived with Gelman at the Rivoli Theater and immediately suffered an attack of stage fright, muttering under his breath, "Oh, brother, this is like fighting a bull for the first time." And when he first appeared on the huge screen, pedaling the old-fashioned bicycle through the streets of London, he gasped, "Here's what this little Indian has been dreaming of all his life." The audience signaled its approval some three hours later with a tremendous round of applause, which they repeated at the end of the animated credits. Later, when television reporters asked him for a comment, Moreno answered nervously—in the true spirit of Cantinflas—with the only English words he could think of, "Merry Christmas!"[7]

That smashing first night marked the beginning of a long triumphal parade in which the movie earned $25 million in rentals and rave reviews from critics. "This mammoth and mad pictorial rendering of the famous old novel of Jules Verne," wrote Bosley Crowther in the *New York Times,* "is a sprawling conglomeration of refined English comedy, giant-screen travel panoramics, and slam-bang Keystone burlesque."[8] Everyone wanted credit for the extraordinary success. Michael Todd Jr. declared that his father's use of cameos had ensured that the producer alone remained the true star of the film. Niven's biographer wrote with convoluted logic that the British actor gave "a performance of sustained charm and elegance, never better than when he is up with Passepartout in the air balloon. . . . That, rather than any single moment with a guest star, was the quintessential image and memory of *Around the World,* and it belonged entirely to David." Mexican reviewers naturally defended their star's honor, announcing that "Cantinflas is the heart of this colossal production."⁹ But a picture as big as that one had ample credit to pass around, and Moreno's share included an open ticket to the film capital of the world.

Hollywood Temptations

Mexican journalists, although proud at first of their countryman's international fame, soon began to show concern as his foreign trips continued. A month after the filming ended, *Cinema Reporter* worried that the actor appeared rather thin from his travels and warned him to take better care to avoid a dangerous competition with the flaco de oro, Agustín Lara. A year later *El Cine Gráfico* observed that Cantinflas was still on his voyage around the world long after the allotted eighty days. These fears about Mexico's leading celebrity reflected a broader concern about the national cinema industry, which had fallen dramatically from the "golden age" of the 1940s. Business magnate William Jenkins, with his powerful political connections, had extended his theater monopoly throughout the country and threatened to strangle domestic production in order to show more Hollywood features. After the deaths of Jorge Negrete and Pedro Infante in the mid-1950s, Mario Moreno seemed uniquely capable of reviving Mexican cinema, and the "mysterious trips" he made to the United States in the late 1950s seemed an ominous warning of his imminent defection. Indeed, between Hollywood tributes and plans for future productions in the United States, Mexico's foremost comedian grew distant from those who had originally supported his career.¹⁰

Expectations ran high in Mexico that Moreno's experience in the United States would boost the entire national cinema industry. In the late summer of 1956, he filmed his first color picture in Mexico, *El bolero de Raquel* (Raquel's bolero), which continued his reputation for high production values but otherwise proved disappointing. The title turned on a predictable pun; Cantinflas worked as a bootblack (*bolero*) to support a girlfriend named Raquel. He also danced to Ravel's "Bolero" with actress Elaine Bruce in an unsuccessful attempt to revive his hilarious Apache dance from *Gran Hotel*. Much of the film was devoted to Cantinflas's antics in Acapulco, and this distance from his pelado origins may account for the low box office revenues, which were less than expected considering the novelty of the color film and the press attention devoted to the international premiere of *Around the World*. Even so, a disappointing effort by Cantinflas still ranked among the year's most profitable films in Mexico, and Moreno seemed unconcerned, preoccupied as he was by parties in the United States, including the gala world premiere in New York and the Los Angeles opening in December.

Even in Mexico, Moreno worked on his Hollywood connections by hosting the marriage ceremony of Michael Todd and Elizabeth Taylor. Having just undergone back surgery in New York, the actress graciously accepted Moreno's assistance at the Mexico City airport, and the wedding party then proceeded to Acapulco, where they stayed hidden from multinational packs of reporters inside the heavily guarded compound of Miguel Alemán. The former president loaned his yacht to the visitors for a cruise on February 2, 1957, and the mayor of Acapulco officiated the ceremony late that afternoon. They finished their champagne dinner as the sun was setting over the bay, then a native group performed exotic torchlight dances. Finally, Moreno offered his wedding present, a spectacular fireworks display culminating with rockets that spelled out the newlyweds' initials.[11]

The accolades continued for *Around the World in 80 Days,* including numerous Mexican tributes to Cantinflas and the Academy Award in Hollywood for best picture. The personal high point for Moreno was his nomination for the Golden Globe award as best comic actor of 1956. Dressed in a smoking jacket and accompanied by the faithful Gelman, he arrived by limousine at the Hollywood Ambassador Hotel on the night of March 12, 1957. The elite of the Los Angeles Mexican colony had all secured seats for the ceremony in the exclusive Coconut Grove Club, while crowds of Mexican Americans waited outside to cheer their hero. Vincent Price served as master of ceremonies, and Elizabeth Taylor announced that the winner of the best comic actor award was Mario Moreno. After a five-minute standing ovation, which nearly brought tears to his eyes, Moreno accepted the award with pride and humility, speaking in excellent English.[12]

This latest international honor triggered another round of public tributes to Moreno in Mexico. Newspapers heralded his recognition in Hollywood as a great national victory and concluded their stories with patriotic cries of "*¡Viva México!*" The nation's leading teacher, José Vasconcelos, spoke in recognition of Moreno's cultural and educational contributions. A reporter from *Mañana* commented hopefully on the "predominant note of unanimity within the entire cinematic family. All the leaders, all the sectors—all are in agreement that Cantinflas is the best." Indeed, the STIC union leader, Salvador Carrillo, had joined the STPC head, Roberto Gavaldón, in a banquet honoring the comedian. Implicit behind all of the talk of "such necessary cinematic unity" was the actual state of disarray within the industry and the hope that Moreno, having led the industry out of such difficulties before, would step forward to do so again. Holding aloft the Golden Globe, the actor affirmed, "This prize, like all that I have achieved, I owe to my people. They have made me what I am."[13]

Nevertheless, within a week, he was back in Beverly Hills for a breakfast press conference with David Niven hosted by Michael Todd. In addition to praising his leading actors, Todd intimated his plans to follow up the success of *Around the World* with another blockbuster production starring the Mexican comedian. Moreno visited the White House in May, although President Dwight D. Eisenhower sent his regrets, as he usually did with Latin American dignitaries, leaving the actor to meet with Vice President Richard Nixon. The comic star continued on to France for the Cannes festival, and for once Mexicans could share in Hollywood's lofty attitude of cultural imperialism. "As one would expect," a reporter noted with equanimity, "the Europeans, who continue resisting New World domination, could find no enthusiasm for our great artist."[14]

Pride yielded to jealousy when it became clear that Mexico would not receive the honor of hosting the Latin American premiere of *Around the World*. Michael Todd announced that the Mexican ticket price ceiling of four pesos (about thirty cents) made it impossible to show a profit after installing the equipment needed to project the film in Todd-AO. The government refused to grant an exception, and the motion picture went instead to Caracas, Venezuela. In a pique, the Mexican producers Oscar Brooks and Ernesto Enríquez announced plans for an all-star film of their own, with all the leading celebrities of Mexican cinema *except* Cantinflas, but nothing came of it. Meanwhile, the Venezuelan general Marcos Pérez Jiménez used the regional premiere of *Around the World* to try to gain a measure of respectability for his military dictatorship. Advertisements promised a waiver of censorship for the special performance, and on opening night, June 26, 1957, Moreno sat among the uniformed figures in the presidential box of the Boyacá Theater. The visit also included a triumphal parade through the city, a comic bullfight for charity, and the inevitable promotions for local businesses.

The refusal to show *Around the World* in Mexico was part of a broader dispute over distribution that divided Posa Films from the official cinema establishment. In 1953, Eduardo Garduño, the director of the national cinema bank, sought to revitalize the national industry and to challenge Jenkins' control over theaters by limiting the importation of foreign films to 150 per year, but the monopolist thwarted his plan. Production stagnated still further when the film union went out on strike the following year. Garduño then tried to reorganize the bank's distribution network, adding a new corporation, Cimex, for the international exportation of films to the existing group of Peliculas Nacionales and Peliculas Mexicanas. These actions threatened Posa's contract with Columbia Pictures, which had been the exclusive international distributor for Cantinflas films since the mid-1940s. When Cimex managers took control of *El señor fotógrafo* and then botched its marketing, Santiago Reachi went over Garduño's head and appealed directly to Angel Carbajal, the minister of gobernación. The cinema bank president accused Moreno of selling out to foreign capital and even threatened a domestic boycott of his films. Nevertheless, Posa had no trouble making arrangements with local theater owners to project films by the most popular star in Mexico, and Columbia soon regained its lucrative international distributorship. Garduño lost his position in 1958 at the end of the Ruiz Cortines administration, having accomplished little to improve Mexican cinema. Indeed, Jenkins had further consolidated his monopoly over domestic theaters in 1957 by buying out his only remaining competitor, Abelardo Rodríguez.[15]

Although Mexican film production remained steady at more than a hundred features annually, the quality had fallen dramatically. Producers churned out ever more formulaic and low-budget churros, such as the lucha libre series starring the masked wrestler Santo. The decadence of the Mexican film industry gave further cause for Moreno to stay in Hollywood, where no shortage of attractive offers awaited him. Michael Todd had already chosen a Hispanic theme for his next major project, a star-filled version of Don Quixote. The idea seemed a sure bet to recapture the magic of *Around the World* and to highlight Moreno's comic talent in the role of Sancho Panza. Todd cast about for a suitable Quixote, finally signing the French comedian Fernandel, and the prospect of Elizabeth Taylor as Sancho's shrewish wife heightened the appeal. But in September 1957, Moreno backed out, explaining that Cervantes's classic novel should not be defiled by celluloid and, anyway, Sancho was not his type. Todd had indeed taken a cavalier attitude toward the project, as his own son complained. His only script was a watercolor painting of Don Quixote tilting at windmills. But such liberties could scarcely have mattered to a master of parody who staged a food fight in *Romeo y Julieta*. More likely, the conflict involved either money or artistic differences, a Hollywood euphemism for a clash of egos. In any event, the film was never made because Todd died in a tragic plane crash on March 23, 1958.[16]

Meanwhile in Mexico, another personality conflict, between Mario Moreno and Santiago Reachi, threatened to end one of the longest-lasting and most-profitable partnerships in Mexican cinema. Reachi had an ongoing struggle with Posa's third partner, Jacques Gelman, and only their mutual friendship with Moreno had held them together. The Russian distributor, reportedly against Reachi's better judgment, had conceived the disastrous plan to dub *Los tres mosqueteros* into French for Cannes. In 1955, Gelman had faithfully followed Moreno during the filming of *Around the World,* while the president of Posa Films worked alone on his longtime dream of establishing an independent film studio, this time in Havana, Cuba. Gelman therefore basked in the reflected glow of the comedian's public tributes, both in Mexico and Hollywood. When Reachi sought to organize a banquet for Moreno in March 1957, industry sources intimated that his offer was rebuffed.[17]

With his celebrity status renewed by *Around the World*, Moreno became the center of attention when tragedy struck on July 28, 1957, in the form of an earthquake that devastated Mexico City. The seismic blast was so powerful it toppled the Angel of Independence from its pillar on Reforma Avenue, where it had stood as a symbol of Mexican nationalism since its construction in 1910. Another structure destroyed by the quake was the Rioma building on Insurgentes Avenue, owned by Mario Moreno. The sensationalist newspaper *La Prensa* published a front-page story about the loss to Mexico's famous comedian and called for the builders responsible for the faulty workmanship to be punished severely. With nearly seventy people dead and $200 million in property losses throughout the city, anger crystallized against the criminal landlords who cut corners on construction and maintenance, profiteering at the expense of human lives. Meanwhile, people waited anxiously as inspectors went round to see if their apartment buildings were unsafe, forcing them to join the large numbers of homeless disaster victims. At this time of loss and uncertainty, the cartoon Cantinflas of the 1930s returned to the pages of *El Universal* as the conscience of the city. Standing before two menacing looking buildings personifying "Crime" and "Scarcity," the pelado informed a police officer, "Those are the ones that should be demolished." But this attempt to revitalize Cantinflas as a symbol of the common people fell flat when it became known that residents of the Rioma building had pressed charges against Moreno personally for damages due to the earthquake.[18]

Notwithstanding disputes over real estate and the local screening of *Around the World,* the Mexican cinema establishment still held out hopes that Moreno might help to revitalize domestic filmmaking. The advent of television had cut into cinema profits worldwide, and Mexico was particularly vulnerable because of union troubles within the studios and Jenkins' stranglehold over the theaters. Insiders even speculated in 1957 that Cantinflas might bolt to the small screen, which could spell the demise of Mexican cinema. The nascent television industry had adopted a variety show format that was particularly well suited to Moreno's background in the carpa theater. Broadcasters also possessed tremendous political clout because of former president Miguel Alemán, who held a large stake in Telesistema Mexicano, SA. Producers could not even take comfort from the highly publicized spat following the performance of *Yo, Colón* at the Insurgentes Theater, because Moreno and Alemán had long since patched up any difficulties.[19]

Yet the television producers, like the cinema studios, remained in the dark as Moreno continued his flirtation with Hollywood. The question of his production plans dominated the Mexican media industry throughout 1957, and reporters grew almost frantic as the year drew to a close without the annual Cantinflas movie. In 1958, he made up for the previous year's absence by filming two Mexican movies, neither of which showed any particular inspiration. The first, *Ama a tu prójimo* (Love your neighbor), was a local version of *Around the World,* filled with celebrity cameo appearances in a series of melodramatic episodes, all thrown together as a charity for the Red Cross. The second, *Sube y baja* (Up and down), lacked even that redeeming feature and provided little more than a vehicle for Cantinflas to frolic as an Acapulco playboy. Moreno was clearly marking time in Mexico while devoting his energies to international plans, one a French coproduction of *Platero y yo,* based on the novel by Juan Ramon Gimenez, and the other a Pan-American venture, *Travel, S. A.,* reportedly costarring Pat Boone and Marilyn Monroe.[20]

Moreno found yet another excuse for travel in the international success of Mexican boxing, long one of his favorite hobbies. The bantamweight world champion, Raul "the Rat" Macías, was a particular favorite because of his highly publicized origins in Tepito, the hometown of Cantinflas. Mario Moreno and María Félix led a pilgrimage of Mexican celebrities to Los Angeles for a title fight on November 6, 1957, then mourned his loss to the Frenchman Alphonse Halimi. Mexico won the right to a rematch through the prowess of José "Tapato" Becerra, and once again celebrities competed for ringside seats in Los Angeles on February 5, 1960. La Doña scored a victory over Agustín Lara by securing front-row tickets with her new husband, the international banker Alex Berger, while the flaco de oro had to settle for seats farther back with his current partner, Vianey Larraga. Moreno watched the fight with the former champion, Raul "the Rat," after reportedly paying top dollar for ringside seats as well. Mexicans everywhere rejoiced when Becerra knocked out Halimi in the ninth, recovering both the championship and national honor.

The mystery surrounding Moreno's next major project was finally resolved in 1959 with the decision to film *Pepe.* In May, he traveled to London, where they had loved him as Passepartout, hoping to collect an international cast. Despite his best efforts, the film collapsed into a Hollywood affair, produced and directed by George Sidney. *Pepe* also entailed the final break with Reachi, who considered the project "simply detestable." The details behind the split remain obscure, for Reachi recorded a bitter, contradictory account in his memoirs and Moreno left no word at all. The master publicist blamed the breakup on the nefarious influence of the "third partner," Gelman, who was a close friend of Sidney. The two producers reportedly convinced Moreno to go ahead with *Pepe* only because they had already invested $400,000 in the film. Reachi had meanwhile suffered another setback when the Cuban studio project collapsed, along with the government of Fulgencio Batista, to Fidel Castro's revolution. Just as the federal government was nationalizing the film distribution industry, taking over the Jenkins cinema chain, Moreno finally bought out Reachi's interest in Posa and, against the advice of his former partner, began work on his second foreign film.[21]

Pepe

Moreno had waited two decades for his Hollywood break, and when it finally came, it was far too easy—the eternal curse of his artistic career. His greatest barrier to success in the United States had always been the difficulty of translating Cantinflas's unique verbal humor, a problem Michael Todd had evaded through the physical comedy of Passepartout. The popularity of *Around the World* made *Pepe* too lucrative to pass up, especially because Latin American revenues were virtually guaranteed to cover the costs of production, making ticket sales in the United States pure profit. Perhaps if he had been gambling his financial future on the outcome, like Todd five years earlier, he might have found a screenwriter gifted enough for the translation of Cantinflas's humor for U.S. audiences. But Moreno had always disdained writers and directors, preferring to trust his own instincts, and *Around the World* gave him no reason to doubt his innate appeal in the United States. Therefore, *Pepe* was written the Hollywood way—by committee—with a formula instead of a plot and stereotypes instead of characters. And so, after years of resistance, Moreno finally succumbed to the seductions of Tinseltown, selling out Cantinflas only to be denied payment when the film bombed at the box office.

Unlike the timeless classic *Around the World in 80 Days, Pepe* was immediately dated to its filming in March 1960. It was not a good time for the movie studios, owing to competition from television, and Columbia Pictures suffered more than most. The film's producer and director, George Sidney, was the son of an MGM vice president and represented precisely that embattled Hollywood establishment. With credits including the musicals *Anchors Aweigh, Showboat,* and *Annie Get Your Gun,* he seemed the logical person to attempt to duplicate Michael Todd's spectacular hit. Again there were plenty of cameo roles, although the stars were drawn from contemporary television rather than classic movies and theater, names such as Donna Reed, Jay "Dennis the Menace" North, and Zsa Zsa Gabor. Primary colors and artificial fog predominated the song and dance routines. Sidney even made a pilgrimage to the Sands Hotel in Las Vegas for a "Meeting at the Summit" with those cool cats, Frank Sinatra, Dean Martin, Peter Lawford, Joey Bishop, and Sammy Davis Jr., otherwise known as the Rat Pack.

For want of a better idea, the script regurgitated a timeworn Hollywood myth as the vehicle for introducing Cantinflas's character to United States audiences. Producers had long encouraged ordinary people to dream of personal celebrity (and to buy more movie tickets) through the legend that stardom was a lottery and that anyone could be "discovered" as the next Marilyn Monroe or Cary Grant. Not that Moreno was discovered; instead, he assisted a young Shirley Jones to make it in the movies. As usual with fairy godmother roles, he played the hired help, a Mexican horse trainer who came to Hollywood when a dissolute filmmaker, Dan Dailey, purchased the prize stallion he thought of as a son. While working as the horse's groom, he turned the director's life around, helping him to stop drinking and film his masterpiece. Pepe convinced Dailey to hire Jones for the lead role then financed the project by taking his piggy bank to Las Vegas and winning big at roulette. Halfway through the filming, in scenic Acapulco, the money ran out and the director sold the horse. Pepe consoled himself on the loss of his "son" with the thought of marrying Jones, but she turned out to be in love with Dailey. In the end, the director finished the movie and married the actress while Pepe lived happily ever after with the horse.

Such a script had little chance of capturing the Mexican character of Cantinflas. Even the name seemed alien to Hollywood moguls, so they substituted Pepe. If that was not enough, one musical number included the lines: "I'll even spell it for you. . . . P. E. P. E. Pepe, that's me!" Moreno lacked the confidence to try fast-talking in English, and throughout the filming he retained his Mexican director, Miguel Delgado, who spoke the language fluently, to coach him through the uninspired dialogue. He shared a few interesting lines in a duet with Bing Crosby, who concluded the cameo appearance by autographing Pepe's taco. The film also tried to convert his urban trickster identity into a Mexican migrant worker entering the United States through the bracero program. But Pepe made it past the border patrol only with a cheap laugh about the ferocity of Mexican cooking. Physical comedy provided a few shadows of his original character: the drooping pants, a bolero dance, and an amusing comic bullfight that finished with Pepe reading a newspaper over the animal's back.

The bulk of the film portrayed crude stereotypes of Mexico as a nation of lazy, drunken charity cases fit only for tourist entertainment. Moreno had settled for the sidekick role in *Around the World,* but he had at least shown some initiative as Passepartout, climbing the balloon rigging and rescuing the princess. In *Pepe,* he jumped out of a rustic bottle, clad in peasant breeches and sombrero, to dance with Debbie Reynolds to the tequila song. Later, when his piggy bank proved insufficient to buy an engagement ring for Shirley Jones, he looked so endearingly despondent that Kim Novak paid for the diamond.

The film seemed shaped primarily to the demands of the tourist industry, with scenes of cliff divers and nightclubs in Acapulco, images of the splendid baroque cathedral in the silver-working town of Taxco, and in Mexico City an illuminated nighttime shot of the Plaza of the Constitution and the luxurious Palace of Fine Arts, where Dailey screened his movie. The few images shown from that supposed cinema masterpiece resembled a tearjerker worthy of Harlequin Romances.

The one negative stereotype absent from *Pepe* was the Mexican bandit portrayed in countless westerns, left out, no doubt, to reassure foreigners that the country was a safe tourist destination. Instead, the producers simply exchanged that stereotype for another: the innocent Mexican, thereby reducing Cantinflas to the level of a mental incompetent. He won at the casino in Las Vegas, for example, not through his street smarts but because of an accident—he did not even know that he was betting. Then he immediately handed the money over to his employer, something the old Cantinflas would have found hilarious indeed. Another sad parody of his earlier work came in a studio encounter with Jack Lemmon, who was dressed in the drag costume he wore for *Some Like It Hot*. Lemmon's transformation from heels and wig to trousers and cigar baffled the innocent Pepe, who had apparently forgotten his own days dressed as the Empress Carlotta.

The film descended to its most infantile level when Pepe learned the difference between romantic love and friendship. He supported Shirley Jones through her lovers' quarrels with Dan Dailey, then wrongly interpreted her affectionate gratitude as romantic interest. In psychological terms, Pepe suffered from childhood Oedipal delusions. This crudely drawn narrative clearly sought to build an identification between the comic star and children, which the studio considered essential to his success in the role of a film clown. At the same time, it reassured adult viewers that Mexico posed no threat to Anglo notions of racial purity. Although the so-called Latin lover might marry the blond in fiction, as depicted by the movie within the movie, in reality—the movie proper—the director easily won the beautiful starlet away from his childlike rival.

The tasteless stereotypes and obvious exploitation appalled critics and viewers alike when the film opened over the Christmas holidays in 1960. "The rare and wonderful talents of Mexican comedian Cantinflas," wrote Bosley Crowther in the *New York Times,* "are pitifully spent and dissipated amid a great mass of Hollywooden dross." Blame for the travesty clearly lay with George Sidney, who had produced and directed the film "about as tastelessly as it could have been done." Revenues were dismal, but a few warm-hearted viewers saw through the studio-induced clutter to establish a rapport with Moreno. One Arthur Murray Aibinder of New York City wrote to President Adolfo López Mateos after seeing *Pepe* to suggest the establishment of a Cantinflas hospital for children in Mexico. Aibinder volunteered his free time working with hospitalized children and offered to contribute to such a center as his limited means made possible. Except for such individual cases, *Pepe* did little to improve understanding between the two countries.[22]

After the disastrous opening in the United States, Columbia Pictures delayed the Latin American release for another two years, and even then it met with an icy, critical reception. *Cinema Reporter* had already complained during production that the only things Mexican about the movie were Acapulco and Mario Moreno. The film's condescending attitude about race made it seem ironic that even relatively favorable reviews in Mexico expressed such an intense disliking for Sammy Davis Jr., who made a cameo appearance in the film. Santiago Reachi delivered the final epitaph, noting with bitter satisfaction that the true star of the picture was not Cantinflas but a trained horse.[23]

With *Around the World in 80 Days,* Mario Moreno finally conquered Hollywood. Unlike his contemporaries Lupe Vélez and Dolores del Río, who had sacrificed their Mexican identity to the demands of cinematic Orientalism, Cantinflas took the role of Passepartout and made it his own. But seeing himself on the wide screen of Todd-AO changed Moreno somehow, even after decades of cinematic fame. During the filming on the yacht *Henrietta,* a Mexican reporter had glimpsed the private individual behind Cantinflas from a casual remark about the crowds. "Mario Moreno looked at me as he never does on screen," the journalist wrote. "And I knew his heart. 'There is nothing comparable to solitude. In the silence we renew ourselves.'"[24] Notwithstanding this desire for solitude, the international acclaim and the Golden Globe drew Moreno relentlessly back to Tinseltown.

The financial rewards of returning to Hollywood were never in doubt. Although the decision split the Posa Films management, ending Moreno's long friendship with the savvy advertising executive Santiago Reachi, the remaining partner, Jacques Gelman, negotiated a highly lucrative contract with Columbia, just as he had previously with Michael Todd. Later in life, Moreno invented a story for interviewers about landing the role in *Around the World* by accident. Todd had approached him for a cameo role, the actor explained, but he knew the book and had always wanted to play Passepartout. Nevertheless, Michael Todd Jr. provided a more realistic version, explaining that his father had offered Moreno the role with an eye on the Latin American market and that months of tough negotiations with Gelman were needed to reach a deal. "Mario got the highest salary of anyone in the film, plus a hefty percentage of the gross film rental from all the Spanish-speaking territories—and he was worth it, if for no other reason than record-breaking grosses in the so-called Cantinflas territories."[25]

Single-minded pursuit of Hollywood gold proved an artistic trap, for Moreno lacked the insider knowledge of the U.S. film industry that might have helped him distinguish the brilliant showman Michael Todd from the studio hack George Sidney. From the beginning, Columbia executives had never imagined Cantinflas as anything more than a children's clown. The Mexican comic's improvisational skills failed to carry an English-language film the way they had in Spanish, and Moreno's talent provided only a glimmer of sincerity in an otherwise leaden production. The disaster of *Pepe* dashed Moreno's hopes of filming again in the United States, and thereafter even his Mexican movies seemed hollow masks of the former Cantinflas.

7

A MODERN QUIXOTE

"I identify myself with Don Quixote and Sancho Panza at the same time," Mario Moreno told reporters in 1972, "but perhaps more with Sancho, because he and Cantinflas are the attitude of the people."[1] He made this statement as part of a publicity campaign for his latest movie, *Don Quijote cabalga de nuevo* (Don Quixote rides again), and some dismissed it as an egocentric association with the great novel. Nevertheless, by the end of his career the Mexican comic had indeed come to share the Spanish hidalgo's madness. The same romantic faith in a chivalrous past that prompted Don Quixote to tilt at windmills blinded Moreno to the failures of the postrevolutionary regime. His final movies attempted to recreate the triumphs of his youth, when Cantinflas truly represented the attitude of a revolutionary people who were subverting social hierarchies to forge a modern nation. Although Moreno imaged himself to be a cavalier of the institutional revolution, which had made his fame and fortune, to the rest of the world, he appeared to be a mouthpiece of authoritarian government. The PRI no longer responded to the changing needs of the common people, who set out in search of new ways of being Mexican only to be lectured by the aging actor for their lack of patriotism. Moreover, by cleansing his films of transgression, Moreno not only lost his comic inspiration, he also trivialized Cantinflas to the level of a childish cartoon character.

Mexico finally seemed to have emerged in the 1960s as a progressive industrial economy, balancing business expansion with growing real wages. Yet far from a triumph for Alemán's development program, this appearance of success was merely a prelude to its utter collapse. The theory of trickle-down growth depended on private enterprise to create jobs for the lower

Knight of La Mancha or of Los Pinos? (Top) *Having earlier sworn not to defile Cervantes's classic, Cantinflas traveled to Spain in 1972 to portray Sancho Panza opposite Fernando Fernán Gómez as Don Quijote. It was a rare box-office failure for the Mexican comedian.* Don Quijote cabalga de nuevo, *production still. Courtesy: Dirección General de Actividades Cinematográficas de la UNAM.* (Bottom) *Mario Moreno honored by José López Portillo, considered by some to have been one of the most corrupt occupants of the presidential residence, Los Pinos, in modern Mexican history. Courtesy: Archivo General de la Nación.*

classes. Unfortunately, the capital-intensive nature of Mexican industrialization functioned precisely in reverse, widening the gap between rich and poor. This disparity of incomes threatened a genuine social crisis as Mexico reached its demographic peak, with population rising at annual rates of up to 3.4 percent during the crucial transition from the countryside to the city. And rather than attempting to resolve the inequalities of income by taxing business, the government financed industrialization through a dangerous reliance on foreign loans.

Even at the height of the boom, the PRI faced challenges to its monopoly of political power. The government had crushed a railroad workers' strike in 1959, justifying the use of force as a necessary response to communist subversion, but the massacre of hundreds of students at Tlatelolco in 1968 demonstrated its inability to co-opt even middle-class dissent. Then the bottom fell out of the economy as a combination of oil price increases and global recession pushed Mexico to the brink of a collapse in 1976. The discovery of offshore petroleum reserves allowed the economy to recover briefly, but rather than recognizing the need for balanced development, the government squandered the windfall on unsustainable industrialization and social programs while borrowing even more heavily in anticipation of future oil revenues. In the early 1980s the oil price dropped by half and Mexico could not even pay the interest on its accumulated foreign debt of nearly $100 billion. As the peso went into free fall, the government began cutting food subsidies for the poor in accordance with an austerity program dictated by the International Monetary Fund (IMF). With nearly 40 percent of the population suffering from malnutrition in the mid-1980s, schisms opened within the official party, which were only contained through electoral fraud by the technocratic elite. The decade of turmoil that followed revealed that the political machine of the PRI was increasingly out of touch with the Mexican people.

Age withered Moreno alongside the institutional revolution that he symbolized. As a young comedian, he had impressed critics with his range of facial expression; indeed, he could scarcely have become a national symbol, the synecdoche for a diverse society, without such adaptability. Public expectations for Cantinflas had always weighed heavily on Moreno, but they became unbearable with the realization that, although his character was eternally young, he was growing old. The actor underwent plastic surgery, which delayed the sagging but accelerated the loss of elasticity in his skin. After the operation he could no longer make the subtle facial gestures that had previously elevated his inane puns to the level of sublime humor. Ultimately, the facelift transformed Moreno into a parody of Cantinflas, tragically confirming Plato's warning to actors, made nearly 2,400 years earlier, that "the mask they wear may become their face."[2]

Family Life

Mario Moreno considered the entire Mexican nation to be his extended family but still felt disappointed not to have children of his own. With great excitement, therefore, he returned home one afternoon in September 1960, accompanied by Jacques and Natasha Gelman, carrying a tightly bundled infant. Depositing the blond-haired baby on the bed, he announced to his wife Valentina, "Rusa, here is your son."[3] Mario Arturo Moreno Ivanova, as they baptized the boy, reveled in the affection of his adoptive parents. Meanwhile, the concerns of fatherhood became apparent in Moreno's filmmaking, uniting the theme of childlike innocence from *Pepe* with a desire to relive the memories of his youth. But the joys of domesticity were shaken by scandal and tragedy a year later when Marion Roberts, the boy's mother and a U.S. citizen, named Moreno as the father and then committed suicide.

By 1960 a sheltered family life looked increasingly attractive to middle-class Mexicans as a refuge from the perceived dangers of social dissolution. Industrial workers, dissatisfied by a decade of charro union leaders, took to the streets demanding better wages and a share of business profits. Meanwhile, with the decline of official agrarian reform in the countryside, impoverished peasants began land invasions under the leadership of a Zapatista veteran, Rubén Jaramillo. President Adolfo López Mateos ordered the federal army to break these incipient revolts and to arrest the radical leaders; Jaramillo and his family were found murdered in 1962. Nevertheless, the authorities could do little to contain the problem of disaffected youths known as *rebeldes sin causa* after the James Dean movie, *Rebel without a Cause* (1955). Newspapers attributed daily acts of random violence to gangs of leather-clad teenagers who listened to loud rock-and-roll music and roamed the streets of Mexico City. Although urban crime had long been a problem, this new menace seemed particularly unsettling, in part because of the gender ambiguities of the teenagers' role models. Graham McCann, in his book *Rebel Males: Clift, Brando and Dean,* has described the revolution in acting style effected in the 1950s by these handsome but troubled young movie stars and their androgynous musician counterparts, such as Elvis Presley. In his classic film, Dean played an emotionally fragile youth performing rebellious acts of bravado to cover his masculine insecurities, just as Cantinflas had in the 1930s.[4]

With rebeldes sin causa taking over his former streetwise, gender-bending image, Moreno adopted the innocent simpleton from *Pepe* as a new identity for Cantinflas. A lack of artifice and sophistication had always been part of his wise fool character, but in *El analfabeto* (The illiterate, 1960), he no longer appeared wise, merely a fool. The film opened with Moreno, in the role of a provincial youth, Inocencio Prieto y Calvo, receiving a letter informing him that he had inherited a fortune from an uncle in Mexico City. Embarrassed by his illiteracy, he put the letter away and enrolled in a school, determined not to discover the contents of the note until he could read it for himself. The decision transformed his life; he began teaching his friends to read, found work as a bank janitor, and courted an equally innocent maid, played by Lilia Prado. Dramatic tension arose from a rival employee, who stole the letter and attempted to claim the inheritance through falsified documents. The movie featured Moreno's strongest supporting cast in decades, including two old mentors, Angel Garasa as the bank president and Carlos Martínez Baena as the teacher, and even a cameo appearance by Sara García, his costar from *Ahí está el detalle*. Although the plotline seemed lifted from the 1940s, the characterizations followed Moreno's bourgeois turn of the 1950s, so that the capitalist represented a benevolent guardian while the antagonist was a jealous fellow worker trying to sabotage his success. The film ended with Inocencio involved in a cheerful blend of modern and traditional symbols: first a mad-dash automobile race to obtain his rightful inheritance and then a church wedding to Lilia Prado.

Moreno's encounter with Marion Roberts, the mother of his adopted son, came as a tragic counterpoint to the happy endings of Cantinflas movies. An attractive blonde from Corpus Christi, Texas, she checked into the Hotel del Prado late in 1959, just short of her twentieth birthday, looking for excitement in Mexico City nightclubs. Her meager savings were quickly exhausted, and the hotel management threw her out on the street, impounding her Buick to guarantee the unpaid bill. When her divorced parents refused to send money, she spent the Christmas holiday with the family of a hotel receptionist, who provided a list of wealthy Mexicans she could ask for assistance. After several failed attempts, she finally found a benefactor in Mario Moreno, who was happy with the thought that he could reunite a helpless young woman with her family, just the sort of thing Cantinflas might do in the movies. She stayed in touch with the millionaire actor and later asked for another loan to open a beauty parlor. In the spring of 1960, while Moreno was filming *Pepe,* she visited the movie set to inform him she was pregnant. He offered to pay a reported $10,000 to adopt the child, keeping the agreement secret from his wife to avoid disappointing her. Marion gave birth on September 1, 1960, in a Dallas hospital, then used the settlement to establish a new life for herself as a Clairol representative. But within a year the money was gone, and in November 1961, she traveled to Mexico City to demand the return of her son. When Moreno refused, she locked herself in a hotel room and took an overdose of barbiturates. A maid discovered her body on the night of November 30, along with a suicide note naming Moreno as the child's father. Police summoned the actor to identify the remains, and *La Prensa* splashed the story on the front page beneath the headline, "Killed herself for Cantinflas." The scandal passed when Moreno denied having had any sexual relations with her and swore on her grave to give the child a good home.[5]

Undeterred by tragic reality, Moreno continued to perpetuate his illusion of helping beautiful young women live fairy tales in his next film, *El extra* (The extra, 1962). He played the title role of a studio extra in a succession of movie scenes recalling the characters of his youth; for example, he practiced the nonsense oratory of "momentous moments" in a French revolutionary setting and made bullfighting passes in an Aztec revival. The film thus served as an homage to both Cantinflas and the Mexican film industry. Moreno preached a conservative view of national history in the movie by inserting references to Pancho Villa and the Mexican Revolution within a monarchist speech in defense of Marie Antoinette and respect for a traditional, hierarchical society. For his next film, *Entrega inmediata* (Immediate delivery, 1963), he revived another character from the past: the unknown gendarme, agent 777. This time, Moreno played a simple mailman forced to become an international spy following the murder of secret agent XU-777. But these movies were little more than diversions while Moreno cast about for a new social cause worthy of Cantinflas.

In Search of a Father for the Children of Sánchez

Mario Moreno built an entire career out of imitating the double talk of pelados, and for even longer than that, intellectuals had presumed to speak for the supposedly inarticulate Mexican masses. But in the mid-1950s, an anthropologist from the United States, Oscar Lewis, finally listened to a family from Tepito and published their stories in a book entitled *The Children of Sánchez: Autobiography of a Mexican Family* (1961). They lived in desperate poverty, but spoke—and in one case wrote—with great eloquence, making the work an instant bestseller. A Spanish edition appeared in 1964 and sold out within two months, engaging a national debate about the condition of poverty in Mexico.[6] Some politicians demanded a democratic opening and the redistribution of income, whereas others sought to turn the clock back on urbanization and recreate a simpler, more traditional society. Moreno entered the fray personally with a motion picture about a progressive cleric, *El padrecito* (The little priest, 1964), which he considered to be, both artistically and socially, the most important of his career.

The trenchant critique of official modernization programs implicit in *The Children of Sánchez* roused both reformist and conservative politicians to search for solutions to the problem of urban poverty. Lewis had begun his anthropological research in a rural community in the late 1930s, but as his subjects began migrating to Mexico City in search of greater opportunities, he shifted his focus to the urban poor in the slums of Tepito. In this way, he observed at firsthand the transformation of Mexico City as it tripled in size from 1.5 to 5 million people during the 1940s and 1950s. His stark ethnographic account portrayed a bleak life in the slums far different from that described in official propaganda, which proclaimed an economic "miracle." Some Mexican politicians and intellectuals responded simply by burying their heads in the sand—demanding government censorship of the offending book—and in 1965 the publisher withdrew it from sale. Nevertheless, the poverty debate inspired political reformers, led by the newly appointed president of the PRI, Carlos Madrazo, to attempt a wholesale regeneration of the ruling party. Madrazo advocated a system of open primaries for local offices, selecting university students to prominent positions within the party, and creating a commission of honor to purge corrupt leaders, all of which encountered fierce opposition from the party establishment. Meanwhile, some conservatives within the PRI, headed by the long-serving regent of the Federal District, Ernesto P. Uruchurtu, believed that the only solution to urban poverty was to stop completely the industrialization of Mexico City. He launched "beautification" campaigns to plant trees along boulevards, impede commuter traffic, arrest vagrants and prostitutes, and even bulldoze impoverished squatter settlements in outlying areas.

Neither the right nor the left of the governing party proved capable of addressing basic social inequalities, and as a result the trickle-down development strategy of Alemán continued unchanged. Adolfo López Mateos, a labor lawyer who had supported the actors' union in 1946, became president in 1958 with the promise to govern "on the extreme left within the constitution." Businessmen took this as a provocation and withdrew $250 million from the economy in a matter of days, threatening the stability of the peso and forcing the new administration to back down from radical change. Six years later, the next president, Gustavo Díaz Ordaz, attempted to reform the tax code by closing loopholes for the rich, but opposition from business leaders once again blocked any real reform. In the end, the new tax law actually was even more regressive than the old. To keep corporate taxes at a minimum, the government began financing its industrial support program by borrowing money from foreign bankers.[7]

Despite these victories for big business, the conservative opposition was divided by the growth of progressive Catholicism. The Second Vatican Council, called by Pope John XXIII in October 1962, attempted to reconcile the Church with the modern world by offering a more prominent place for women in the Church and by using vernacular languages instead of Latin for Mass. Most radical of all was a change in Catholic beliefs about sin, which was now viewed as a social problem resulting from oppression and injustice and not simply as failings of personal behavior and morality. These new doctrines helped transform the Church in Latin America from an instrument of the rich to an ally of the poor.[8]

Even before the bishops' conference had concluded, Mario Moreno endorsed their progressive doctrines as the answer to Mexican poverty. *El padrecito* told the story of a young priest assigned to his first parish in the picturesque colonial town of San Miguel de Allende, where Moreno owned considerable real estate. The entire community rejected him at first, starting with the resident priest, played by Angel Garasa, who feared being displaced from his congregation. The corrupt municipal president, wanting no challenge to his control over the town, sent a gang of bandits on horseback to shoot up the bus in an attempt to scare off the padrecito. Ordinary people shunned him in the streets, but he gradually gained their trust through humor and optimism. He knelt down with children to shoot marbles and rocked the cathedral by imitating Chuck Berry on the organ. The townspeople finally embraced him without reservation when he saved their fiesta after the regular bullfighter failed to show up. Doffing the curial robes to reveal his signature drooping pants, the padrecito gave a comic bullfight, all cape work and dash, with none of the bloodshed of picadors or banderilleros. As shouts of "olé" echoed through the arena, the town notables attempted to retrieve a letter they had sent to the Archbishop demanding his removal. The mail had already been picked up, so the boss sent his masked henchmen to hold up the bus and carry off the petition. The motion picture thus took stereotypes of Mexico as a traditional country ruled by political bosses and conservative clerics, with bloody bullfights and dangerous bandits, and refashioned them into the humorous folklore of a modern nation.

Moreno also used the film as a vehicle for lecturing Mexicans about their duties in this progressive society. The sacraments, which brought people in contact with the church throughout their lives, allowed him to comment on the lack of discipline he perceived in the modern world. When a young couple asked to be married, he quizzed the bride on her recipe for *chilaquiles,* a simple breakfast dish made of leftover tortillas and chile sauce. The nervous woman left out the onion, and he insisted that she wait to get married until she had mastered *chiles en nogada* (stuffed chile peppers in walnut sauce), one of the most difficult preparations of Mexican cuisine. The padrecito likewise refused to baptize a child when the parents wanted to pass on the father's old-fashioned name, Nepomuceno, and confession provided the opportunity to berate a young Romeo for chasing the daughters of various local dignitaries.

The padrecito even immersed himself in politics, violating the Constitution of 1917 but nevertheless remaining moderate in his calls for social reform. He financed school supplies for a catechism class by rolling dice with the local merchant, then he taught the children of hacienda workers that salaries should be proportional to work, prompting their parents to demand higher wages. When accused of spreading communism, he responded by quoting the Mexican constitution as well as the 1891 papal encyclical *Rerum Novarum,* which first advocated social Catholicism. He used the collection plate as a practical means of redistributing wealth by demanding more from the political boss and then refunding money to a poor widow. Nevertheless, his progressivism fell far short of the liberation theology that later emerged from Vatican II in other Latin American countries such as Colombia, where radical priests became martyrs in a guerrilla war for social justice. The padrecito ostensibly attacked the municipal president in a sermon, but at the same time he declared it a sin to take part in politics, scarcely a call for democratic action. Moreover, he gave his approval to closed-door machinations, winning concessions from the boss by cutting a deck of cards rather than by leading the people to liberate themselves.

Even the limited reforms of the padrecito alarmed many conservative Mexicans. Some complained that the film ridiculed the priesthood and the faith, for example, by covering up a cross-eyed saint with the sunglasses that had become part of

Mario Moreno's celebrity image. Nevertheless, the actor assured reporters of his deep respect for religion and of the great care he had taken so that "the message would be only positive, constructive, happy, human, Christian."[9] At least some within the Church agreed, for a Latin American seminary student in Rome wrote to inform the actor that five hundred of his fellows had gone to see a special exhibition at the height of the historic council meeting. The priests declared the movie to be the finest sermon of the modern era. "You are not alone," they proclaimed. "With you is all of the new Church, rejuvenated by this Vatican Council; with you are all of the young priests of 'the new wave'; with you are all of us who wish to live the authentic evangelization to its ultimate consequences."[10]

Such youthful enthusiasm was largely doomed to frustration, for Mexico had one of the most conservative Catholic establishments in Latin America, and the bishops quickly reined in the zeal of younger clerics. The promise of greater democracy likewise proved hollow. Although the conservative opposition party, Partido de Acción Nacional (PAN), was allowed to win a few municipal elections in the mid-1960s, the government invalidated PRI losses at the state and national level. Carlos Madrazo, who was forced to resign the party presidency in 1965 after his attempt at internal reforms, carried on his campaign for political openness outside the PRI until he was killed in a mysterious plane crash in 1969. President Díaz Ordaz likewise refused to tolerate Uruchurtu's reactionary challenge to the official development program and used a notorious bulldozing of a squatter settlement as an excuse to fire him, allowing the capital to continue its unrestrained growth. Meanwhile, Moreno adopted an ever more conservative stance in response to Mexico's changing social conditions.

"¿Pelados? ¡Peludos!"

Pelados or hippies? That was the question for Mexican middle-class youth in the 1960s. The folkloric national identity of their parents, based on popular culture icons of the 1930s and 1940s—the pelado Cantinflas, the mariachi Jorge Negrete, the Bohemian musician Agustín Lara, and the Indian flower girl

Dolores del Río—seemed old-fashioned by comparison with the youth protest movement sweeping Europe and the United States. But students who embraced such international symbols of rebellion as the Beatles and Che Guevara were attacked by their elders for selling out the patria to foreign imperialists. The Mexican counterculture attempted to subvert this PRI monopoly over nationalist ideology by fashioning an alternative authenticity in the guise of the *jipiteca,* an indigenous version of the hippie. Mario Moreno, enraged by this challenge to his status as the representative of the Mexican people, proceeded to berate the hippies in a succession of movies in the late 1960s and early 1970s. Simultaneously, he redoubled his efforts to identify with young children and thereby ensure that Cantinflas lived on in the national consciousness. But far from restoring his youthful image, these films revealed him as the aging spokesman of a sclerotic political establishment.

Moreno began his campaign against middle-class protesters with *El señor doctor* (Mr. Doctor, 1965), produced as an object lesson in professional responsibility at a time when medical interns were on strike for better working conditions in Mexico City hospitals. Cantinflas appeared as a provincial doctor returning to Mexico City ostensibly to update his medical training but also to remind urban doctors of traditional values. Once again Moreno trumpeted the benefits of the institutional revolution, this time extolling the virtues of Seguro Social, the national health insurance program, while overlooking that it did not cover the poorest segments of Mexican society. The film was no more realistic in its portrayal of an innocent country doctor reuniting elderly mothers with wayward sons, preventing the divorce of a sick child's parents, and performing brain surgery without prior training.

Moreno's condescending lectures on caring for patients must have seemed particularly galling to the interns working at the Veinte de Noviembre Hospital. They had gone on strike at the end of 1964 to protest the withholding of their traditional Christmas bonus and to demand better working conditions. In a gesture of reconciliation, the newly inaugurated president, Díaz Ordaz, granted some concessions to the strikers. Then in April 1965, immediately after Moreno completed filming, a dissident faction of young doctors walked out again. This time the government took a hard line, forcing them back to work. When they struck one more time in August, riot police took over the hospital, jailing a number of prominent sympathizers. The premiere of *El señor doctor* in October doubtless seemed bitter medicine to the more than two hundred strikers who were fired in the aftermath.[11]

Moreno's life had likewise become a medical tragedy since his wife Valentina was diagnosed with bone cancer early in 1964. *El señor doctor* therefore functioned at one level as Moreno's attempt at wish fulfillment, to be the doctor who could save her life. Nevertheless, after nearly two years of therapy, she passed away on January 6, 1966, leaving the grieving actor as a single parent to his adopted child, Mario Arturo.

Business affairs, like social commentary, demonstrated a growing egocentrism in the millionaire actor. He still jealously defended his control over Cantinflas, although with perfect legitimacy. For example, he took legal action against Eloy Poire Hernández, who attempted to distribute his films without permission. Despite the break with his former partner Santiago Reachi, Moreno remained close to the advertising industry through his friendship with Eulalio Ferrer, one of Mexico's leading publicists. Nevertheless, when Pepsico offered him a million dollars for a global advertising campaign in 1966, Moreno held out for 5 percent of the multinational corporation's stock, worth more than $30 million at the time. He justified this outrageous demand by claiming that "it would be the first advertising campaign using Cantinflas as a testimonial and actor and for that his participation has no price." Pepsico raised its bid to $1.5 million, but Moreno refused even that unprecedented sum. His ostensible refusal to sell out Cantinflas to foreign capital appeared less convincing because of the advertisements he had made for General Motors and Canada Dry thirty years earlier and his more or less constant presence in the publicity business ever since.[12]

His megalomania reached even greater heights in the arena of international politics as he lectured world leaders in his next film, *Su excelencia* (Your excellency, 1966). Moreno played a petty diplomat from the Central American republic of Los Cocos responsible for stamping tourist visas in the communist bloc country of Pepeslavia. This embassy clerk suddenly acquired global significance when first a Cold War peace conference gathered in the capital of Pepeslavia and then a succession of palace revolutions in Los Cocos elevated him to the rank of

ambassador extraordinary and minister plenipotentiary. With
Cantinflas holding the deciding vote between Eastern and Western powers, Pepeslavia assigned a beautiful secret agent to seduce him, but the blond spy got drunk at an embassy party and
went to bed with the wrong diplomat, an odd plot twist for a
film made less than a year after the death of Moreno's Russian
wife. Cantinflas refused in the end to cast his vote for either
side and spent a full fifteen minutes haranguing the rival powers in the name of world peace; nevertheless, he lost the moral
high ground of nonalignment through his blatant anticommunism. The New York premiere, attended by U.N. Secretary General U Thant, scored a box office victory over Charlie Chaplin's
last film, *The Countess of Hong Kong,* which opened the same
week. The revenues indicated not the spread of Moreno's appeal to Anglo audiences but rather the huge population of
Puerto Rican migrants who had moved to East Harlem in the
postwar era and retained their affection for Cantinflas. Three
years later, Moreno published a novelization of the movie without giving credit to the screenplay's coauthor, humorist Marco
Almazán, a former diplomatic clerk. Finally, in a curious example of reality imitating art—or at least cinema—in the mid-
1970s, Mexican president Luis Echeverría made an unsuccessful
bid for the position of head of the United Nations.[13]

Domestically, the PRI recognized the need to buy off middle-
class voters to preserve the social peace in the 1960s, but material gains seemed only to prompt demands for a corresponding
political voice. Many ostensible welfare projects for the poor, in
Mexico as in the United States, actually benefited the middle
classes, particularly federal bureaucrats and industrial workers
with CTM connections. These subsidies included comfortable
apartment buildings, such as the Unidad Tlatelolco surrounding
the historic Plaza of Three Cultures, and free tuition at the Universidad Nacional Autónoma de México or the Instituto Nacional Politécnico. Unfortunately, jobs in government and
industry did not keep pace with the number of graduates, disil-
lusioning even those with prestigious engineering and legal de-
grees. Moreover, the political system remained dominated by
conservative, middle-aged bureaucrats, to the disgust of Mexican young people, who joined in their dissatisfaction with the
youth of Europe and the United States.

Perhaps most stifling of all to Mexican youth was the weight of official nationalism that had been constructed by the ruling party around the myths of the Revolution of 1910 and the icons of "golden age" cinema. The movie industry had forced the radical pachuco humor of Tin Tan into the stifling mold of Cantinflas, while the PRI had channeled peasant demands for land into empty ceremonies bastardizing the memory of Emiliano Zapata. In the 1950s the rebeldes sin causa had rejected such outdated dogma in favor of black leather, Elvis Presley, and James Dean. The continued invasion of Anglo-Saxon popular culture, together with the physical presence in Mexico of large numbers of hippies from the United States evading the Vietnam draft and searching for the fabled hallucinogenic mushrooms of Huautla de Jiménez, Oaxaca, led to the creation in the mid-1960s of a local counterculture, La Onda (the wave). The official establishment condemned the rebellious youth for selling out the national culture by listening to such English-language rock musicians as the Beatles, the Rolling Stones, and Jimi Hendrix, although Mario Moreno ironically chose this moment to film *Por mis pistolas* (For my pistols, 1968), an imitation of Sergio Leone's spaghetti westerns. But participants in La Onda fashioned their own alternative authenticity as jipitecas, adopting indigenous clothing, haircuts, and spirituality, or at least creative reconstructions of pre-Hispanic cultures.[14]

The diverse elements of the student movement joined together in the summer of 1968 to form the National Strike Action Committee, with representatives from 128 schools ranging from secondary students in vocational schools to aspiring politicians from the national law school. Fearing a disruption of the Olympic Games, scheduled to begin in October, President Díaz Ordaz ordered riot police to repress the student demonstrations with extreme force, in one case using a bazooka to blast through the doors of a prep school. On October 2, army troops surrounded a peaceful gathering of several thousand students at the Plaza of Three Cultures in Tlatelolco. A military helicopter dropped flares onto the crowd as a signal for the attack, then machine gunners began raking the speakers' platform while police infiltrators worked through the fleeing crowds, arresting student leaders. Foreign journalists reported that more than three hundred died in the brutal massacre, and ten times that number were wounded or arrested and tortured. The national media, by contrast, tended to minimize the losses and to support government claims that the military response had been justified by the danger of social unrest.[15]

Mario Moreno joined in the attempt to restore the ruling party's legitimacy by condemning the students as a threat to the nation. He had already denounced the local counterculture in *El señor doctor* by showing the provincial doctor and his nurse girlfriend in a nightclub filled with drugged-out beats. In 1965 the Mexican police had just conducted a series of raids against music clubs, and the movie scene ended with police arresting the medics and revealing drug paraphernalia and concealed weapons among the youths—thus seeking to justify the official repression.[16] By 1968, Moreno had tied his personal image to the Olympic Games through a series of television commercials for the local organizing committee. The personal embarrassment caused by the student protests became palpable in his first film after the Tlatelolco massacre. *Un Quijote sin mancha* (A "spotless" knight, 1969), punning Don Quixote de la Mancha, featured Moreno as a legal cavalier dedicated to defending the residents of a poor neighborhood. The movie recycled the nightclub scene from *El señor doctor,* although two years after the summer of love the youth wore hippie fringe instead of beat turtlenecks and danced go-go instead of jazz.[17] Following the obligatory police raid, which conspicuously revealed the presence of drugs, switchblades, and brass knuckles, the lawyer proceeded to lecture the jipitecas in jail. His opening line, "¿Pelados? ¡Peludos!" asserted a claim of nationalist authenticity in a generational struggle between the "hairless" lumpenproletariat of the 1930s and the shaggy middle-class protesters of the 1960s. But in berating the jipitecas for smoking dope instead of working, Moreno reversed the roles of his earlier movie, *Ahí está el detalle,* conceding to them the carefree youthful spirit of Cantinflas while he became the stodgy establishment figure played by Joaquín Pardavé. After all, the detalle had formerly referred to a marijuana cigarette.

Moreno now spoke across the generations primarily as a father figure for small children. The prevalence of violence, nudity, and bad language in contemporary cinema made the transgressions of his early films appear tame by comparison, ideal fare for holiday matinees. In 1970, following a heart attack, he made *El profe* (The teacher), the juvenile adventures of a small-town schoolmaster, which was his biggest success in years, playing for a record twenty-two weeks at first-run theaters. His next film, the Spanish coproduction of *Don Quijote cabalga de nuevo,* proved a complete failure both critically and at the box office, in Europe and the Americas. Nevertheless, Spanish producers used his visit to create an animated "Cantinflas Show," broadcast in Mexico by Televisa, with peace signs and little airplanes, a Hispanic version of the Beatles' *Yellow Submarine* (1968) but without all the psychedelic imagery.

Moreno's career had reached a terminal decline when reduced to such a cartoon parody of his former self. In *Un Quijote sin mancha,* he tried to relive the triumphant courtroom scene from *Ahí está el detalle;* but where in 1940 Cantinflas had subverted the entire courtroom with his fast-talking nonsense, the best he could manage in 1969 was to accuse the prosecutor of vacationing in Acapulco with a bilingual secretary. Attempts to restore his youthful complexion through heavy makeup, particularly in *El señor doctor,* made him look more like a puppet than a person, nor did it help to put his increasingly bulky frame next to the white-haired but still slim Angel Garasa. Most pathetic of all was his desire to have his youthful cake and eat it too by disguising himself in a mop-top wig and wire-rimmed glasses to dance with a go-go girl before lecturing the jipitecas. He appeared, in the end, like an ambivalent old parson, simultaneously seduced by the sins of youth and terrified for his immortal soul. While venting his wrath on middle-class youth, he also lost touch with the changing reality of the urban poor, always his most loyal audience.

After the Pelado

Cantinflas sprang from the gaping fissures of Mexican culture that divided country and city, tradition and modernity, but by 1970 even those fundamental distinctions had lost much of their validity. Modernity seemed on the verge of triumph in even the most remote villages through the arrival of television, soccer, and Pepsi Cola, just as the city itself succumbed to an invasion of

The pelado from the 1930s confronts hippies in the 1960s as part of a struggle to represent Mexico's national identity. Although Cantinflas triumphed over the hippies on screen, many young people considered him a momiza *(square).* Conserje en condominio, *production still. Courtesy: Dirección General de Actividades Cinematográficas de la UNAM.*

shantytowns from the countryside. The increasingly homogeneous conditions of poverty experienced in both town and country forced Mexico to confront its multiethnic nature and to question the myth of the cosmic race as a path to national unity. Meanwhile, the political certainties of a one-party state unraveled as the PRI began to split into technocratic and populist wings. All of these changes took place in a climate of perpetual crisis as the economy built by Miguel Alemán collapsed under its own weight. Confronted by such monumental challenges, Mexicans grasped instinctively for familiar icons. On the eve of the millennium, the Virgin of Guadalupe made apparitions in the subway, Zapatistas took to the hills of Chiapas, and a Cárdenas was elected mayor of Mexico City. But attempts to resuscitate Cantinflas failed, and the nation mourned as it undertook the laborious task of forging a new identity without the familiar old pelado, who had formerly offered comfort through laughter.

Mexican politicians were so captivated by the country's impressive economic growth in the 1960s that they failed to notice the far more significant growth in population. Expanding at an annual rate of up to 3.4 percent, as fast as virtually any country in Africa or Asia, Mexico's population rose to nearly fifty million by 1970. Young people had little hope of making a living in the countryside because of the capital-intensive nature of agricultural development and the lack of further land reform; therefore, nearly two million of them migrated to Mexico City in the 1960s alone. Only a small fraction could find housing in the tenements of Tepito, and most settled in primitive shacks on marginal land outside the city. By 1970 such outlying shantytowns housed fully half of Mexico City's nine million inhabitants, while inner-city slums accounted for only about 6 percent of the urban population. These shantytowns bore a striking resemblance to poor rural villages even though half of the residents had moved to them from other parts of the Federal District. Households commonly included a few chickens or a pig as a means of supplementing meager incomes and of recycling all available scraps. Few residents found factory jobs in the formal economy, and the vast majority were either self-employed as street vendors or performed service work in middle-class neighborhoods.[18]

Although the growth of shantytowns appalled the former mayor, Uruchurtu, subsequent administrations encouraged such settlements as an escape valve for an otherwise ungovernable metropolis. Public housing projects tended to benefit middle-class families and could not, in any event, keep pace with the rapidly growing population. Instead of bankrupting the city with such investment, officials turned a blind eye to illegal land invasions. Self-help housing provided an outlet for unemployed workers, while penny capitalism offered such people a precarious livelihood. The official party established mechanisms for tapping political support from such marginal populations, thereby incorporating the informal sector of society alongside the more established labor unions and peasant organizations. Political fixers known as "coyotes" arranged the invasions in the first place, and officials then gradually, capriciously, provided city services, legitimized land titles, and protected small-scale vendors in exchange for continued loyalty to the PRI. These informal arrangements paradoxically encouraged both conservatism and disgruntlement. On the one hand, reliance on self-help stabilized the system, for penny capitalists were ill-equipped to organize mass strikes, and homeowners who had invested years of their own work making improvements were unlikely to become urban terrorists. Nevertheless, the frustration of city dwellers at the vagaries of city bureaucracy made a powerful bloc of voters with little attachment to the official party, awaiting the emergence of democratic political movements willing to address their local concerns.

Mario Moreno recognized this widespread feeling of frustration, but his intimate connections to the political elite undermined his desire to identify with common people. In *El ministro y yo* (The minister and I, 1975), he played an *escribano,* a notary public sitting in the plaza of Santo Domingo, a few blocks north of the Zócalo, typing letters for illiterate citizens. The film began with a friend asking his assistance in obtaining a permit from the land census bureau, appropriately the destination of squatters hoping to regularize land titles. The notary public went through a series of frustrating encounters with city functionaries, which doubtless struck familiar chords with the audience. But the movie became sheer fantasy when his letter of protest gained him a personal audience with the cabinet minister, who even more unrealistically appointed him to reform the inefficient bureaucracy. He then proceeded to demonstrate, using fast-motion photography and slow, tedious lectures, how he thought public officials should function in a democracy. Finally, he resigned the official position and returned to the plaza to write letters for common people. The audience may have appreciated some of his barbs; for example, when a superior asked if he had ever held a position in the bureaucracy, the escribano replied, "No, I've always worked . . . independently." Nevertheless, Moreno lost all credibility by portraying the cabinet minister as a compassionate man willing to invite a humble escribano home for dinner in order to learn about the needs of common people. Having dined in the homes of many top PRI officials, the millionaire actor may have believed that they dedicated themselves to public service, but it seemed uncharitable, at best, to blame all of Mexico's troubles on underpaid and overworked functionaries.

As Moreno lost touch with the common people, the mantle of the Mexican country bumpkin passed from Cantinflas to the more socially relevant character of "La India María." Played by María Elena Velasco, she first appeared on Televisa's variety show "Siempre en Domingo" (Always on Sunday) about 1970, just as middle-class residents of Mexico City grew concerned about the large numbers of women in the city wearing indigenous costume and engaged in petty commerce or begging. There was nothing new about seeing poor people in the streets of the capital, but city officials since Porfirian times had at least enforced dress codes to assure that pelados wore European-style clothing, however tattered. The appearance of the "Marías," as the indigenous women were derisively known, together with the growth of shantytowns, challenged the modern self-image cultivated by progressive Mexicans.[19]

La India María became the most popular comedian of her day by bridging the divisions of Mexican society and identifying with the poor without threatening the rich, just as Cantinflas had thirty years earlier. She made the transition from television to motion pictures with *Tonta tonta pero no tanto* (Foolish but not that much, 1971), *La madrecita* (The little mother, 1973), and *La presidenta municipal* (The municipal president, 1974). Although La India played the wise fool with many of the same puns and sight gags as Cantinflas, she represented a Mexico that had become simultaneously more cosmopolitan and more provincial. The pelado was the product of an assimilationist nationalist project dedicated to forging a cosmic race by annihilating native culture, and he retained his original ethnicity only by negation, the failure to speak correct Spanish or even to grow a proper mustache. La India also emerged from a hybrid culture, but rather than destroying her indigenous culture, exposure to global mass media gave her the sophistication to play multiple roles and thus to preserve her Native American identity. She cheerfully added tennis shoes and a Texas hat to the braids and shawl of her village costume. And as was common in the 1970s, she supported herself through penny capitalism, selling fake pre-Hispanic curios to gringo tourists. Unlike Cantinflas, La India felt at home in her native community, being elected municipal president in one film. She even survived a trip to Los Angeles in *Ni de aquí ni de allá* (Neither from here nor there, 1987), although the Immigration and Naturalization Service deported her in the end, along with so many of her compatriots.[20]

Moreno responded to competition from La India María by pathetically selling out his beloved old gendarme character to the power elite in *Patrullero 777* (Patrolman 777, 1977). Having gone thick in the middle at the age of sixty-six, he fit poorly in a police uniform; drooping pants had become completely unthinkable. But advanced years did not stop him from carrying out his duties of karate chopping drug pushers, rescuing fallen women, and lecturing hippies. The combination seemed all the more absurd as corruption reached new heights within the Mexico City police department under Arturo "El Negro" Durazo. Appointed chief of police by his childhood friend, José López Portillo, who had been elected president in 1976, Durazo was already under indictment in the United States for narcotics trafficking. His determination to consolidate his hold over the cocaine trade became apparent when rival Colombian dealers turned up dead in the Tula River. Not even law-abiding citizens of Mexico City could escape his grasp, for patrolmen regularly cruised the crowded expressways during rush hour collecting bribes for imaginary infractions in order to feed Durazo's relentless demands. The irony was not lost on reviewers, who described the film as "a contribution to making the abominable and feared 'blues' [of the capital's police force] sympathetic."[21]

Another member of the López Portillo administration to benefit from Moreno's filmmaking was the Federal District regent, Carlos Hank González. A multimillionaire with experience as director of the state welfare agency CONASUPO and governor of Mexico State, he conceived elaborate plans to make the capital more livable through highway construction to ease commuting times for middle-class drivers and reforestation to reduce the air pollution caused by excessive cars and factories. Moreno was such a close personal friend of the mayor that he dedicated his last Cantinflas film, *El barrendero* (The street sweep, 1981), to support this urban beautification campaign. The film also attempted to recreate Moreno's earlier work as a union activist by featuring a struggle against a corrupt boss, perhaps symbolizing his equally fossilized rival, Fidel Velázquez, who still headed the CTM.

Also in 1981, about the time *El barrendero* was released, Moreno appeared in a massive publicity campaign for the credit card Carnet. Billboards and television commercials featured the aging actor standing in front of a portrait of a young Cantinflas, painted in the early 1950s, with the slogan, "Carnet goes with my personality!" In an interview, journalist Enrique Maza asked about the implications of using the pelado to advertise a credit card that was out of the reach of ordinary Mexicans. Moreno saw no contradiction, insisting that the slogan came from him, the millionaire, speaking to the common man, Cantinflas. "I never imagined that one might think it wrong to urge the people to get rich," he explained, apparently without giving much thought to the general lack of social mobility in Mexico. This episode illustrated once again that, even at this advanced age, people still expected the actor to live up to his character.[22]

With his credit card endorsement, Moreno came to symbolize one of Mexico's gravest problems in the 1980s, the massive foreign debt contracted by the government in an attempt to bolster the faltering economy. Borrowing had begun on a large scale in the late 1960s to finance a balance of payments deficit, which grew even worse during the global recession following the first oil price shock in 1973. Three years later, at the end of his term in office, President Luis Echeverría let the peso float—"like a rock," as Mexicans wryly observed. The 40 percent devaluation threatened the entire postwar development program until the state petroleum company, Pemex, announced the discovery of offshore reserves amounting to as much as 200 billion barrels. President José López Portillo mortgaged future oil revenues to finance massive infrastructure and social programs, such as the road building and reforestation of Carlos Hank González. Then in 1981, as the national debt reached $80 billion and petroleum exports accounted for three-fourths of foreign revenue, the price of oil collapsed. With the Mexico City government near bankruptcy and pollution even worse than when the mayor took office, people began referring to the mayor as "Genghis" Hank. The presidency of Miguel de la Madrid, from 1982 to 1988, proved to be one long economic crisis, during which the foreign debt peaked at nearly $100 billion and the peso fell to a rate of 2,300 to the dollar before finally bottoming out in 1990 at 3,000 to the dollar.[23]

A long-time relationship with Columbia Pictures cushioned Moreno from the peso's collapse by providing a regular source of dollar income. In fact, the desperate conditions in Mexico during the 1980s may actually have increased Moreno's film and video rental receipts by driving greater numbers of migrant workers across the border to the United States. His last movie, *El barrendero,* reportedly grossed $3.5 million in Texas and California alone. And like many other wealthy Mexicans, he hedged against domestic inflation by investing in United States real estate, including a penthouse apartment in Houston's Warwick Tower and a mansion in Century City, California.[24]

Moreno made a few final attempts in the 1980s to revitalize Cantinflas, to make him relevant to new generations. In 1983, he agreed to record an album, *Con los niños del mundo* (With the children of the world), as an outgrowth of the animated Cantinflas show, despite his almost complete lack of musical talent. Produced by Carlos Avila for RCA Victor, and with one song, "Cantinfleando," written personally by Moreno, the album proved a commercial failure. The selection of Mexico to host the World Cup soccer championship in 1986 offered another opportunity to restore Cantinflas as a modern symbol of national identity. The president of the Mexican soccer federation, Rafael del Castillo, declared the comic character to be the official mascot in a 1985 ceremony, but objections immediately arose that Moreno had no relationship with soccer other than as an investor in the prominent professional team América. The issue soon exploded into a national debate as prominent academics publicly denounced Cantinflas as a backward and inappropriate symbol of the Mexican people. Sociologist Jacqueline Avramov explained that "the myth of Cantinflas has no support in the [current] social situation. He is not what we Mexicans are, much less what we would want to be." Psychiatrist Alberto Cuevas, the brother of avant-garde artist José Luis Cuevas, dismissed him as a "momiza" (square). Stung by the attacks, Moreno withdrew Cantinflas as the mascot, to be replaced by Pique, a cartoon jalapeño pepper in a sombrero.[25]

The decline of his public status coincided with the disintegration of his personal life. Having lectured Mexicans for more than a decade about the problems of undisciplined youth, he had to admit his own failure as a father by sending his adopted son to the Betty Ford clinic for drug and alcohol addiction. On April 22, 1988, after finishing treatment, Mario Arturo married a former Miss Guanajuato, Araceli Abril del Moral, in a ceremony witnessed by such luminaries as Carlos Hank González. The couple gave Moreno two grandchildren, Valentina and Mario, but domestic troubles continued. On the second anniversary of his marriage, in 1990, police arrested Mario Arturo in an Acapulco disco for the possession of narcotics, and a few years later, the prodigal son left his wife for another woman, Sandra Bernat.[26]

Meanwhile, Moreno became embroiled in a bizarre legal scandal of his own when a Texas woman, Joyce Jett, sued him for divorce from an alleged common law marriage. He had met her in April 1968 while purchasing building materials for a new house from the electrical supply business she ran in Houston. Moreno was just beginning a public affair with a Spanish actress, Irán Eory, which never culminated in marriage because of her refusal to give up her career. Nevertheless, he continued to see Jett in Houston during the frequent medical checkups following his heart attack in 1970. She eventually won his trust, and, in return for loans and gifts, she came to manage his affairs in the United States, even checking in on Mario Arturo during his treatment at the Betty Ford clinic. At Mario Arturo's insistence, Jett stood at the wedding as mother of the groom, but her relationship with Moreno had already become strained. A year later, in 1989, she sued him for divorce under Texas's antiquated common law marriage statute, which was repealed by the state legislature before the end of the year. Her lawyers offered a weak case, but Moreno's attorney made the mistake of first accepting the court's jurisdiction over a Mexican citizen, even though marriage laws differed between the two countries, and then failing to refute the charges. A Houston judge ruled in favor of Jett, awarding her half of the actor's reputed net worth of $52 million. The legal trauma finally ended on May 3, 1990, when she accepted a settlement check for $700,000, in addition to half of his continuing royalties from Columbia Pictures and $600,000 she had made by selling his Houston apartment.

Mario Moreno made a final visit to Houston in February 1993 after doctors diagnosed him with lung cancer from a lifetime of cigarette smoking. He stayed for a month of radiation and chemotherapy, then returned to Mexico City to spend his last days among family and friends, including carpa actors Jesús Martínez "Palillo" and Delia Magaña. On the evening of April 20, Abraham Zabludovsky, the manager of Televisa, appeared visibly shaken when he interrupted the regularly scheduled soap opera to inform Mexico that Mario Moreno had passed away. The station then broadcast *El gendarme desconocido* as a tribute to the beloved comic actor. The wake, at the Jorge Negrete Theater of the National Association of Actors, was attended by famous names and old friends such as director Miguel M. Delgado, cinematographer Gabriel Figueroa, actress Silvia Pinal, politician Carlos Hank González, media magnate Miguel Alemán Velasco and his wife Christiane Martell, boxer Raul "the Rat" Macías, and Moreno's old theater partner, Manuel Medel. Condolences also arrived from throughout the Hispanic world, including the presidents of Venezuela, Peru, and Honduras, and King Juan Carlos of Spain. The PRI, having received so many endorsements from the comic actor, sought to make one last association with Cantinflas as President Carlos Salinas de Gortari joined Mario Arturo in a guard of honor.

However closely Moreno had become tied to the political elite, the common people remained loyal to the end, turning out in mass for his funeral. In addition to the political elite, there also stood an alternative, working-class guard of honor, comprising ordinary street clowns and headed by Superbarrio, the former professional wrestler and activist for poor and homeless residents of Mexico City. Some sixty-five thousand people lined the streets as motorcycle police and a patrol car hastily painted with the number 777 accompanied the hearse across town to Tacuba, former site of the Carpa Valentina, to the resting place of Moreno's wife Valentina in the Spanish pantheon. Officials had suggested to Moreno on his deathbed a state burial alongside his old friend Agustín Lara in the Rotunda of Illustrious Men, but he declined the offer with the protestation that while not at all illustrious, he was indeed rotund. He left as an epitaph an appropriately cantinflasque enigma: "It would appear that he's gone, but it's (not) certain."[27]

CONCLUSION

The dual biography of Mario Moreno and Cantinflas forms a substantial chapter in the history of Mexico from the 1930s through the 1980s. The tensions that existed between the millionaire comedian and his working-class character mirrored the social contradictions of the Institutional Revolutionary Party, which employed populist rhetoric to legitimize the co-optation of the popular sectors while following an economic program of "trickle-down" development favoring wealthy capitalists. But critics who denounced Moreno for selling out his plebeian origins overlooked the fact that Cantinflas was never simply the creation of a single individual. The pelado had sprung from the realm of popular culture, and although the character was nurtured by a media industry that profited from his image, he nevertheless remained the communal property of the Mexican people. Attempts by the ruling party and its unofficial spokesman, Mario Moreno, to trick the masses through cantinfladas into unquestioning acceptance of an authoritarian government could only succeed through the complicit reception of the people themselves, and the maundering medium of Cantinflas's speech invariably subverted this hegemonic message.

Ambiguity permeates the historical memories of Mario Moreno and Cantinflas. The actor first entered politics from the carpa stage in the 1930s through an elaborate parody of the Marxist rhetoric of Vicente Lombardo Toledano. The celebrity status he gained in part through a mock debate with the powerful labor leader propelled him a decade later into an actual union conflict for self-determination within screen actors' guild, which in turn helped resolve a broader contest for union democracy in the postwar era. Both Moreno and Lombardo had originally championed the rights of workers to negotiate contracts

211

freely and to strike when dissatisfied, only to repudiate the slogan of "trapitos al sol" in favor of behind-the-scenes negotiations within the union bureaucracy. Meanwhile, an ironic reversal of roles culminated with the actor as a presidential confidant and the politician as an exile from government. In the early 1950s, the status of Cantinflas as a national treasure was being debated on the floor of the Senate. He received nominations for political office and even proposals that he be named the official party's presidential candidate.[1] Nevertheless, these joking campaigns reflected not a widespread belief in his statesmanlike qualities but rather a cynical view of democracy in Mexico. Even after Mario Moreno had come to resemble a "dinosaur" politician, Cantinflas continued to challenge the system in the popular imagination.

The extreme loyalty of ordinary Mexicans for Cantinflas was reciprocated by the pelado's embodiment of the national identity, notwithstanding Mario Moreno's sellout to Hollywood by filming the stereotypes in *Pepe.* While Chaplin's tramp assumed pretensions of gentility, Cantinflas remained a simple pelado and forced the world to change around him. In *El mago,* for example, when Cantinflas left Mexico to become sultan of a distant land, he brought along a Native American woman to make fresh tortillas. Mexicans also scored vicarious nationalist triumphs through the actor's adventures abroad. Cinema reporter Roberto Cantu ironically informed readers that the philanthropic Moreno had contributed $25 to the city of Los Angeles in the form of a speeding ticket. "Naturally, communication was difficult between Cantinflas and the motorcycle officer, besides the complications of his dialect, Mario spoke no English while the policeman did not wish to learn Spanish."[2] In this exchange, Moreno inverted the usual power relations between Anglo policemen and Mexican residents in the United States. Unlike most Mexicans, who came to work, the actor traveled on vacation. And although Mexicans usually suffered if they did not speak English, Moreno could jabber away with impunity. He even broke the law, speeding freely down the highway, and a ticket that would have imposed an onerous financial burden on migrant workers was dismissed as an act of charity.

Even rich and powerful Mexicans could enjoy the humble pelado's victories over the Colossus of the North. Politicians shared the laugh when Cantinflas satirized a diplomatic initiative from the United States by asking, "Why worry about a shortage of *pan* (bread) when we have so much Pan-Americanism?"[3] Moreno's Golden Globe–winning performance in *Around the World in 80 Days* also brought pride to Mexico's elite, as did his visits to the White House and his receipt of an honorary doctorate from the University of Michigan. Indeed, the only time that Mexican critics accepted the low-brow comedian was in the role of national champion, either when he won the applause of foreigners or when he was attacked by outside critics, such as the French at Cannes. The Mexican cultural elite thus acknowledged, in a backhand way, Moreno's embodiment of the national identity, a point never doubted by the masses. And despite the unfortunate *Pepe,* he ultimately conquered film audiences in the United States on his own terms, through the migration of millions of Hispanics north of the Rio Grande.

Cantinflas bequeathed an ambiguous masculine legacy despite the best efforts of Mario Moreno to force his character into more conventional gender behavior. The destabilization of gender roles was an essential element of his early character, not limited to the masculine one-upmanship of albures but as part of a wider current of homosexuality within the carpa theater. For commercial success in the cinema, Moreno tamed the cross-dressing and homoerotic embraces in the 1940s, and contented himself with mocking the extremes of masculine posturing. By the 1960s, even his playful androgynous gestures had hardened into the stereotypical macho behavior that Moreno had formerly parodied to such devastating effect. In *El padrecito,* for example, when challenged by the political boss's son, he ended the contest immediately with a simple one-two punch, apparently having forgotten the deliriously funny slapstick boxing skills of his youth. Yet Cantinflas had the last laugh once again as biographers posthumously disputed Moreno's virility. Miguel Angel Morales claimed that he had an illegitimate son by an Argentine actress in the 1940s, while Guadalupe Elizalde quoted an intimate friend of the actor saying that he was unable to have children.[4]

The multiple ambiguities of Cantinflas reflected the equally uncertain legacy of Mexico's quest for modernity. The mantras of progress, urbanization, industrialization, and nation building, which had carried Mexico through the years of the miracle, sounded hollow by the 1970s. The ostensibly revolutionary government succeeded in constructing the facade of a modern industrial society, but it turned out to be a ghastly parody of the original plan. Immigration from the countryside overwhelmed the feeble attempts to construct decent housing and transformed Mexico City into a metropolis of primitive shanties. Unable to find regular work in factories, migrants survived on the exploitative wages of service jobs or through the self-exploitation of petty commerce. But contrary to the ideals of the "cosmic race," these newcomers retained elements of their rural, often indigenous identity, and the new cultural forms they did adopt tended to come from transnational media rather than from the ruling party's stock of national icons. These hybrid cultures, increasingly common on the margins of globalization, even emerged from the Mexican media industry; for example, Mario Moreno's refusal to hire a decent screenwriter was a relic of his origins in the audience-centered carpa theater. By contrast, the supposedly spontaneous humor of the former vaudeville player, Groucho Marx, was in fact carefully scripted by the Hollywood studios, a point he deeply resented and rarely acknowledged.[5] Those who praise Groucho while scorning Cantinflas thus offer a perhaps unknowing compliment to the advances of industrial rationalization in the United States at the expense of Mexican modernity.

The critics' view of Moreno, that he had sold out his popular character to the political elite, is at once both an obvious fact and a fundamental misinterpretation, as with so many generalizations about the carnivalesque Cantinflas—obvious because of the enormous wealth and conservative political stances he held by the end of his career, and a fundamental misinterpretation because the carpa was always an audience-driven theater and Moreno remained steadfast in his pursuit of popular applause, even at the expense of critical acceptance. The experimentation of his early films represented a search for the broadest possible market, and in that Cantinflas succeeded beyond all expectations, both in Mexico and throughout the Hispanic world. For a brief moment, about 1941, popular opinion coincided with that of Mexico's cultural elite, in part from nationalist pride at the comedian's global fame. But the logic of social distinction separating high- and lowbrow culture made such universal acceptance impossible to maintain.[6] Moreno was soon, inevitably, forced to choose between the masses and the critics, and it was not money alone that determined his artistic direction.

The strains of a lifetime spent fulfilling public expectations for Cantinflas left Mario Moreno with a serious case of what Will Kaufman termed "irony fatigue," the psychic exhaustion resulting from his inability to say what he meant without the comedian's inevitable proviso, "Just kidding, folks."[7] Samuel Clemens and Mark Twain represent the most famous example from United States literature of the tension inherent in being a social critic masquerading as a comic. Throughout his life, Clemens longed to repudiate his alter ego and be a spoilsport, but audience demands and financial necessity kept drawing him back to the ironic voice of Twain. Mario Moreno was actually quite serious in private, and his family remembered him playing the part of Cantinflas only in a very good mood.[8] He spent the second half of his life trying to tame his fictional identity and transform the footloose pelado into a respectable bourgeois by toning down his scripts and advertising consumer products. His late attempts to sanitize the pelado into a children's cartoon character revealed how age had magnified the tension between Cantinflas and Moreno. As the actor explained, "The face of Cantinflas is always the same because Cantinflas has no age"—an ironic statement given his own loss of facial movement as a result of advancing age and plastic surgery.[9] Far from being tamed by Moreno, in some ways Cantinflas swallowed up his progenitor.

The genius of Cantinflas was his ability to destabilize situations, making the question of audience reception problematic. From the very beginning critics complained that one could scarcely hear the jokes because of the thunderous laughter filling the theater.[10] The cultural elite found this no great loss, considering his movies to be terribly lowbrow. When *Romeo and Juliet* played on a Mexico City stage a few years after the Cantinflas version, even the former fan and scriptwriter Salvador Novo observed, "What a lamentable trauma these parodies have inflicted on unwitting minds. A youth at one of these functions asked: 'When does the funny stuff start? That Cantinflas movie was really hilarious.'"[11] Carlos Monsiváis found social relevance in his early films, at least through *El gendarme desconocido,* but considered the rest to have been cultural industry–grade sequels. Cantinflas had exchanged his tattered gabardine for the emperor's new clothes, still provoking laughter without having told any jokes.[12] Certainly Mario Moreno's political views, always relatively conservative, became increasingly reactionary as he made personal friendships with high officials of the ruling party such as Miguel Alemán and Carlos Hank González. Yet one should not overestimate the power of mass media to shape public opinion in a uniform manner. After all, Fernando de Fuentes's brilliant, historically revisionist film, *¡Vamanos con Pancho Villa!,* failed at the box office in 1936 partly because people resisted efforts to manipulate their heroic image of the revolutionary general.[13] Moreover, the argument that early Cantinflas films conditioned the reception of all later ones fails to account for successive generations, who laughed without having seen Cantinflas first in such works as *Ahí está el detalle.*

From the very beginning, people interpreted Cantinflas movies in radically different ways. True, many people remembered his movies simply as wholesome entertainment, an agreeable way to spend an afternoon with the children.[14] Nevertheless, the subversive edge of the pelado survived long after that supposed "golden age" for countless viewers; for example, one of the Cuban revolutionaries who fought with Fidel Castro in the Sierra Maestra Mountains adopted Cantinflas as his nom de guerre.[15] The most popular Venezuelan comic at the end of the millennium, Emilio Lovera, admitted, "If only I could be a copy of Cantinflas, to have lived in his time and had his spontaneity, which was his basic strength and genius to make people laugh."[16] The film *Star Maps* (1997), by Puerto Rican director Miguel Arteta, used Cantinflas as a spiritual guide to a troubled woman. Cantinflas even appeared as an ironic Buddha, complete with the third eye of wisdom, in a piece called *Infinito Botanica NYC 2000* contributed to the Biennial Exhibition of American Art at the Whitney Museum by San Antonio artist Franco Mondini-Ruiz.

The test of Cantinflas's influence ultimately lay in asking to whom the cantinfladas belonged, the speaker or the listener. The simple-minded and disjointed humor that critics found appalling may actually have been the secret to Cantinflas's great success in that it provided such wide latitude for interpretation by individual viewers. Each member of the audience could find—or invent—different jokes within his rambling discourses, for his wordplay derived from the Mexican genius for albures. Even the meaning of the name Cantinflas was open to exegesis, because Moreno wisely refused to explain it definitively. One cannot overlook a certain coercive element to his double entendres: the fear that a person who did not understand the joke was, by definition, its object. But in the end, Cantinflas's humor was always more procedural than substantive, emphasizing a method of inverting social hierarchies rather than any particular joke. As a result, Moreno's endorsement of the authoritarian regime may have sounded to many viewers like just another meaningless cantinflada. Witness Che Guevara; according to Paco Ignacio Taibo II, when late in life the revolutionary commander "wanted to transform himself, when he wanted not to take himself seriously, he cultivated a resemblance to Cantinflas."[17]

One final glance back at the comedian's career can be taken in the looking glass of caricature. Mexicans love a good caricature, one that reflects a person like a fun house mirror, exaggerating the features to reveal the soul. The country's most influential artist of the nineteenth century, José Guadalupe Posada, recorded an entire era through satiric woodcuts of everyone from street corner pelados to the dictator Porfirio Díaz. A generation later, revolutionary president Alvaro Obregón paid with his life for his fondness of caricature when an assassin's pistol lurked behind a young artist's pad. Cantinflas was born from a caricature, Chupamirto, and as his cinematic fame grew, he swallowed up his comic strip model. Artist Jesús Acosta gradually modified the character, with Mario Moreno's encouragement, into a replica of Cantinflas and finally took a job drawing movie posters for Posa Films.[18] At first sketch artists transmogrified Mario Moreno into a monkey, the better to shock bourgeois complacency in the 1930s. Those early caricatures also revealed the feminine features of Cantinflas, his curving hips emphasized all the more by drooping pants. But the youthful face ultimately became an artificial mask when drawn on movie posters in the 1970s. As a symbol of the Mexican nation, Cantinflas was always just a caricature, but no less beloved because of it.

NOTES

Introduction, Pages xv–xxvi

1. René Cisneros, "The Comic Verbal and Nonverbal Expression in the Mario Moreno Cantinflas Film: Meaning and Illocutionary Force" (Ph.D. diss., University of Texas, Austin, 1978), 89 (unless otherwise noted, all ellipses are in the original *cantinfladas*). The difficulty of translating the ambiguous, slang-filled humor of Cantinflas into English was always the comic's greatest barrier to success in the United States, and it has proven no easier for this biographer. As the footnotes reveal, I have drawn on a variety of sources, although responsibility for all translations is ultimately my own.

2. Quoted by John Mraz, "Mario Moreno Reyes (Cantinflas)," in *Encyclopedia of Mexico: History, Society and Culture,* ed. Michael S. Werner, 2 vols. (Chicago, 1997), 2:951.

3. Emilio García Riera, *El cine mexicano* (Mexico, 1963), 77.

4. For a discussion of gender in the films of Cantinflas, see María Paz Balibrea Enríquez, "Cantinflas: ¿Dónde está el detalle?" *Revista de Cultura: El Acordeón* 15 (September–December 1995): 5–14.

5. Salvador Novo, *Nueva grandeza mexicana: Ensayo sobre la ciudad de México y sus alrededores en 1946* (Mexico, 1992), 41.

6. "La polémica del siglo: Cantinflas vs. Morones!" *Todo,* August 12, 1937.

7. Carlos Monsiváis, *Mexican Postcards,* trans. John Kraniauskas (London, 1997), 99–100.

8. Roger Bartra, *The Cage of Melancholy: Identity and Metamorphosis in the Mexican Character,* trans. Christopher J. Hall (New Brunswick, NJ, 1992), 129.

9. "Cantinflas es un burgues," *Todo,* September 19, 1940. Cantinflas's attacks on the labor leader Vicente Lombardo Toledano demonstrated the conservatism of Moreno's politics already evident in the 1930s.

10. R. Larriva Urias [Carlos Rivas Larrauri], "Cantinflas íntimo," *Todo,* October 28, 1937.

11. Marshall Berman, *All That Is Solid Melts into Air: The Experience of Modernity* (New York, 1982).

12. Miguel Covarrubias, "Slapstick and Venom: Politics, Tent Shows and Comedians" *Theater Arts* 22 (August 1938): 587–96.

13. Quoted by Filo Blanco de la Hoz, "Celebridades comerciales," *Todo,* January 9, 1941.

14. Adolfo Fernández Bustamante, "Mexicanismos y dichos mexicanos," *Todo,* January 1, 1942.

15. Pedro Granados, *Las carpas de México,* (Mexico, 1984), 19–25, 48.

16. "La autocandidatura presidencial de Cantinflas en 1938," *Proceso,* April 27, 1993.

17. Quoted by Will Kaufman, *The Comedian as Confidence Man: Studies in Irony Fatigue* (Detroit, 1997), 40. See also the theoretical discussion in William H. Beezley, "Recent Mexican Political Humor," *Journal of Latin American Lore* 11, no. 2 (Winter 1985): 195–223.

18. Mikhail Bakhtin, *Rabelais and His World,* trans. Hélène Iswolsky (Cambridge, MA, 1968).

19. How many suburban fans of "gangsta" rap music really understand the lyrics—either in Orange County, California, or Osaka, Japan?

20. This transnational cinema is described by the essays in Ann Marie Stock, ed., *Framing Latin American Cinema* (Minneapolis, 1998).

21. Mraz, "Mario Moreno," 2:952; Ilan Stavans, *The Riddle of Cantinflas: Essays on Hispanic Popular Culture* (Albuquerque, 1998), 31–52; Monsiváis, *Mexican Postcards,* 105.

22. Duende Filme [Angel Alcántara Pastor], "Nuestro cinema," *El Universal,* September 12, 1943.

23. *Jueves de Excélsior,* September 16, 1943.

Chapter 1, Pages 1–32

1. Juan Pedro Viqueira Albán, *Propriety and Permissiveness in Bourbon Mexico,* trans. Sonya Lipsett-Rivera and Sergio Rivera Ayala (Wilmington, DE, 1999), 97–103.

2. Magnus Mörner, *Race Mixture in the History of Latin America* (Boston, 1967); R. Douglas Cope, *The Limits of Racial Domination: Plebeian Society in Colonial Mexico City, 1660–1720* (Madison, WI, 1994).

3. Gabriel Haslip-Viera, "The Underclass," in *Cities and Society in Colonial Latin America,* ed. Louisa Schell Hoberman and Susan Migden Socolow (Albuquerque, NM, 1986), 285–312.

4. Michael C. Scardaville, "Alcohol Abuse and Tavern Reform in Late Colonial Mexico City," *Hispanic American Historical Review* 60, no. 4 (November 1980): 643–71; John E. Kicza, "The Pulque Trade of Late Colonial Mexico City," *The Americas* 37, no. 2 (October 1980): 193–216.

5. Linda A. Curcio, "A Position of Disrepute: Perception of the Acting Profession in Colonial Mexico," paper presented at the Rocky Mountain Council on Latin American Studies, Santa Fe, New Mexico, March 21, 1996.

6. Silvia Marina Arrom, "¿De la caridad a la beneficencia? Las reformas a la asistencia pública desde la perspectiva del Hospicio de Pobres de la ciudad de México, 1856–1871," in *Ciudad de México: Instituciones, actores sociales y conflicto político, 1774–1931,* ed. Carlos Illades and Ariel Rodríguez Kuri (Zamora, Michoacán, 1996), 21–53; Haslip-Viera, "The Underclass," 302–6.

7. Michael Johns, *The City of Mexico in the Age of Díaz* (Austin, TX, 1997), 13–14, 48–57, quote from 55.

8. Octavio Paz, *The Labyrinth of Solitude*, trans. Lysander Kemp (New York, 1961), 29–46.

9. Carleton Beals, *Mexican Maze* (Philadelphia, 1931), 238.

10. See the excellent essays in Lyman L. Johnson and Sonya Lipsett-Rivera, eds., *The Faces of Honor: Sex, Shame, and Violence in Colonial Latin America* (Albuquerque, NM, 1998); Robert McCaa, "*Calidad, Clase*, and Marriage in Colonial Mexico: The Case of Parral, 1788–90," *Hispanic American Historical Review* 64, no. 3 (August 1984): 477–502.

11. John M. Ingham, *Mary, Michael, and Lucifer: Folk Catholicism in Central Mexico* (Austin, TX, 1986), 144.

12. Cheryl English Martin, "Popular Speech and Social Order in Northern Mexico, 1650–1830," *Comparative Studies in Society and History* 32, no. 2 (1990): 305–24; Sonya Lipsett-Rivera, "*De obra y palabra:* Patterns of Insults in Mexico, 1750–1856," *The Americas* 54, no. 4 (April 1998): 511–39.

13. Sergio Rivera Ayala, "Lewd Songs and Dances from the Streets of Eighteenth-Century New Spain," in *Rituals of Rule, Rituals of Resistance: Public Celebrations and Popular Culture in Mexico,* ed. William H. Beezley, Cheryl English Martin, and William E. French (Wilmington, DE, 1994), 34.

14. Francisco Rosete Aranda, *Al compania de titeres de los Rosete Aranda* (Tlaxcala, 1993), 75–77.

15. Juan Manuel Aurrecoechea and Armando Bartra, *Puros cuentos: La historia de la historieta en México, 1874–1934* (Mexico, 1988), 238–40. Quote from *El Universal,* September 20, 1927.

16. Raúl Béjar Navarro, "Ensayo pa' balconear al mexicano desde un punto de vista muy acá," in *El mexicano: Aspectos culturales y psico-sociales* (Mexico, 1983), 201–37; Luis Fernando Lara, "Mexican Spanish," in *Encyclopedia of Mexico,* ed. Michael S. Werner (Chicago, 1997) 2:873–77; Bartra, *The Cage of Melancholy,* 127–28; Armando Jiménez, *Vocabulario prohibido de la picardía mexicana* (Mexico, 1976).

17. Fernández Bustamante, "Mexicanismos y dichos mexicanos."

18. Irving A. Leonard, *Baroque Times in Old Mexico* (Ann Arbor, MI, 1959), 138.

19. Lara, "Mexican Spanish," 2:876. The foremost modern authority on popular humor, Armando Jiménez, has described the albur as the "principal self-defense for well-bred Mexicans." See his *Sitios de rompe y rasga en la Ciudad de México* (Mexico, 1998), 213.

20. Clifford Geertz, *Negara: Theater State in Bali* (Princeton, NJ, 1980); Jürgen Habermas, *The Structural Transformation of the Public Sphere: An Inquiry into a Category of Bourgeois Society,* trans. Thomas Burger (Cambridge, MA, 1989); Dena Goodman, *The Republic of Letters: A Cultural History of the French Enlightenment* (Ithaca, NY, 1994); James H. Johnson, *Listening in Paris: A Cultural History* (Berkeley, CA, 1996).

21. M. A. Campero report, May 8, 1866, 800/385, Archivo Histórico de la Ciudad de México (hereafter cited as AHCM); Viqueira Albán, *Propriety and Permissiveness,* 78.

22. Armando de Maria y Campos, *El teatro de género chico en la revolución mexicana* (Mexico, 1996), 27, 46, 66, 81.

23. Ibid., 90–97; John B. Nomland, *Teatro mexicano contemporáneo [1900–1950]* (Mexico, 1967), 147.

24. Maria y Campos, *El teatro de género chico,* 115–16.

25. José Clemente Orozco, *An Autobiography,* trans. Robert C. Stevenson (Austin, TX, 1962), 45.

26. Maria y Campos, *El teatro de género chico,* 256.

27. Ibid., 302; Covarrubias, "Slapstick and Venom," 587.

28. Orozco, *An Autobiography,* 45.

29. Covarrubias, "Slapstick and Venom," 588.

30. Arnaldo Córdova, *La Revolución en crisis: La aventura del maximato* (Mexico, 1995), 40–44.

31. Josephus Daniels to Secretary of State, February 27, 1934, box 661, Josephus Daniels Papers, Manuscripts Division, Library of Congress, Washington, DC; "Lo cómico y lo patrio," *La Nación,* July 8, 1944.

32. Heather Fowler-Salamini and Mary Kay Vaughan, eds., *Creating Spaces, Shaping Transitions: Women of the Mexican Countryside, 1850–1990* (Tucson, AZ, 1994).

33. Anne Rubenstein, *Bad Language, Naked Ladies, and Other Threats to the Nation: A Political History of Comic Books in Mexico* (Durham, NC, 1998); Nomland, *Teatro mexicano contemporáneo,* 159.

34. Granados, *Carpas de México,* 19–22; Max Miller, *Mexico Around Me* (New York, 1937), 143–56.

35. Maria y Campos, *El teatro de género chico,* 208.

36. Stage homosexuality was prevalent in New York at exactly this time. George Chauncy, *Gay New York: Gender, Urban Culture, and the Making of the Gay Male World, 1890–1940* (New York, 1995).

37. Orozco, *An Autobiography,* 46. See also Maria y Campos, *El teatro de género chico,* 52.

38. Hipólito Amor report, August 29, 1922, 812.1708, AHCM; Susan E. Bryan, "Teatro popular y sociedad durante el porfiriato," *Historia Mexicana* 33, no. 129 (1983): 130–69.

39. *Jueves de Excélsior,* November 20, 1941.

40. Socorro Merlín, *Vida y milagros de las carpas. La carpa en México, 1930–1950* (Mexico, 1995), 43–59; quote from Beals, *Mexican Maze,* 253.

41. Henry Jenkins, *"What Made Pistachio Nuts?" Early Sound Comedy and the Vaudeville Aesthetic,* (New York, 1992), 71.

42. R. Larriva Urias [Carlos Riva Larrauri], "Cantínflas íntimo," *Todo,* October 28, 1937.

43. Miguel Angel Morales, *Cantinflas: Amo de las carpas,* 3 vols. (Mexico, 1996), 1:16–21.

44. Quoted in Miguel Angel Morales, "La primera entrevista a Cantinflas," *El Nacional,* June 25, 1992. See also Guadalupe Elizalde, *Mario Moreno y Cantinflas . . . Rompen el silencio* (Mexico, 1994), 239–42.

45. Miguel Angel Morales, *Cómicos de México* (Mexico, 1987), 148; Granados, *Carpas de México,* 112–14.

46. Elizalde, *Mario Moreno y Cantinflas,* 242–43.

47. Miguel Léon-Portilla, ed., *Native Mesoamerican Spirituality* (New York, 1980), 158.

48. Julie Greer Johnson, *Satire in Colonial Spanish America: Turning the New World Upside Down* (Austin, TX, 1993).

49. José Joaquín Fernández de Lizardi, *The Itching Parrot,* trans. Katherine Anne Porter (Garden City, NY, 1942), 158.

50. *El Universal,* September 25, 1927.

Chapter 2, Pages 33–64

1. Granados, *Carpas de México,* 56–60, 86; Morales, *Cómicos de México,* 89, 149.

2. Nomland, *Teatro mexicano contemporáneo,* 175; *Todo,* October 28, 1937.

3. Armando Jiménez, *Sitios de rompe y rasga en la Ciudad de México* (Mexico, 1998), 235–36; Granados, *Carpas de México,* 124.

4. Covarrubias, "Slapstick and Venom," 594–95; Maria y Campos, *El teatro de género chico,* 389; Miguel Ángel Morales, "Ahí está el detalle: Ruta teatral de Cantinflas," *El Nacional,* August, 12, 1993.

5. Andrew G. Wood, *La Hora Azul: Agustín Lara and Modernity in Mexico* (Wilmington, DE, forthcoming); Julia Tuñón, *Mujeres de luz y sombra en el cine mexicano: La construcción de un imagen 1939–1952* (Mexico, 1998), 47; Granados, *Carpas de México,* 28.

6. *Todo,* November 3, December 22, 1936; Nomland, *Teatro mexicano contemporáneo,* 177.

7. Samuel Ramos, *Profile of Man and Culture in Mexico* (Austin, TX, 1962), 58–59.

8. Ingham, *Mary, Michael, and Lucifer,* 144–45. On the pelado, Cantinflas, as a symbol of national assimilation, see Balibrea Enríquez, "Cantinflas," 6–7.

9. Xavier Villaurrutia, *Crítica cinematográfica* (Mexico, 1970), 242.

10. William B. Taylor, *Drinking, Homicide, and Rebellion in Colonial Mexican Villages* (Stanford, 1979), 82.

11. Quoted in Eduardo de la Vega Alfaro, *Arcady Boytler* (Guadalajara, 1992), 172.

12. Ibid., 116.

13. *El Universal,* September 12, 1943.

14. John Mraz, "Photographing Political Power in Mexico," in *Citizens of the Pyramid: Essays on Mexican Political Culture,* ed. Wil G. Pansters (Amsterdam, 1997), 147–80.

15. Nomland, *Teatro mexicano contemporáneo,* 162.

16. Adrian Bantjes, *As If Jesus Walked on Earth: Cardenismo, Sonora, and the Mexican Revolution* (Wilmington, DE, 1998); John W. Sherman, *The Mexican Right: The End of Revolutionary Reform* (Westport, CT, 1997), 59.

17. Nomland, *El teatro contemporáneo,* 161; Maria y Campos, *El teatro de género chico,* 382.

18. Morales, *Cómicos de México,* 156.

19. Alfonso Taracena, *La revolucíon desvirtuada,* 7 vols. (Mexico, 1968), 5:177–78; Salvador Novo, *La vida en México en el periodo presidencial de Lázaro Cárdenas* (Mexico, 1994), 82.

20. "The Polemic of the Century: Cantinflas vs. Morones," *Todo,* August 12, 1937.

21. Novo, *La vida en México,* 122; Carlos Monsiváis, *Amor perdido* (Mexico, 1977), 284.

22. "La autocandidatura presidencial."

23. Quoted in Carlos Bonfil, ed., *Cantinflas: Aguila o sol* (Mexico, 1993), 24.

24. "La autocandidatura presidencial," 22.

25. Ibid.

26. Merlín, *Vida y milagros,* 19.

27. Urias, "Cantínflas íntimo."

28. Quoted in Bonfil, *Cantinflas: Aguila o sol,* 43.

29. Urias, "Cantinflas intimo."

30. Maria y Campos, *El teatro de género chico,* 394.

31. "Teatro," *La Nación,* January 24, 1942.

32. Villaurrutia, *Crítica cinematográfica,* 253.

33. Monsiváis, *Amor perdido,* 265–96.

34. Emilio García Riera, *Historia documental del cine mexicano* (hereafter cited as HDCM), 17 vols. (Guadalajara, 1992), 2:96.

35. Matthew Gutmann, *The Meanings of Macho: Being a Man in Mexico City* (Berkeley, CA, 1996), 124.

36. Chris Straayer, "Redressing the 'Natural': The Temporary Transvestite Film," *Wide Angle* 14 (January 1992): 36–55.

37. Orozco, *An Autobiography,* 46.

Chapter 3, Pages 65–96

1. Juan Bustillo Oro, *Vida cinematográfica* (Mexico, 1984), 185–86.

2. Pierre Bourdieu, *Distinction: A Social Critique of the Judgement of Taste,* trans. Richard Nice (Cambridge, MA, 1984).

3. *Todo,* January 13, 1938.

4. *El Cine Gráfico,* April 18, 1943, June 27, 1943.

5. Santiago Reachi, *La Revolución, Cantinflas, y JoLoPo* (Mexico, 1982), 157–60. See also the advertisements in *Hoy,* July 3, 1943, January 8, 1944.

6. García Riera, HDCM, 2:159.

7. Bustillo Oro, *Vida cinematográfica,* 186.

8. Translation, slightly modified, from Cisneros, "Comic Verbal and Non-verbal Expression," 34–38.

9. *El Universal,* September 6, 1940.

10. Cisneros, "Comic Verbal and Nonverbal Expression," 42–56.

11. García Riera, HDCM, 2:160.

12. *Jueves de Excélsior,* June 5, 1941.

13. Reachi, *La Revolución, Cantinflas, y JoLoPo,* 174; Elizalde, *Mario Moreno y Cantinflas,* 171.

14. Elizalde, *Mario Moreno y Cantinflas,* 120.

15. The importance of Moreno's improvisational ability becomes readily apparent in an examination of the script, which included none of the film's best jokes—particularly the gendered humor—and often merely indicated, "Cantinflas executes his 'danzón' in his own style with all of his comic detalles as appropriate." Jaime Salvador, *El gendarme desconocido,* 586/11887, Propiedad Artisticas y Literarias, Archivo General de la Nación (hereafter AGN).

16. "Luces y sombras," *Todo,* September 19, 1941.

17. Elizalde, *Mario Moreno y Cantinflas,* 49.

18. *Cinema Reporter,* October 17, 1941, December 5, 1941.

19. Tuñón, *Mujeres de luz y sombra,* 44–58, quote from 45.

20. *El Cine Gráfico,* June 27, 1943; *Cinema Reporter,* January 16, 1942; "Cantinflas se encumbra," *Todo,* January 1, 1942; "Luces y sombras," *Todo,* October 1, 1942.

21. *El Cine Gráfico,* January 3, 1943.

22. García Riera, HDCM, 2:262.

23. "Cine," *La Nación,* September 5, 1942. See also "Luces y sombras," *Todo,* July 30, 1942; *El Universal,* August 29, 1942; "Ultimos estrenos," *Hoy,* September 5, 1942.

24. Villaurrutia, *Crítica cinematográfica,* 306. See also *Cinema Reporter,* August 20, 1943; *Jueves de Excélsior,* September 16, 1943.

25. Humberto Olguin Hermida, "El teatro de México," *Hoy,* September 26, 1942.

26. González, "Teatro," *La Nación,* December 11, 1943, December 18, 1943; *Jueves de Excélsior,* January 1, 1942; *Cinema Reporter,* August 20, 1943.

27. Quoted in García Riera, HDCM, 3:49.

28. Duende Filme, "Nuestro cinema."

29. *New York Times,* March 18, 1939.

30. *El Cine Gráfico,* March 14, 1943.

31. *New York Times,* June 17, 1944.

32. *El Mundo* (San Juan), April 27, 1944.

33. "Luces y sombras," *Todo,* March 12, 1942; *El Cine Gráfico Anuario,* 1945–1946.

34. Douglas Butterworth and John K. Chance, *Latin American Urbanization* (Cambridge, England, 1981), 51–72.

35. Elizalde, *Mario Moreno y Cantinflas,* 307.

36. *Todo,* April 10, 1943; Ignacio Arizmendi, "No tenemos policia," *Todo,* July 3, 1941, August 14, 1941.

37. Natalio Burstein, "Dos fiestas bancarias," *Hoy,* October 10, 1942.

38. *Jueves de Excélsior,* February 6, 1941.

39. Ibid., June 5, 1941.

Chapter 4, Pages 97–127

1. Ernest Gruening, *Mexico and Its Heritage* (New York, 1936), 371.

2. Sarah García et al. to Manuel Avila Camacho, April 11, 1944, 432/64-2, Ramo Presidentes, Manuel Avila Camacho, AGN.

3. Ibid.

4. Jesús Grovas to Avila Camacho, December 24, 1940, 432/64-1, AGN; *Hoy,* September 13, 1941.

5. Quoted in Friedrich E. Schuler, *Mexico between Hitler and Roosevelt: Mexican Foreign Relations in the Age of Lázaro Cárdenas, 1934–1940* (Albuquerque, NM, 1998), 174.

6. Quoted in Jorge Mejía Prieto, *Fidel Velázquez: 47 años de historia y poder* (Mexico, 1980), 24.

7. Luis Medina, *Del cardenismo al avilacamachismo,* vol. 18 of *Historia de la Revolución Mexicana* (Mexico, 1978), 287.

8. Ibid., 177, 291, 302.

9. *Hoy,* April 1, 1944.

10. Sarah García et al. to Avila Camacho, April 11, 1944, Enrique Solís to Avila Camacho, April 21, 1944, 432/64-2, AGN; "Cine," *La Nación,* February 24, 1945.

11. *Diario de la Marina* (Havana), April 11, 1944.

12. Enrique Solís to Avila Camacho, July 27, August 6, August 8, 1944, 432/64-2, AGN.

13 . Elena Poniatowska, *La mirada que limpia: Gabriel Figueroa,* vol. 3 of *Todo México* (Mexico, 1996), 58.

14. *Hoy,* February 17, 1945.

15. Poniatowska, *La mirada que limpia,* 61.

16. Fidel Cortés to Avila Camacho, February 16, 1945, 432/64-2, AGN.

17. *El Universal Gráfico,* February 15, 1945.

18. Fidel Velázquez to Francisco Trujillo Gurría, February 27, 1945, 432/64-3, AGN.

19. *El Universal Gráfico,* February 27, 1945.

20. Rosa Castro, "Cinematicas," *Hoy,* March 3, 1945; "Cine," *La Nación,* March 17, 1945.

21. Salvador Carrillo et al. to Avila Camacho, March 3, 1945, 432/64-3, AGN.

22. "Intergremiologia," *Hoy,* March 24, 1945.

23. Ibid.

24. "Cine," *La Nación,* March 17, 1945.

25. "Escenas de la asamblea de actores en el frontón," *Cine Mexicano,* March 24, 1945.

26. Roberto Soto to Avila Camacho, June 30, 1945, 432/64-3, AGN; "El líder Palillo habla de trompudolucto," *La Nación,* April 21, 1945.

27. "Cine," *La Nación,* May 12, 1945. See also León Zedillo et al. to Avila Camacho, May 15, 1945, 432/64-3, AGN; *El Universal Gráfico,* May 10, 1945; *Cinema Reporter,* May 12, 1945.

28. *El Universal Gráfico,* July 30, 1945; *Cinema Reporter,* July 28, 1945; *Hoy,* September 1, 1945.

29. Mario Moreno to Fidel Velázquez, September 6, 1945, 432/64-3, AGN.

30. "Trabajo," *La Nación,* September 15, 1945.

31. Jesús González Gallo to Fidel Velázquez, September 11, 1945, 432/64-3, AGN.

32. Lester D. Langley, *Mexico and the United States: The Fragile Relationship* (Boston, 1991), 29.

33. *Hoy,* February 9, 1946; *El Universal Gráfico,* February 20, 1946, March 5, 1946, "Política," *La Nación,* March 9, 1946.

34. *El Universal Gráfico,* February 2, 1946.

35. Mario Pavón Flores to Avila Camacho, February 12, 1946, 432/64-3, AGN.

36. Salvador Novo, *La vida en México durante el periodo presidencial de Manuel Avila Camacho* (Mexico, 1994), 499.

37. *El Universal Gráfico,* March 7, 1946.

38. *Excélsior,* March 10, 1946.

39. *El Universal Gráfico,* March 9, 1946.

40. Transcript of STPC Assembly, March 11, 1946, 432/64, AGN, pp. 13–14.

41. *La Prensa,* March 14, 1946.

42. *El Nacional,* March 15, 1946; *El Universal Gráfico,* March 12, 1946.

43. *El Universal Gráfico,* March 29, 1946.

44. "Historia gráfica exclusiva del conflicto intergremial," *La Nación,* March 30, 1946.

45. See Seth Fein, *Transnational Projections: The United States in the Golden Age of Mexican Cinema* (Durham, NC, forthcoming); idem, "From Collaboration to Containment: Hollywood and the International Political Economy of Mexican Cinema after the Second World War," in *Mexico's Cinema: A Century of Film and Filmmakers,* ed. Joanne Hershfield and David R. Maciel (Wilmington, DE, 1999).

46. Gonzalo N. Santos, *Memorias* (Mexico, 1984), 836. The author did not record Moreno's reaction to this remark.

Chapter 5, Pages 129–161

1. "Les films et les acteurs au festival de Cannes," *Le Figaro,* September 22–23, 1946; Henri Magnan, "Première journée du festival de Cannes," *Le Monde,* September 22–23, 1946.

2. "Cantinflas en Cannes," *El Universal,* October 24, 1946; *Cinema Reporter,* October 26, 1946.

3. "Habla Cantinflas," *La Nación,* May 25, 1946.

4. *Cinema Reporter,* November 12, 1949.

5. Stephen R. Niblo, *War, Diplomacy, and Development: The United States and Mexico, 1938–1954* (Wilmington, DE, 1995).

6. Ibid., 176, 215, 230; García Riera, HDCM, 4:205.

7. Carl J. Mora, *Mexican Cinema: Reflections of a Society, 1896–1988*, rev. ed. (Berkeley, CA, 1989), 76; García Riera, HDCM 4:107, 6:158.

8. Miguel Contreras Torres, *El libro negro del cine mexicano* (Mexico, 1960), 269; Niblo, *War, Diplomacy, and Development*, 229; *Cinema Reporter*, October 12, 1946.

9. García Riera, HDCM, 4:191; Tuñón, *Mujeres de luz y sombra*, 55, 57; Mora, *Mexican Cinema*, 99; J. Villegas, *La industria cinematográfica nacional* (Mexico, 1945), 24, 61–65.

10. *Cinema Reporter*, July 10, 1948.

11. Contreras Torres, *El libro negro*, 269; García Riera, HDCM, 4:107, 5:7–8; Villegas, *La industria cinematográfica*, 66.

12. Claudia de Icaza, *Gloria y Jorge: Cartas de amor y conflicto* (Mexico, 1993), 120.

13. *Excélsior*, April 5, 1953.

14. Niblo, *War, Diplomacy, and Development*, 119.

15. *Cinema Reporter*, October 4, 1947.

16. Ibid., December 18, 1948.

17. Ibid., February 19, 1949.

18. Luis Medina, *Civilismo y modernización del autoritarismo*, vol. 20 of *Historia de la Revolución mexicana* (Mexico, 1979), 120–32.

19. Ibid., 159; Monsiváis, *Amor perdido*, 289.

20. García Riera, HDCM, 5:72.

21. Medina, *Civilismo y modernización*, 36.

22. Ibid., 62–67.

23. *Hoy*, February 9, 1952.

24. Ibid., July 12, 1952.

25. Daniel Cosío Villegas, *La sucesión presidencial* (Mexico, 1975), 139.

26. John Mraz, "Germán Valdés (Tin Tan)," in *Encyclopedia of Mexico: History, Society and Culture*, ed. Michael S. Werner, 2 vols. (Chicago, 1997), 2:1516.

27. *Hoy*, September 14, 1946.

28. Diego Rivera, *My Art, My Life* (New York, 1960), 282.

29. Maria y Campos, *El teatro de género chico*, 454.

30. "Teatro," *La Nación*, May 10, 1953.

31. *Novedades*, May 5, 1953, quoted in Maria y Campos, *El teatro de género chico*, 454; *Mañana*, June 6, 1953, quoted in Elizalde, *Mario Moreno y Cantinflas*, 64.

32. Quoted in *El Cine Gráfico*, September 16, 1956. See also *Cinevoz*, May 15, 1949; *Cinema Reporter*, January 4, 1947.

33. *Cinema Reporter*, November 9, 1946.

34. "Mano a mano Cantinflas-Mariles," *La Nación*, February 28, 1949; "Habla Cantinflas," *La Nación*, May 24, 1946.

35. "Están destruyendo a Cantinflas," *Siempre*, October 5, 1954.

36. *Hoy*, March 20, 1948.

37. Benito Riaño, "Cantinflas en el pais de las hadas," June 7, 1940, 566/10930; Fernando Mendez García, "El Gendarme," June 4, 1940, 566/10917; Francisco Colmenero y Cruz, "Cantinflas Detective," August 16, 1951, 979/

12583; Maximiliano Gómez Zavala, "Cantinflas marinero," August 15, 1951, 982/12839, Propiedad Artisticas y Literarias, AGN.

38. Paco Ignacio Taibo II, *Ernesto Guevara, también conocido como El Che* (Mexico, 1996), 106.

39. J. M. Taylor, *Eva Perón: The Myths of a Woman* (Chicago, 1979), 105.

40. *La Prensa,* January 3, 1953, January 4, 1953.

41. Ibid., January 6, 1953.

42. García Riera, HDCM, 7:11.

Chapter 6, Pages 163–183

1. Sheridan Morley, *The Other Side of the Moon: The Life of David Niven* (New York, 1985), 195.

2. Michael Todd Jr., *A Valuable Property: The Life Story of Michael Todd* (New York, 1983).

3. Thomas Renzi, *Jules Verne on Film* (Jefferson, NC, 1998), 23–24.

4. See the insightful discussion in Ella Shohat, "Gender and Culture of Empire: Toward a Feminist Ethnography of the Cinema," *Quarterly Review of Film and Video* 13, nos. 1–3 (1991): 45–84.

5. Quoted in Todd, *A Valuable Property,* 300.

6. Ibid., 315.

7. Morales, *Cantinflas,* 2:39, 42.

8. *New York Times,* October 18, 1956.

9. Morley, *Other Side of the Moon,* 194; *Cinema Reporter,* February 20, 1957; "Nuestro cinema," *El Universal,* September 13, 1957.

10. *Cinema Reporter,* March 21, 1956, August 27, 1958; *El Cine Gráfico,* July 14, 1957.

11. C. David Heymann, *An Intimate Biography of Elizabeth Taylor* (New York, 1995), 157; cf. Todd, *A Valuable Property,* 329.

12. *Cinema Reporter,* March 13, 1957.

13. Quotes from *Mañana,* March 2, 1957; March 16, 1957. See also Homenaje program dated March 7, 1957, 135.2/663, Ramo Presidentes, Adolfo Ruiz Cortines, AGN.

14. *Cinema Reporter,* March 27, May 8, May 15, 1957.

15. Santiago Reachi to Angel Carbajal, December 8, 1955, 703.4/984, Presidentes, Ruiz Cortines, AGN; Contreras Torres, *El libro negro,* 192, 268, 321.

16. Todd, *A Valuable Property,* 355–56; *El Cine Gráfico,* September 8, 1957.

17. Reachi, *La Revolución, Cantinflas y JoLoPo,* 181–84; *Cinema Reporter,* March 20, 1957; *El Universal,* March 12, 1957.

18. *La Prensa,* August 1, 1957; *El Universal,* August 9, August 26, 1957. I thank Michael Meyer for these citations.

19. *Cinema Reporter,* January 30, May 8, 1957.

20. See the nine-volume first edition of Emilio García Riera's *Historia documental del cine mexicano* (Mexico, 1969–1978), 7:19; *Cinema Reporter,* May 3, 1959.

21. Reachi, *La Revolución, Cantinflas y JoLoPo,* 171–81, 194–97; *La Prensa,* May 4, 1959.

22. *New York Times,* December 22, 1960; Arthur Murray Aibinder to Adolfo López Mateos, December 27, 1960, 425.1/148, Ramo Presidentes, Adolfo López Mateos, AGN.

23. *Cinema Reporter,* February 17, 1960; "Nuestra Cinema," *El Universal,* May 4, 1962; Reachi, *La Revolución, Cantinflas y JoLoPo,* 180.

24. *El Cine Gráfico,* February 26, 1956.

25. Todd, *A Valuable Property,* 276; *Los Angeles Times,* February 5, 1984.

Chapter 7, Pages 185–210

1. Quoted in García Riera, HDCM, 16:112.

2. Quoted in Mendel Kohansky, *The Disreputable Profession: The Actor in Society* (Westport, CT: Greenwood Press, 1984), 179.

3. Quoted in Elizalde, *Mario Moreno y Cantinflas,* 304.

4. McCaan, *Rebel Males,* 2–16.

5. Elizalde, *Mario Moreno y Cantinflas,* 275–304.

6. Jean Franco, *Plotting Women: Gender and Representation in Mexico* (New York, 1989), 160.

7. Roger D. Hansen, *The Politics of Mexican Development* (Baltimore, 1971), 169; Peter H. Smith, "Mexico since 1946," in *Latin America since 1930: Mexico, Central America, and the Caribbean,* vol. 7 of *The Cambridge History of Latin America,* ed. Leslie Bethell (Cambridge, England, 1990), 119.

8. Roderic Ai Camp, *Crossing Swords: Politics and Religion in Mexico* (New York, 1997), 85–86.

9. Enrique Maza, "El Cantinflas de *El Padrecito* y el Mario Moreno de Carnet," *Proceso,* April 26, 1993.

10. Quoted in the final volume of the first edition of García Riera, HDCM, 9:27.

11. Smith, "Mexico since 1946," 126.

12. Morales, *Cantinflas,* 3:29–30. See also *Excelsior,* April 19, 1963.

13. García Riera, HDCM, 13:115; Duende Filme, "Nuestro cinema," *El Universal,* May 4, 1967.

14. Eric Zolov, *Refried Elvis: The Rise of the Mexican Counterculture* (Berkeley, CA, 1999).

15. Colin M. MacLachlan and William H. Beezley, *El Gran Pueblo: A History of Greater Mexico* (Upper Saddle River, NJ, 1999), 407; Judith Adler Hellman, *Mexico in Crisis,* 2d. ed. (New York, 1983), 173–86.

16. Zolov, *Refried Elvis,* 101.

17. The juxtaposition of women in shifts and go-go boots (1963–1966) and men in hippie fringe and wire-rimmed glasses (1967–1970) reveals an interesting Mexican confluence of styles that were quite distinct in Britain and the United States.

18. Susan Eckstein, *The Poverty of Revolution* (Princeton, NJ, 1977), 54–57; Butterworth and Chance, *Latin American Urbanization,* 91–99.

19. Lourdes Arizpe, *Indígenas en la ciudad: El caso de las "Marías."* (Mexico, 1975); William H. Beezley, *Judas at the Jockey Club and Other Episodes of Porfirian Mexico* (Lincoln, NE, 1987), 112.

20. Mora, *Mexican Cinema,* 162; Nestor García Canclini has described this cultural blending in *Hybrid Cultures: Strategies for Entering and Leaving Modernity* (Minneapolis, 1996).

21. David G. LaFrance, "The Myth and the Reality of 'El Negro' Durazo: Mexico City's Most-Wanted Police Chief," *Studies in Latin American Popular Culture* 9 (1990): 237–48. Quotes from Leopoldo Meraz, "La Película," *El Universal Gráfico,* May 3, 1978.

22. Maza, "El Cantinflas," 18.

23. Clark W. Reynolds, "Why Mexico's 'Stabilizing Development' Was Actually Destabilizing," *World Development* 6 (1978): 1005–18; Alan Riding, *Distant Neighbors: A Portrait of the Mexicans* (New York, 1986), 374.

24. Gregg Barrios, "Little Rich Poor Guy, *"Los Angeles Times,* February 5, 1984.

25. Morales, *Cantinflas,* 3:26–35.

26. Ibid., 3:41; Elizalde, *Mario Moreno y Cantinflas,* 373–76; Carlos Puig, "Espectáculos," *Proceso,* July 30, 1990.

27. "Parece que se ha ido, pero no es cierto." Differences in punctuation between sources compound the ambiguity. Compare Morales, *Cantinflas,* 3:53, with Bonfil, *Cantinflas: Aguila o sol,* 143.

Conclusion, Pages 211–217

1. García Riera, HDCM, 5:16; Carlos A. Oquendo to Adolfo Ruiz Cortines, June 24, 1957, 606.3/22, AGN.

2. *Cinema Reporter,* May 23, 1941.

3. Victor H. Bernstein, "Como los E.E.U.U. boycotean a la democracia en México," *Hoy,* April 1, 1944; Justo Sierra, "Mario Moreno, embajador," *Revista de Revistas,* May 3, 1993.

4. Morales, *Cantinflas,* 1:53; Elizalde, *Mario Moreno y Cantinflas,* 281.

5. Stefan Kanfer, *Groucho: The Life and Times of Julius Henry Marx* (New York, 2000).

6. Bourdieu, *Distinction,* 56–58, 230–49.

7. Kaufman, *The Comedian as Confidence Man,* 11–18, 35–40.

8. Elizalde, *Mario Moreno y Cantinflas,* 263.

9. Quoted in Javier Castelazo, *Cantinflas. Apología de un humilde* (Mexico, n.d. [c. 1970]), 67.

10. "Ultimos estrenos," *Hoy,* September 5, 1942.

11. Salvador Novo, *La vida en México en el periodo presidencial de Miguel Alemán* (Mexico, 1994), 297.

12. Monsiváis, *Mexican Postcards,* 105.

13. Ilene V. O'Malley, *The Myth of the Revolution: Hero Cults and the Institutionalization of the Mexican State, 1920–1940* (New York, 1986), 110.

14. José Bohr interviewed in *Cuadernos de la cineteca nacional: Testimonios para la historia del cine mexicano,* 7 vols. (Mexico, 1975–1976), 1:42.

15. Jon Lee Anderson, *Che: A Revolutionary Life* (New York, 1997), 258.

16. Angel Méndez, "Emilio Lovera, el mejor cómico de la TV," *Horizontes* 105 (1999): 56.

17. Taibo, *Ernesto Guevara,* 106.

18. Aurrecoechea and Bartra, *Puros cuentos,* 2:425.

BIBLIOGRAPHICAL ESSAY

Two biographies of Mario Moreno have appeared since his death, Miguel Ángel Morales, *Cantinflas: Amo de las carpas*, 3 vols. (Mexico, 1996) and Guadalupe Elizalde, *Mario Moreno y Cantinflas . . . rompen el silencio* (Mexico, 1994). Carlos Bonfil edited a commemorative volume, *Cantinflas: Aguila o sol* (Mexico, 1993). Mexico's most distinguished modern cultural critic, Carlos Monsiváis, included an essay on Cantinflas in the collection *Mexican Postcards*, trans. John Kraniauskas (London, 1997), 88–105, and his many as yet untranslated works have also been useful, particularly *Amor perdido* (Mexico, 1977). Another discussion of Cantinflas can be found in Roger Bartra's excellent study of national identity and cultural hegemony in Mexico, *The Cage of Melancholy: Identity and Metamorphosis in the Mexican Character* (New Brunswick, NJ, 1992). The most succinct but insightful sketch of the comedian is by John Mraz, "Mario Moreno Reyes (Cantinflas)," in *Encyclopedia of Mexico: History, Society and Culture*, 2 vols. (Chicago, 1997), 2:951. Ilan Stavans examined the comic's social *habitus* in *The Riddle of Cantinflas: Essays on Mexican Popular Culture* (Albuquerque, NM, 1998), 31–52. For a perspective on gender, see María Paz Balibrea Enríquez, "Cantinflas: ¿Dónde está el detalle?" *Revista de Cultura: El Acordeón* 15 (September–December 1998): 5–14. Finally, a linguistic analysis of his humor was performed by René Cisneros, "The Comic Verbal and Nonverbal Expression in the Mario Moreno Cantinflas Film: Meaning and Illocutionary Force" (Ph.D. dissertation, University of Texas at Austin, 1978).

For the theatrical roots of Cantinflas, start with the brief sketch of the carpa theater by Mexican artist Miguel Covarrubias, "Slapstick and Venom: Politics, Tent Shows and Comedians," *Theater Arts* 22 (August 1938): 685–96. Invaluable chronicles were recorded by Armando de Maria y Campos, *El teatro de género chico en la revolución mexicana* (Mexico, 1996); Pedro Granados, *Carpas de México: Leyendas, anécdotas e historia del teatro popular* (Mexico, 1984); Miguel Ángel Morales, *Cómicos de México* (Mexico, 1987); and Armando Jiménez, *Sitios de rompe y rasga en la Ciudad de México* (Mexico, 1998). Academic studies include John B. Nomland, *El teatro mexicano contemporáneo [1900–1950]* (Mexico, 1967); and Socorro Merlín, *Vida y milagros de las carpas. La carpa en México, 1930–1950* (Mexico, 1995).

The indispensable first source for any study of Mexican cinema is Emilio García Riera, *Historia documental del cine mexicano*, 18 vols. (Guadalajara, 1992), which provides production data, plot synopses, and commentaries on every feature film made in Mexico before 1976. For excellent thematic surveys, see Paulo Antonio Paranaguá, ed., *Mexican Cinema*, trans. Ana M. López (London, 1995); and García Riera, *El cine mexicano* (Mexico, 1963). Insightful synthetic works include Aurelio de los Reyes, *Medio siglo de cine mexicano* (Mexico, 1987); and Carl J. Mora, *Mexican Cinema: Reflections of a Society, 1896–1988*, rev. ed. (Berkeley, 1989). For excellent studies of gender in Mexican cinema, see Julia Tuñón, *Mujeres de luz y sombra en el cine mexicano: La construcción de una imagen, 1939–1952* (Mexico, 1998); Joanne Hershfield, *Mexican Cinema/Mexican Woman, 1940–1950* (Tucson, AZ, 1996); and Ana M. López, "Tears of Desire: Women and Melodrama in the 'Old' Mexican Cinema," in *Mediating Two Worlds: Cinematic Encounters in the Americas*, ed. John King, Ana M. López, and Manuel Alvarado (London, 1993). An invaluable study of Moreno's formative director is provided by Eduardo de la Vega Alfaro, *Arcady Boytler*, vol. 2 of *Pioneros del cine sonoro* (Guadalajara, 1992). For film reviews by the leading critic of the "golden age" of Mexican cinema, see Xavier Villaurrutia, *Crítica cinematográfica* (Mexico, 1970). Also helpful was the oral history compilation *Cuadernos de la cineteca nacional: Testimonios para la historia del cine mexicano*, 7 vols. (Mexico, 1975–1976). For the filming of *Ahí está el detalle*, see Juan Bustillo Oro, *Vida cinematográfica* (Mexico, 1984). On *Around the World in 80 Days*, see Michael Todd Jr., *A Valuable Property: The Life Story of Michael Todd* (New York, 1983).

Useful comparative works on early cinema include Steven J. Ross, *Working-Class Hollywood: Silent Film and the Shaping of Class in America* (Princeton, NJ, 1998); Leo Charney and Vanessa R. Schwartz, eds., *Cinema and the Invention of Modern Life* (Berkeley, 1995); David Robinson, *Chaplin: His Life and Art* (New York, 1985); and Stefan Kanfer, *Groucho: The Life and Times of Julius Henry Marx* (New York, 2000). Henry Jenkins has written an excellent history of the vaudeville roots of Hollywood comedy entitled, *"What Made Pistachio Nuts?" Early Sound Comedy and the Vaudeville Aesthetic* (New York, 1992). For an exemplary reading of the importance of ethnicity in film comedy, see Mark Winokur, *American Laughter: Immigrants, Ethnicity, and 1930s Hollywood Film Comedy* (New York, 1996). Cinematic representations of masculinity are described with great insight by Graham McCann, *Rebel Males: Clift, Brando and Dean* (New Brunswick, NJ, 1993). Interpretations of cross-dressing appear in Annette Kuhn, "Sexual disguise and cinema," in *The power of the image: Essays on representation and sexuality* (London, 1985); Marjorie Garber, *Vested Interests: Cross Dressing and Cultural Anxiety* (London, 1992); and Chris Straayer, "Redressing the 'Natural': The Temporary Transvestite Film," *Wide Angle* 14 (January 1992): 36–55.

The classic ethnography of Mexican humor is Armando Jiménez, *Picardía mexicana* (Mexico, 1958). For theoretical perspectives, see William H. Beezley, "Recent Mexican Political Humor," *Journal of Latin American Lore* 11, no. 2 (Winter 1985): 195–223. See also Julie Greer Johnson, *Satire in Colonial Spanish America: Turning the New World Upside Down* (Austin, TX, 1993). The humor of albures is analyzed most famously by Octavio Paz, *The Labyrinth of Solitude: Life and Thought in Mexico,* trans. Lysander Kemp (New York, 1961). See also John M. Ingham, *Mary, Michael, and Lucifer: Folk Catholicism in Central Mexico* (Austin, 1986); Sonya Lipsett-Rivera, *"De obra y palabra:* Patterns of Insults in Mexico, 1750–1856," *The Americas* 54, no. 4 (April 1998): 511–39; Cheryl English Martin, "Popular Speech and Social Order in Northern Mexico, 1650–1830," *Comparative Studies in Society and History* 32, no. 2 (1990): 305–24; Raúl Béjar Navarro, "Ensayo pa' balconear al mexicano desde un punto de vista muy acá," in *El mexicano: Aspectors culturales y psico-sociales* (Mexico, 1983), 201–37; and Agustín

Basave Fernández del Valle, "Ingenio festivo y humor satírico en los mexicanos," in *Vocación y estilo de México: Fundamentos de la Mexicanidad* (Mexico, 1989), 481–93. Carnivalesque humor is brilliantly analyzed by Mikhail Bakhtin, *Rabelais and His World* (Cambridge, MA, 1968). For a Bakhtinian reading of *bato* word-play—the borderlands' counterpart of pelado albures—see José E. Limón, *Dancing with the Devil: Society and Cultural Poetics in Mexican-American South Texas* (Madison, WI, 1994). Other useful comparative studies of humor were Will Kaufman, *The Comedian as Confidence Man: Studies in Irony Fatigue* (Detroit, 1997); and Robert M. Torrance, *The Comic Hero* (Cambridge, MA, 1978).

For the cultural background of the pelado in colonial taverns, see Juan Pedro Viqueira Albán, *Propriety and Permissiveness in Bourbon Mexico,* trans. Sonya Lipsett-Rivera and Sergio Rivera Ayala (Wilmington, DE, 1999). On the colonial honor complex, see Lyman L. Johnson and Sonya Lipsett-Rivera, eds., *The Faces of Honor: Sex, Shame, and Violence in Colonial Latin America* (Albuquerque, NM, 1998). Excellent social histories of race and class in colonial Mexico include R. Douglas Cope, *The Limits of Racial Domination: Plebeian Society in Colonial Mexico City, 1660–1720* (Madison, WI, 1994); and Magnus Mörner, *Race Mixture in the History of Latin America* (Boston, 1967). The continuation of this popular culture to the modern era is described by William H. Beezley, *Judas at the Jockey Club and Other Episodes of Porfirian Mexico* (Lincoln, NE, 1987); and Michael Johns, *The City of Mexico in the Age of Díaz* (Austin, TX, 1997). For an excellent examination of the pelado in criminal discourse, see Robert M. Buffington, *Criminal and Citizen in Modern Mexico* (Lincoln, NE, 2000).

The historiography of the Revolution of 1910 is thick, but for the Maderista period, start with Charles C. Cumberland, *Mexican Revolution: Genesis under Madero* (Austin, TX, 1952). On the 1920s, see John W. F. Dulles, *Yesterday in Mexico: A Chronicle of the Revolution, 1919–1936* (Austin, TX, 1961); Arnaldo Córdova, *La Revolución en crisis: La aventura del maximato* (Mexico, 1995); John W. Sherman, *The Mexican Right: The End of Revolutionary Reform* (Westport, CT, 1997); and Marjorie Ruth Clark, *Organized Labor in Mexico* (Chapel Hill, 1934). For an excellent overview of interpretations of the Revolution under

Lázaro Cárdenas, see Adrian Bantjes, *As If Jesus Walked on Earth: Cardenismo, Sonora, and the Mexican Revolution* (Wilmington, DE, 1998). Other useful works include Friedrich E. Schuler, *Mexico between Hitler and Roosevelt: Mexican Foreign Relations in the Age of Lázaro Cárdenas, 1934–1940* (Albuquerque, NM, 1998); Robert P. Millon, *Mexican Marxist: Vicente Lombardo Toledano* (Chapel Hill, NC, 1966); and Joe C. Ashby, *Organized Labor and the Mexican Revolution under Cárdenas* (Chapel Hill, NC, 1967).

The intellectual history of the pelado turns around the national self-analysis by Samuel Ramos, *Profile of Man and Culture in Mexico,* trans. Peter G. Earle (Austin, TX, 1962). Academic studies include Martin S. Stabb, *In Quest of Identity: Patterns in the Spanish American Essay of Ideas, 1890–1960* (Chapel Hill, NC, 1967); and Henry C. Schmidt, *The Roots of Lo Mexicano: Self and Society in Mexican Thought, 1900–1934* (College Station, TX, 1978). A trenchant critique of this literature is provided by Bartra's *The Cage of Melancholy* cited earlier.

Studies of Mexico after 1940 have tended to describe the "Peace of the PRI" from a social scientific rather than strictly historical perspective. The classics of this genre are Pablo González Casanova, *Democracy in Mexico* (New York, 1970); and Frank R. Brandenburg, *The Making of Modern Mexico* (Englewood Cliffs, NJ, 1964). On industrial policy, see Roger D. Hansen, *The Politics of Mexican Development* (Baltimore, 1971); and Roderic Ai Camp, *Entrepreneurs and Politics in Twentieth-Century Mexico* (New York, 1989). An excellent account of labor politics is provided by Kevin J. Middlebrook, *The Paradox of Revolution: Labor, the State, and Authoritarianism in Mexico* (Baltimore, 1995). Historical studies include several volumes of the Colegio de México's series, *Historia de la Revolución mexicana,* particularly volumes 18 and 20 by Luis Medina, *Del cardenismo al avilacamachismo* (Mexico, 1978) and *Civilismo y modernización del autoritarismo* (Mexico, 1979); and volume 22 by Olga Pellicer de Brody and José Luis Reyna, *El afianzamiento de la estabilidad política* (Mexico, 1978). Stephen R. Niblo gives an insightful account of the myths and realities of the economic "miracle" in *War, Diplomacy, and Development: The United States and Mexico, 1938–1954* (Wilmington, DE, 1995). The outlines of a cultural history of postrevolutionary

Mexico are emerging in the volume edited by Gilbert M. Joseph, Anne Rubenstein, and Eric Zolov, *Fragments of a Golden Age: The Politics of Culture in Mexico Since 1940* (Durham, NC, forthcoming).

Social scientists have also produced a rich literature on urbanization in contemporary Mexico City, beginning with Oscar Lewis, *The Children of Sánchez: Autobiography of a Mexican Family* (New York, 1961). The scandal surrounding the first Mexican edition, published and withdrawn by the Fondo de Cultura Económica, is recounted in the preface to Editorial Grijalbo's version, *Los hijos de Sánchez* (Mexico, 1982). The next generation of urban studies produced such classics as Larissa Adler Lomnitz, *Networks and Marginality: Life in a Mexican Shantytown*, trans. Cinna Lomnitz (New York, 1977); Lourdes Arizpe, *Indigenas en la ciudad: El caso de las "Marías."* (Mexico, 1975); Wayne A. Cornelius, *Politics and the Migrant Poor in Mexico City* (Stanford, CA, 1975), Susan Eckstein, *The Poverty of Revolution: The State and the Urban Poor in Mexico* (Princeton, NJ, 1977); and Carlos Vélez-Ibañez, *Rituals of Marginality: Politics, Process, and Culture in Central Urban Mexico, 1969–1974* (Berkeley, CA, 1983). An excellent summary of this literature is provided by Douglas Butterfield and John K. Chance, *Latin American Urbanization* (Cambridge, England, 1981). For an insightful view of changing masculine identity within this urban environment, see Matthew C. Gutmann, *The Meanings of Macho: Being a Man in Mexico City* (Berkeley, CA, 1996).

INDEX

Latin American Silhouettes
Studies in History and Culture

William H. Beezley and
Judith Ewell
Editors

Volumes Published

Silvia Marina Arrom and Servando Ortoll, eds., *Riots in the Cities: Popular Politics and the Urban Poor in Latin America, 1765–1910* (1996). Cloth ISBN 0-8420-2580-4 Paper ISBN 0-8420-2581-2

Roderic Ai Camp, ed., *Polling for Democracy: Public Opinion and Political Liberalization in Mexico* (1996). ISBN 0-8420-2583-9

Brian Loveman and Thomas M. Davies, Jr., eds., *The Politics of Antipolitics: The Military in Latin America*, 3d ed., revised and updated (1996). Cloth ISBN 0-8420-2609-6 Paper ISBN 0-8420-2611-8

Joseph S. Tulchin, Andrés Serbín, and Rafael Hernández, eds., *Cuba and the Caribbean: Regional Issues and Trends in the Post-Cold War Era* (1997). ISBN 0-8420-2652-5

Thomas W. Walker, ed., *Nicaragua without Illusions: Regime Transition and Structural Adjustment in the 1990s* (1997). Cloth ISBN 0-8420-2578-2 Paper ISBN 0-8420-2579-0

Dianne Walta Hart, *Undocumented in L.A.: An Immigrant's Story* (1997). Cloth ISBN 0-8420-2648-7 Paper ISBN 0-8420-2649-5

Jaime E. Rodríguez O. and Kathryn Vincent, eds., *Myths, Misdeeds, and Misunderstandings: The Roots of Conflict in U.S.-Mexican Relations* (1997). ISBN 0-8420-2662-2

Jaime E. Rodríguez O. and Kathryn Vincent, eds., *Common Border, Uncommon Paths: Race, Culture, and National Identity in U.S.-Mexican Relations* (1997). ISBN 0-8420-2673-8

William H. Beezley and Judith Ewell, eds., *The Human Tradition in Modern Latin America* (1997). Cloth ISBN 0-8420-2612-6 Paper ISBN 0-8420-2613-4

Donald F. Stevens, ed., *Based on a True Story: Latin American History at the Movies* (1997). Cloth ISBN 0-8420-2582-0 Paper ISBN 0-8420-2781-5

Jaime E. Rodríguez O., ed., *The Origins of Mexican National Politics, 1808–1847* (1997). Paper ISBN 0-8420-2723-8

Che Guevara, *Guerrilla Warfare*, with revised and updated introduction and case studies by Brian Loveman and Thomas M. Davies, Jr., 3d ed. (1997). Cloth ISBN 0-8420-2677-0 Paper ISBN 0-8420-2678-9

Adrian A. Bantjes, *As If Jesus Walked on Earth: Cardenismo, Sonora, and the Mexican Revolution* (1998; rev. ed., 2000). Cloth ISBN 0-8420-2653-3 Paper ISBN 0-8420-2751-3

Henry A. Dietz and Gil Shidlo, eds., *Urban Elections in Democratic Latin America* (1998). Cloth ISBN 0-8420-2627-4 Paper ISBN 0-8420-2628-2

A. Kim Clark, *The Redemptive Work: Railway and Nation in Ecuador, 1895–1930* (1998). ISBN 0-8420-2674-6

Joseph S. Tulchin, ed., with Allison M. Garland, *Argentina: The Challenges of Modernization* (1998). ISBN 0-8420-2721-1

Louis A. Pérez, Jr., ed., *Impressions of Cuba in the Nineteenth Century: The Travel Diary of Joseph J. Dimock* (1998). Cloth ISBN 0-8420-2657-6 Paper ISBN 0-8420-2658-4

June E. Hahner, ed., *Women through Women's Eyes: Latin American Women in Nineteenth-Century Travel Accounts* (1998). Cloth ISBN 0-8420-2633-9 Paper ISBN 0-8420-2634-7

James P. Brennan, ed., *Peronism and Argentina* (1998). ISBN 0-8420-2706-8

John Mason Hart, ed., *Border Crossings: Mexican and Mexican-American Workers*

(1998). Cloth ISBN 0-8420-2716-5 Paper ISBN 0-8420-2717-3

Brian Loveman, *For* la Patria: *Politics and the Armed Forces in Latin America* (1999). Cloth ISBN 0-8420-2772-6 Paper ISBN 0-8420-2773-4

Guy P. C. Thomson, with David G. LaFrance, *Patriotism, Politics, and Popular Liberalism in Nineteenth-Century Mexico: Juan Francisco Lucas and the Puebla Sierra* (1999). ISBN 0-8420-2683-5

Robert Woodmansee Herr, in collaboration with Richard Herr, *An American Family in the Mexican Revolution* (1999). ISBN 0-8420-2724-6

Juan Pedro Viqueira Albán, trans. Sonya Lipsett-Rivera and Sergio Rivera Ayala, *Propriety and Permissiveness in Bourbon Mexico* (1999). Cloth ISBN 0-8420-2466-2 Paper ISBN 0-8420-2467-0

Stephen R. Niblo, *Mexico in the 1940s: Modernity, Politics, and Corruption* (1999). Cloth ISBN 0-8420-2794-7 Paper (2001) ISBN 0-8420-2795-5

David E. Lorey, *The U.S.-Mexican Border in the Twentieth Century* (1999). Cloth ISBN 0-8420-2755-6 Paper ISBN 0-8420-2756-4

Joanne Hershfield and David R. Maciel, eds., *Mexico's Cinema: A Century of Films and Filmmakers* (2000). Cloth ISBN 0-8420-2681-9 Paper ISBN 0-8420-2682-7

Peter V. N. Henderson, *In the Absence of Don Porfirio: Francisco León de la Barra and the Mexican Revolution* (2000). ISBN 0-8420-2774-2

Mark T. Gilderhus, *The Second Century: U.S.-Latin American Relations since 1889* (2000). Cloth ISBN 0-8420-2413-1 Paper ISBN 0-8420-2414-X

Catherine Moses, *Real Life in Castro's Cuba* (2000). Cloth ISBN 0-8420-2836-6 Paper ISBN 0-8420-2837-4

K. Lynn Stoner, ed./comp., with Luis Hipólito Serrano Pérez, *Cuban and Cuban-American Women: An Annotated Bibliography* (2000). ISBN 0-8420-2643-6

Thomas D. Schoonover, *The French in Central America: Culture and Commerce, 1820–1930* (2000). ISBN 0-8420-2792-0

Enrique C. Ochoa, *Feeding Mexico: The Political Uses of Food since 1910* (2000). ISBN 0-8420-2812-9

Thomas W. Walker and Ariel C. Armony, eds., *Repression, Resistance, and Democratic Transition in Central America* (2000). Cloth ISBN 0-8420-2766-1 Paper ISBN 0-8420-2768-8

William H. Beezley and David E. Lorey, eds., *¡Viva México! ¡Viva la Independencia! Celebrations of September 16* (2001). Cloth ISBN 0-8420-2914-1 Paper ISBN 0-8420-2915-X

Jeffrey M. Pilcher, *Cantinflas and the Chaos of Mexican Modernity* (2001). Cloth ISBN 0-8420-2769-6 Paper ISBN 0-8420-2771-8

Victor M. Uribe-Uran, ed., *State and Society in Spanish America during the Age of Revolution* (2001). Cloth ISBN 0-8420-2873-0 Paper ISBN 0-8420-2874-9

Andrew Grant Wood, *Revolution in the Street: Women, Workers, and Urban Protest in Veracruz, 1870–1927* (2001). ISBN 0-8420-2879-X

Charles Bergquist, Ricardo Peñaranda, and Gonzalo Sánchez G., eds., *Violence in Colombia, 1990–2000: Waging War and Negotiating Peace* (2001). Cloth ISBN 0-8420-2869-2 Paper ISBN 0-8420-2870-6

William Schell, Jr., *Integral Outsiders: The American Colony in Mexico City, 1876–1911* (2001). ISBN 0-8420-2838-2

John Lynch, *Argentine Caudillo: Juan Manuel de Rosas* (2001). Cloth ISBN 0-8420-2897-8 Paper ISBN 0-8420-2828-6

Samuel Basch, M.D., ed. and trans. Fred D. Ullman, *Recollections of Mexico: The Last Ten Months of Maximilian's Empire* (2001). ISBN 0-8420-2962-1